# DOPE KINGS OF LONDON

## BRILLIANT CHANG, EDDIE MANNING, AND THE SECRET HISTORY OF THE FIRST WAR ON DRUGS

### JOHN LUCAS

# Contents

Foreword ...................................................................... 1

Drug Laws Timeline ........................................................ 6

1. New Laws ................................................................. 10

2. Snow Queens ............................................................ 33

3. Big Maxie ................................................................. 41

4. The Worst Man In London .......................................... 67

5. The Clever Dancer ..................................................... 98

6. The Limehouse Spider ............................................... 104

7. Downfall .................................................................. 131

8. Busted! .................................................................... 151

Illustrations ................................................................ 157

9. The Black Sheep ....................................................... 176

10. Law and Disorder ..................................................... 194

11. Death in a Hotel Room ............................................. 212

12. Death on the Nile ..................................................... 224

13. Broken ................................................................... 231

15. Duke of Hazards ...................................................... 246

16. A Dangerous International Adventurer ......................... 261

17. The Wrong Powder .................................................... 305

18. Problem Solved? ....................................................... 318

Index ......................................................................... 327

# FOREWORD

The global illicit drugs trade is now worth about £350 billion a year. To put that in perspective, the annual revenue generated by Apple, one of the world's most successful companies, is around £220 billion. Drugs like heroin, cannabis and — especially — cocaine, are by weight some of the most valuable substances on the planet. As you might expect from such a lucrative trade, it has produced at least two household name billionaires in Pablo Escobar and Joaquin 'El Chapo' Guzman. But how did the industry begin just over one hundred years ago?

When drugs like cocaine and opium were officially made illegal in Britain in 1920, the resulting black market was open to professional criminals and amateurs alike. Yet in fact, drug dealing and particularly large-scale supply was an area many established underworld players avoided or could not break into because they lacked the necessary international contacts. Often, it was shipping magnates and merchants, and well-connected or well-travelled businessmen, who found themselves at the vanguard of this illicit industry. Such people didn't necessarily consider themselves to be full-time crooks when they invested in quantities of cocaine, cannabis, heroin or other drugs. It was just another facet of their business.

On the street dealing side, it was usually those on the very lowest rungs of society — immigrants and itinerant workers — who hit the headlines as opposed to traditional criminal gangs. The Press frequently described such men as "Cocaine Kings," or "Opium Kings," or the all-encompassing "Dope Kings". On some occasions the title was deserving, on others, probably not. Journalists, industrialists and a host of other characters also established themselves in a criminal enterprise not yet dominated by ruthless cartels and all-powerful drug lords.

Much of the language used to report such cases was racist and I've made the editorial decision to censor the most offensive slurs. We all know what they are and they don't need to be visible in print for us to understand their meaning.

It's worth pointing out right at the start that this is a book about people, not policy. It focuses on the criminal and law enforcement characters involved in what was effectively the first war on drugs, rather than the wider societal issues such as drugs subculture, law making and so on. I've largely kept away from the lives of the consumers, apart from where they cross paths to a significant extent with their suppliers. For example, there are already dozens of books about the Bright Young Things (the upper-class Bohemians famous in peacetime for their fast living and drink and drug-induced antics), so I've mentioned them only in passing.

Likewise, this book only touches peripherally on the drugs situation in North America, and even then only as it relates to Canada, a British territory. The situation in the United States was complicated by the parallel prohibition of alcohol and most of the major players in the drugs market, such as Lucky Luciano, are already very well known as a result.

I've also veered away from dealing in-depth with those other amoral suppliers of narcotics: doctors. Keeping on top of the era's 'script doctors' was a major part of the law enforcement approach to the drugs issue, but their activities could not truly be described as organised crime and have little to no relevance today, unless in an argument about returning to the 'British System' of medicinal supply to addicts. Again, this isn't a book about policy so the subject has been largely avoided. In any case, both topics are well-covered in Christopher Hallam's study *White Drug Cultures and Regulation in London 1916-1960*, which I used as a handy reference guide.

I make no apology for being a muckraker. I am a journalist first and foremost and therefore interested in people, their personalities and (why not?) their peccadillos. As a result, this book contains many hitherto unknown details about the lives of some notorious characters who have been written about before, such as Brilliant Chang and Eddie Manning. But it also discusses in great detail two unusual cases that have rarely — if ever — been explored, those of Richard Cadbury Butler and Johannes Steel.

Both investigations achieved wildly different outcomes (one of the men was convicted, the other was never even arrested), but share in common the fact that if the full details had been known at the time, they would have caused a public sensation. Therefore, with those involved having escaped ignominy in life, I see no reason why we shouldn't have a nose around their questionable public and private activities now that they are long dead.

Unless otherwise stated, most of the information in this book has come from painstaking research of files at the National Archives, as well as newspapers stored at the British Library and on the online British Newspaper Archive. Most of those newspapers are referenced within the text.

In addition, several books have acted as indispensable guides to the period and oeuvre. *Dope Girls*, by Marek Kohn, is the definitive account of the Billie Carleton case. *Empire of Crime*, by Tim Newark, provided much needed context on organised crime within the wider British Empire and pointed me in the direction of several lesser-known cases, while Christopher Hallam's above-mentioned work provided an education on the subjects of script doctors and early regulation of narcotics. *Webs of Smoke*, by Kathryn Meyer and Terry Parssinen, and *Cannabis Britannica* by James H Mills, were also useful texts focusing on the global drugs trade of the early twentieth century. The histories of MI5 and MI6, written by Christopher Andrew and Keith Jeffery respectively, provided essential background context for the chapters on Johannes Steel. Other works are referenced within the text.

# FOREWORD

The first British war on drugs might seem somewhat tame compared with the carnage caused by the parallel prohibition of alcohol in the United States. There, entire criminal and even political dynasties were founded on the profits of booze and the blood of rival gangsters. Professional criminals like Al Capone and Lucky Luciano dominated the illicit marketplace, leaving a staggering body count in their ruthless pursuit of profit.

Those on the criminal side of the British drug war were considerably more genteel, although sometimes equally flamboyant. Perhaps the most marked difference is this — when it became apparent that in-demand substances such as cocaine and heroin could now be sold at a premium thanks to new drug laws, Britain's established professional criminal class mostly left the industry alone. Violent underworld forces such as London's Sabini gang continued to restrict themselves to gambling, general racketeering, and drinking dens. Instead, the trade attracted a colourful collection of chancers and businessmen, who saw the growth of narcotics as an opportunity like any other. These included, as we shall see, Eddie Manning, a jazz drummer, Brilliant Chang, a restaurateur, Richard Cadbury Butler, a wealthy playboy, and Johannes Steel, a journalist and spy. For them, the risks were worth taking.

# DRUG LAWS TIMELINE

Although this book does not deal in-depth with policy, the actions of the world's first drug dealers were shaped by the emerging legislative landscape, both domestically and internationally, as new laws created black markets and pushed suppliers from one territory to another. The key laws and treaties mentioned in this book are below:

## UK Pharmacy Act 1868

Designed to control distribution of poisons such as strychnine, potassium cyanide and ergot. Opium and its derivatives were added later.

## International Opium Convention 1912

First discussed in Shanghai in 1909, the treaty was signed by the United Kingdom, Germany, the United States, China, France, Italy, Japan, Holland, Persia, Portugal, Russia and Siam. All powers agreed to "use their best endeavours to control, or to cause to be controlled, all persons manufacturing, importing, selling, distributing, and exporting morphine, cocaine, and their respective salts, as well as the buildings in which these persons carry such an industry or trade." Some nations, such as the UK, did not implement the agreement until it was incorporated into the Treaty of Versailles.

## US Harrison Act 1914

Federal law regulated and taxed the production, importation, and distribution of opiates and coca products, creating one of the first drugs black markets outside of the Far East.

## Defence of the Realm Act (DORA) 40B

Wartime emergency regulation made it illegal to sell cocaine and opium-based products to military personnel, unless for official medical reasons. It also criminalised possession for anyone not connected with the medical or veterinary professions, and created the stipulation that the drugs could only be dispensed to patients who had a non-reusable prescription signed by their doctors.

## UK Dangerous Drugs Act 1920

Ratified the International Opium Convention and codified the DORA 40B restrictions, which were redundant after the conflict ended. Later amendments to the Act increased sentencing limits and added cannabis to the list of banned substances.

## International Opium Convention 1925

Introduced a statistical control system to be supervised by a Permanent Central Opium Board under the League of Nations, making it harder for legitimate manufacturers in Europe to supply black marketeers and drug smugglers. Criminals subsequently moved their base of operations to Turkey and parts of Eastern Europe.

## Convention for Limiting the Manufacture and Regulating the Distribution of Narcotic Drugs 1931

Created a quota system for the world's estimated supply among the manufacturing countries, France, Germany, India, Italy, Japan, Holland, Switzerland, Turkey, Britain, the USSR and the US, geared towards the needs of each country. Theoretically, it meant only the official quantities needed for each country could be produced. It shifted production centres to China and parts of Latin America and all but ended the involvement of legitimate business in the illicit marketplace.

## Convention for the Suppression of Illicit Traffic 1936

Pushed by the US to criminalise the cultivation, production, manufacture and distribution, as well as the use of opium, coca and cannabis for non-medical and non-scientific purposes. In the end, the Convention restricted itself to trafficking. The US ultimately refused to sign it because it was too weak. It had little effect and was soon made obsolete by World War Two.

# TIMELINE

# 1. NEW LAWS

**B**ritain was at war, but the market rarely allows such things to get in the way of a good product. The advert in *The Times,* on December 9, 1915, began with the eye-catching gambit, "A useful present for friends at the front." And it certainly did sound very handy.

The pocket medicine case, small enough to sit comfortably in a soldier's top pocket, was made by the chemists to the King, Savory & Moore, and contained twelve gelatine sheets, or lamels, each divided into twenty-one small squares, "so that an accurate dose of any particular medicine required can be cut or torn off like a postage stamp and taken without the least trouble or risk". Alongside treatments for malaria and ulcers, this "complete supply of medicines" also contained sheets of coca extract and morphine, two extremely addictive drugs.

The packs, the advert added, "are highly praised by all who use them, and are proving of the greatest possible service to officers on Active Service". Perhaps, many had begun to think, they were being too highly praised. It would have been impossible to know at the time, but the reaction to this seemingly innocuous advert in a national newspaper would help to shape Britain's attitude to drugs for the next century, and beyond.

It sounds trite to say that World War One changed the British way of life forever. Of course it did — nearly one million men did not make it home, and its untidy aftermath fuelled an even more devastating conflagration, engulfing another generation, just two decades later. Yet other consequences of the war are still felt today, long after the living memory of the conflict itself has faded, including the legal status of drugs like cocaine and heroin.

At the start of the war, morphia and coca products had long been sources of abuse and addiction in Britain. The pharmaceutical giant Bayer practically invented heroin and marketed it as a "non-addictive morphine substitute" which could be used by the public to treat coughs and sore throats. Meanwhile, coca, the exotic leaf with extraordinary properties, had been widely touted as a healthy ingredient in tonics for decades, with some companies even going so far as to label their cocaine-infused confections "child restorers" or "brain feeders".

In much the same way that morphia products, such as opium, had been regularly used as a painkiller, cocaine had for years been a common ingredient in medicines to treat hay fever, thanks to its ability to cleanse the respiratory tract. One of the most popular products, Ryno's Hay Fever, consisted of 99.9 percent cocaine — stronger than any version of the drug you would find on the street today. Ryno's was an American import, but Britain had its own brands, chief among them

Tabloid cocaine tablets, marketed for public speakers and singers who wanted to improve their voice, again because of its supposed decongestant attributes. The effects of the drug on the long-term health of human beings were believed to be as negligible as those of tobacco (thought harmless at the time) although some products did carry the minor warning that they could be "habit forming".

For decades, legislators saw little reason to bring these drugs under government control. One early victory for campaigners, and one of the very first drug laws in the world, was Britain's 1868 Pharmacy Act, a piece of legislation designed principally to control the distribution of poisons such as strychnine, potassium cyanide, and ergot. After the law was passed, controlled drugs could only be sold if the buyer, or their intermediary, was known to the seller. It also stipulated that the drugs had to be sold in containers featuring the seller's name and address. Later, opium and its derivatives were added to the schedule of controlled substances. The law was hailed as being responsible for a fall in the opium death rate of more than one third (from 6.4 per million population in 1868 to 4.5 in 1869), although the rate was back to the starting point by the end of the century, partly because over-the-counter sales were still allowed. The 1908 Poisons and Pharmacy Act tightened up the regulations and added several substances to the schedule, including coca.

The catalyst for coca's inclusion had been the high-profile deaths of two actress sisters, Ida and Edith Yeoland, in July 1901. Edith, twenty-eight, had been out of work for more than a month at the time of her death and was later described as "sensitive" by witnesses at her inquest. Ida, twenty-five, was equally downbeat about her career — she had been jobless for twice as long. Edith had once told her landlady, Sarah Callaghan, "Don't be surprised if you come into our room one day and find us dead." In the event, it was indeed Mrs Callaghan who had the horrific experience of stumbling upon their corpses. The sisters' deaths, and the discovery of several bottles of cocaine in their rooms, suggesting a long-standing habit, contributed to a new public debate about drug control.

By that point, the problem had become particularly acute because, unlike today, there was little social stigma attached to drug use. Even when things went desperately wrong, as they had in the case of the tragic sisters, sympathy, rather than scorn, was usually the order of the day. This was no doubt partly thanks to cocaine's popularity amongst the educated classes, which included writers, artists, doctors and politicians. For example, both Sigmund Freud and the (albeit fictional) detective Sherlock Holmes were high profile examples of cocaine aficionados. And as we shall see, among the privileged Bright Young Things of London's Bohemian 1920s party scene, drug use was positively celebrated.

One article in *The Referee* described how the "habit grows rapidly" after a legitimate introduction to the drug:

> A mild ten percent solution obtained at a chemist to cure a toothache has given many people a first taste of the joys and horrors of cocaine. The first effect of a dose is extreme exhilaration and mental brilliancy. The imagination becomes aflame. The after-effects — reaction, utter loss of moral responsibility, a blotched complexion, and lunatic asylum or death. Yet any chemist will tell you that it has been increasingly in demand by women of late years.

It wasn't just cocaine users who were spared approbation, morphia products could also be taken acceptably in polite society. A report in the *British Medical Journal* from the time described upper-class tea parties in Paris where, in addition to drinks and cakes, the hostess would whip out a hypodermic syringe and inject her guests with drugs. Meanwhile, the attraction of young, privileged men to the Chinese opium dens of Limehouse Causeway and Pennyfields, in London's East End, had been a source of controversy for decades.

Concerns over the twin issues of opium and cocaine abuse accelerated as the world hurtled towards conflict. In the East End, the Chinese population had been expanding since the turn of the century and with it the number of Chinese-run businesses — mainly laundries, restaurants, and gambling and drug dens. At the same time, the growth of the West End's theatre and clubland catered for a generation of actresses, singers, dancers and hostesses who worked hard and stayed up late to party with aristocrats and society's elite. Within their stimulant-hungry ranks, cocaine was an increasingly useful friend to have. Then, in July 1914, war broke out in Europe.

The campaign for tougher drug laws began almost immediately, thanks to the practice among soldiers of packing their own supplies of cocaine and morphine to see them through the horrors of the front. As well as the now notorious Savory & Moore advert in *The Times*, Harrods also promoted small packages of morphine and cocaine complete with a syringe and spare needles. Both were among firms soon fined for selling cocaine and morphine outside of the Pharmacy Act regulations.

Despite profiting from the adverts, *The Times* quickly took a lead in suggesting that supplying soldiers with addictive drugs could undermine the combat effectiveness of the British Army. Nevertheless, girls seeing off their sweethearts at the train station continued to slip them cocaine tablets or tonics as one last token of their love.

It wasn't long before the issue escalated into a full-blown moral panic. In 1916, a Canadian major stationed in Folkestone, Kent, discovered a man named Horace Dennis Kingsley and a London prostitute named Rose Edwards were both selling cocaine to his troops. Edwards later admitted sourcing the drug from a man in a West End pub who usually sold the drug to actresses, prostitutes and other female drug users. Kingsley said he simply bought the drug from chemists and sold it on to his soldier friends. "It makes you most keen on what you are doing," he said of cocaine's effects.

The Pharmacy Act, however, did not cover the activities of Kingsley and Edwards, because they were not regulated chemists. Instead, they were both handed sentences of six months' hard labour for the offence of "selling a powder to members of HM Forces, with intent to make them less capable of performing their duties". In the course of their trial it emerged that some forty men in a local camp had developed a drug habit. As a result of the case, *The Times* excitedly labelled cocaine a danger even "more deadly than bullets".

Hyperbole abounded. One article, in the *Daily Chronicle*, suggested drug-addled soldiers were literally crawling into chemists' shops to get their fix. The paper said cocaine "is driving hundreds of women mad. What is worse, it will drive, unless the traffic in it is checked, hundreds of soldiers mad".

It was further reported that suppliers in the West End had taken to using Soho prostitutes, known as 'cocaine girls' or 'dope girls,' to sell their wares to soldiers, who often became aggressive and insubordinate, some even murderous. As the fighting in Europe intensified, the prospect of the Army descending into anarchy thanks to "cocaine-mania" became ever more terrifying. As *The Times* insisted, "Most cocaine-o-maniacs carry revolvers to protect themselves from imaginary enemies." It was even suggested that Germany, a leading power in the legitimate worldwide cocaine market, could be behind an organised plot to undermine Britain's military. This was unlikely, but chillingly plausible to readers.

But still the authorities were hampered by the strictures of the Pharmacy Act. In April 1916, police launched an investigation into a typical Soho cocaine ring. Up to ten young mostly Jewish men were involved. They sold their "snow" to girls around Shaftesbury Avenue and from the Palace Tavern in Charring Cross Road. One of the men, Alfy Benjamin, sourced the drug from a chemist in Lisle Street and sold it on to a one-legged former porter and convicted thief named Willy Johnson, who then dealt the small boxes on the street. Each box contained about one penny's worth of cocaine, estimated to be about one-tenth of a gram, but sold for two-and-sixpence, making Johnson a ninepence profit. While the amount of cocaine was tiny compared with a typical deal today, the content could have been up to one hundred percent pure.

But yet again, the Pharmacy Act only regulated shopkeepers, and allowed for a maximum fine of £5. What's more, it only applied to the sale, not possession, of controlled substances. While Willy Johnson was eventually arrested in possession of eleven boxes of cocaine the officers had not seen him actually sell anything, so he was acquitted in court.

Until the war, the British Establishment had been largely ambivalent when it came to drugs, beyond recognising the need to keep dodgy doctors and chemists in check. It had only been a few years since the government of colonial India garnered most of its revenue by selling opium to China, phasing out the trade in 1907. Even as recently as 1914, the Director of Supplies of the British Expeditionary Force had been told to keep six thousand Sikhs from the Indian army who had landed in France topped up with the drug daily, because they were used to their rations of so-called 'Indian treacle'. But now politicians were keen to act. Chief among them was Sir Malcolm Delevingne, the undersecretary of state at the Home Office.

Delevingne was a mild-mannered career civil servant, but could also be described as the godfather of British drugs control. He was a founding member of the League of Nations' Opium Advisory Committee, giving him a front row seat, and a powerful voice, as international drug control agreements were gradually built over the next two decades. Another key figure in the drive to ban drug use was Sir Francis Lloyd, a general in command of the London district. "I am told that this evil practice is exceedingly rife at the present time," he once said. "It is doing an immense amount of harm, I am told. They say that it is so ingrained that once you take it you will not give it up."

Most historians have since concluded that the evidence used to back up the widespread horror stories about drugs that played out in the Press as war raged in Europe was largely anecdotal and hysterical, but nevertheless the logic of wanting to restrict drug use among troops during a time of crisis was inescapable.

As a result, one of the world's first anti-drugs laws was put into place. On May 11, 1916, the Army Council issued an order banning any unauthorised sale or supply of psychoactive substances, which included cocaine, codeine, hemp, heroin, morphine, and opium, to any member of the armed forces, except for prescribed medical reasons. Breaking the rule could see violators locked up for six months. On July 28, the edict was codified under the 1914 Defence of the Realm Act (DORA) 40B, which allowed the government to dictate wartime measures.

Many of the rules under DORA were draconian. For example, Britons could no longer fly kites, start bonfires or feed bread to wild animals. The law had also allowed the government to institute a system of censorship and limit the production of alcohol. Now, citizens could not sell cocaine and opium-based products to military personnel (although heroin was excluded), unless for official medical reasons. It also criminalised possession for anyone not connected with the medical or veterinary professions, and stipulated that the drugs could only be dispensed to patients (whether military or civilian) who had a non-reusable prescription signed by their doctors.[1]

It was the first time the British state had put drugs under such close control, but prosecutions under the regulation were few and far between, with most being brought against Chinese opium addicts. A most unwelcome side-effect of the law was that people who needed painkillers for genuine reasons could no longer get them. For example, many dentists, especially those who operated in poor communities, were unregistered. As a result, hundreds of patients had to endure procedures without the most common anesthetic — cocaine. Meanwhile, the now illicit nature of the drug only served to increase its popularity on the West End party scene.

If successive wars and natural disasters have proved one thing, it's that you can't stop the British people yearning for their pubs. Yet the domestic restrictions imposed by DORA turned the country into a virtual police state, with the pub trade drastically curtailed.

For example, before the conflict there had been almost no rules on opening hours, with most hostelries serving booze from as early as 5am and closing after midnight, just long enough to turf out the drunks, mop the floor and catch a few hours' sleep. After DORA, pubs were forced to close in the afternoons and call last orders at 9.30pm (and the changes remained in some form for decades). Limits were also placed on the production of beer because it was feared too many men and women would drink themselves into a stupor as the country faced its greatest crisis. London nightclubs tried to continue unabated, but were hit with the Clubs (Temporary Provisions) Act in 1915, which enforced a midnight curfew at weekends, until their operating times were brought into line with pubs. As a result, the war augured the birth of an underground nightclub scene, with at least one hundred and fifty illegal venues popping up in Soho alone.

By the end of the conflict, two of the most famous nightclub owners were Dalton Murray and Kate Meyrick. Their first venture together, Dalton's, in Leicester Square, was famous for hosting both London's underworld and nobility, and drugs and women of questionable virtue were always on the menu.

Dalton's was raided by police and ultimately shut down, branded a "sink of iniquity" and a "noxious fungus growth upon our social system" by a judge. Meyrick went on to open a string of other clubs, including The Forty Three, at 43 Gerrard Street, Soho, and Brett's, a basement dance hall famous for its lurid pink and gold decor on the Charring Cross Road. It was there that a young "dance instructress" named Freda Kempton would later find work.[2]

As London's nascent clubland grew, its clientele became more diverse. Refugees from Europe and tens of thousands of servicemen and civilians from America, India and the Caribbean arrived in the capital. The streets of the West End could at times be teeming with an array of men and women in different uniforms walking together arm-in-arm. This new London upset stuffy Establishment figures but invigorated the club scene in ways they could never understand.

For example, wartime restrictions on alcohol meant party-goers looked for other chemical aids. Cocaine was already popular among the thousands of Canadian soldiers stationed in Britain, so they passed their habits on to the locals. When the jazz craze really took hold in the 1920s, the West End served as a stomping ground for a loose network of upper-class Bohemians and socialites, dubbed the Bright Young Things by the Press. Out of this group would emerge several serious drug addicts, most notably the actress Brenda Dean Paul, who went on to pick up several convictions.

The gossip columnist of the *Evening News*, Quex, wrote about the "dark stories" coming out of "West End Bohemia" in early 1915. "Still more prevalent is that exciting drug cocaine," he wrote. "It is so easy to take — just snuffed up the nose; and no-one seems to know why the girls who suffer from this body and soul racking habit find the drug so easy to obtain."

Another publication, *The Umpire*, said cocaine was "driving hundreds mad" and labelled its aficionados "snow snifters". Americans as well as Canadians were to blame, with Yanks also setting up "hop joints" for opium parties around Leicester Square, Charring Cross Road and Seven Dials. *Umpire* pointed out that in America, cocaine "had been a cause of a great deal of the bloodshed between the black and white races". It was a sign that, as the years went on, cocaine would continue to be seen as a drug used mostly by lower-class women and black men.

Yet the most famous drugs case of the period, and perhaps the most famous accidental overdose of all time, was that of a white actress, Billie Carleton, whose fatal dose was supplied by an upper class, white, male friend.

The actress Billie Carleton was born Florence Leonara Stewart, in Bloomsbury in September 1896. On the birth certificate, her mother listed her profession as "actress", but her father's name was left blank. Today, we might draw our own conclusions from such scant information.

By the age of sixteen, Billie was herself a chorus girl and companion to the much older and wealthier John Darlington Marsh, who gave her large sums of money via another friend, Dr Frederick Stuart, who managed her bank account. At one point, Billie had at least £5,000 of savings, a huge sum equivalent to around £280,000 in today's money.

Billie's big break came in the musical Watch Your Step, at the Empire Theatre in Leicester Square. When the leading lady, Ethel Levey, left her role, the impresario Charles B Cochrane allowed Billie to take her place. Cochrane later described Billie as "a young girl of flower-like beauty, delicate charm, and great intelligence". Unfortunately, she also had an insatiable taste for both opium and cocaine, principally supplied by her favourite costume designer, the flamboyant Reggie De Veulle.

In 1916, rumours of her drug use wrecked Billie's career under Cochrane, but she soon found work elsewhere with another leading revue producer, Andre Charlot. In one production, The Boy, Billie played an early iteration of a flapper — an excitable teenage girl or young woman given to wearing short skirts and having fun on the town. The term would only really come into its own with the post-war explosion of the jazz scene. But the role made her name and by September 1918 Billie was starring in Freedom of the Seas at the Haymarket, making her the youngest leading lady in the West End, picking up £25 per week, nearly £1,500 in today's money.

As is so often the case where youth, fame and excess wealth are combined, there was also the continual lure of drugs. Billie was now hopelessly addicted to cocaine and received regular finger-wagging lectures from Dr Stuart, while at the same time he willingly topped her up with regular shots of morphine, supposedly to manage the pain of wisdom teeth.

De Veulle, meanwhile, was the primary source of her snow (although in the years following her death other names, such as Brilliant Chang and Eddie Manning, would be mentioned). Dr Stuart would pay her bills and De Veulle, who organised her shopping, would tack on a hidden surcharge for the cocaine. At one point, as Billie's personal life deteriorated, she made the toxic decision to move in with her friend De Veulle.

De Veulle habitually purchased cocaine from a Chinese man, Lau Ping Yau and his Scottish wife Ada, who lived in Limehouse. Another source was the film actor Lionel Belcher, based in Notting Hill. Belcher bought the powder from a Lisle Street chemist, Wooldridge's, and sold it to De Veulle at twice the price. Billie also became fast friends with Belcher and accompanied him to opium parties in Limehouse. Ada Lau Ping even provided and cooked the drug during gatherings at Billie's flat in Dover Street.[3]

Ironically, the drug-addled Reggie De Veulle might not have survived the war years if not for his dependence on narcotics. In September 1918 De Veulle was called up, even though he was by now in his late thirties. Dr Stuart gave evidence at his draft tribunal, revealing that his friend was a cocaine addict and therefore unfit to serve his country. De Veulle celebrated his reprieve with gusto. Two months later, on November 11, the whole country erupted in joy as peace was declared. But by then De Veulle had repeatedly ignored the pleas of Dr Stuart and other friends to stop giving cocaine to Billie Carleton.

Just one week before a Victory Ball at the Albert Hall on November 27 — for which De Veulle was to design a stunning costume for his friend — the pair went on an all-night bender which infuriated his wife, Pauline, and led to an embarrassing public argument between the two women. Pauline did not approve of her husband's drug-taking or the outward appearance of his friendship with Billie, platonic as it surely was.

The day of the ball, Billie found herself on her uppers. She had just over £9 in the bank and had to visit a pawnbroker with John Darlington Marsh to retrieve more than £1,000 worth of jewellery. Still, more money was on the horizon — she had just signed her first movie deal and was due to rake in £50 a day during shooting. Billie performed that evening in Freedom of the Seas. It was to be her final appearance on the stage.

The Victory Ball was a glitzy affair, with the cream of London society decked out in breathtaking fancy dress costumes, many referencing the might of the British Empire or the wartime Allied nations, such as France, Belgium and the United States. Pauline De Veulle went as France, while her mischievous husband dressed as a harlequin. Reggie and Billie each spent much of the night in dark corners and the toilets snorting cocaine from small metal boxes.

Billie arrived back at her rooms in the Savoy Court, behind the Savoy Hotel, at around 3am. Lionel Belcher and his girlfriend, Olive Richardson, joined her, as did the dancer Irene Castle. The group partied well into the early hours and dined on bacon and eggs ordered up by Billie, before the guests eventually left her happy, sitting up in bed alone at 6am. By

10am, obviously feeling the worse for wear, Billie phoned a friend to cancel an afternoon meeting, postponing it until the evening. Her maid arrived at 11.30am and could hear her mistress loudly snoring. She went about her work, but when the snoring stopped at 3.30pm, she checked on Billie and failed to wake her. Dr Stuart was called. He gave her mouth-to-mouth and injected her with brandy and strychnine, but Billie Carleton was dead. A small gold box next to her bed was still half full of cocaine.

By the time of Billie's death, detectives at Scotland Yard had already been investigating Reggie De Veulle for several weeks. While there was some initial speculation that the actress had died as a result of the ongoing Spanish Flu pandemic, which killed at least 250,000 in Britain, the theory was soon discounted. Reggie was brought in for questioning. Lionel Belcher also armed himself with a solicitor and went to question De Veulle himself, in the hope that his answers might put him in the clear. But the designer insisted he had not been the source of supply and nobody would be able to say otherwise.

At the inquest, De Veulle's assistant, Mary Hicks — who De Veulle had nicknamed McGinty — gave evidence against him. Belcher made a statement to the police in which he admitted his role in the cocaine ring. He also told the inquest how he was "more addicted to heroin than anything else" and said of his drug dealing via the chemist, "I don't look upon it as any more despicable than selling a bottle of whisky at an over-charged rate, after time". His attitude was indicative of the way many people, both consumers and suppliers, felt about drugs at the time.

# DOPE KINGS OF LONDON

The inquest jury found that Billie Carleton had died from an accidental overdose of cocaine, given to her by Reggie De Veulle "in a culpable and negligent manner". Utterly dismayed, De Veulle was arrested and remanded in Brixton Prison ahead of a trial at the Old Bailey, where he was defended by the legendary barrister Huntly Jenkins.

At trial, Jenkins argued that it was doubtful whether "people accustomed to taking drugs thought that they were doing anything very grave, because it was only since the war that cocaine and opium had been prohibited drugs. Until then, drug-taking was not a crime. It might have been a mortal sin, but it was not a crime." In any case, he pointed out, the experts could not prove beyond doubt that Billie had died as a result of a cocaine overdose, therefore even if Reggie had supplied the drugs, he could not be found culpable for her death.

Thanks to the lawyer, De Veulle was found not guilty of manslaughter, but he pleaded guilty to conspiracy to supply cocaine, along with Ada Lau Ping. De Veulle was given a sentence of eight months in prison, without hard labour, owing to health problems.

Even though the judge accepted that De Veulle had not supplied the drugs to Billie Carleton for profit, he was given the country's longest drugs sentence yet. "Traffic in the deadly drug is a most pernicious thing," he ruled. "It leads to sordid, depraved, and disgusting practices. There is evidence in this case that, following the practice of this habit are disease, depravity, crime, insanity, despair and death."

Other theories have since emerged about the true cause of Billie Carleton's death. Marek Kohn, who wrote the seminal account of the affair, *Dope Girls*, in 1992, argued that the actress may have taken heroin supplied by Lionel Belcher accidentally or, more likely, a barbiturate or a sleeping tablet to help her sleep after such a stimulating day. Both of which could have accounted for the heavy snoring heard by the maid. Deaths from cocaine, in contrast, tend to be fast and violent as the body's organs rapidly collapse.

In any case, the scandal drew even more public attention onto the issue of drugs, cocaine in particular. At the end of the trial, Judge Salter held up a phial of the drug and remarked on how little was needed to cause death. "I thought some mistake had been made," he said, "when it was stated this was a fatal dose of cocaine. But it was not a mistake, and to take the drug in such casual manner between the finger and thumb makes it amazing to me that accidents do not happen much more frequently."

Following the case, the Press again began to write about the dangers of narcotics. There were new warnings of a German plot to undermine the nation by flooding it with cocaine, with young women its particular victims. As an article in the *Daily Express* had it, "You will find the woman dope fiend in Chelsea, in Mayfair, and Maida Vale. An obscure traffic is pursued in certain doubtful teashops. The sale of certain beauty specifics is only a mask for the illicit traffic in certain drugs. The queer, bizarre, rather brilliant bachelor girl is a frequent victim to the insidious advances of the female dope fiend."

The *Daily Mail*, insisting that cocaine was indeed more of a problem for women than men, said the drug was "a fashionable habit, an artificial war product which will disappear with the return of more normal conditions". Nevertheless, it was clear that the problem could not be solved in the coming years by relying on the now-defunct wartime regulations of DORA 40B.

While the issue of drugs legislation caused some fairly intense political debate before, during and after the war — many considered new laws to be completely unnecessary — the strictures of the Hague Convention of 1912, otherwise known as the International Opium Convention, had to be ratified after being incorporated into the Treaty of Versailles. Until that point, the United Kingdom had chosen not to follow the United States, Holland and China, among others, by implementing the agreement it had signed up to before the conflict. To comply with the peace agreement, it was made law under the sweeping Dangerous Drugs Act 1920, which also incorporated the DORA 40B restrictions.

The new Act applied not only to military personnel, but to all citizens and covered cocaine, heroin, morphine, raw opium, and some barbiturates. Offences under the act included unlawful production, import, export, possession, sale and distribution of the drugs. The Act created a new black market for drugs, but was targeted at large drugs companies as well as minor criminals. For example, the London firm T Whiffen & Sons had in 1916 made around £469,000, mostly by supplying some 650,000 ounces of morphine to smugglers who sold it on the illicit Chinese market. By 1922, earnings from morphine had dropped to just £21,000 on sales of about fifty thousand ounces. As we shall see, legitimate manufacturers in Europe would quickly become major drivers of the illegal trade.

The legislation would be the last major drugs law to be introduced until the Dangerous Drugs Act 1964 — some forty-four years later — and marked the start in earnest of a war on drugs that would have its greatest intensity between 1920 and 1925, after which the gradual decline of the club scene coupled with the effects of the Great Depression reduced drug use and pushed addicts and their suppliers deeper into the shadows.

There were a handful of amendments. Tougher penalties and new search powers for the police were granted in 1923; controls on the importation of coca leaf and cannabis were introduced in 1925; and the possession of cannabis was banned in 1928. The drugs classification system that we know today, separating narcotics by their danger levels in classes A-C, was not created until the 1971 Misuse of Drugs Act. That is symptomatic of the fact that many people (police, legislators and journalists included) were confused about the different effects of 'dope' — a word used interchangeably to cover almost all types of illicit substances. For example, there were some examples in newspaper reports of women using cocaine to drug men asleep before stealing their possessions. Such a plot using a powerful stimulant like cocaine would be almost impossible to carry out.

The drugs war was by no means total. The Act still allowed doctors to prescribe morphine, cocaine and heroin to addicts (on the advice of the Departmental Committee on Morphine and Heroin Addiction, chaired by Sir Humphrey Rolleston, then President of the Royal College of Physicians. The body was known as the Rolleston Committee), so long as it was done under a course of treatment rather than merely to satiate the addiction. This became known, for the next forty years, as the "British System" an almost unique approach to the drugs issue. It was, of course, exploited by a string of unscrupulous medics and bringing them to justice was sometimes just as difficult as dealing with organised crime gangs.

For example, one of the first cases brought to court under DORA 40B had been that of Dr Reginald Nitch Smith. The West End physician had been supplying heroin to Deborah Platt, the wife of an officer in the Coldstream Guards, and had found himself under the spotlight after she was charged with shoplifting to fund her habit. Nitch Smith ultimately faced no criminal penalty, but he was struck off in 1917. Another medic, Samuel Grahame Connor, was investigated for more than seven years (at times by the scourge of the drugs underworld, Detective Inspector Walter Burmby) before he was brought to court in 1926 for failing to keep proper records in his Dangerous Drugs Register. He was found guilty and sentenced to six months in prison, although that was overturned on appeal and he paid a £200 fine. Connor was, however, stripped of his license to dispense drugs and consequently went out of business.

Another grey area was that just because somebody was buying, shipping and selling narcotics, it didn't necessarily make them a criminal. While today almost everybody who comes into contact with narcotics is involved in some sort of crime, when the Dangerous Drugs Act was brought into force, legitimate medicinal products containing cocaine and morphia were still being made in European factories, notably in Hamburg and Rotterdam, as well as in France and Switzerland. Independent traders could legitimately purchase these goods and export them from the country. In many cases, the law was only broken once they were shipped to a location where the person in possession of the drugs was not authorised to have them. It was a loophole exploited by criminals for more than a decade before the League of Nations finally agreed to implement further international controls. Even then, as we shall see, drug traffickers found ways around the law.

In terms of enforcement in Britain, the entire drugs issue was overseen by the Home Office 'Drugs Branch' (although no such official title existed until the 1930s) under Sir Malcolm Delevingne and his chief expert, MD Perrins. The Metropolitan Police's Criminal Investigation Department (CID) carried out its own independent investigations, often led by Detective Inspector Walter Burmby.

While there was no centralised Drugs Squad as such, the main stations overseeing Soho and Mayfair, Vine Street and Marlborough Street, did have specialist officers, some of whom regularly took on the dangerous task of going undercover. There was also, based at Vine Street, a Vice Squad, which was for decades riddled with corruption.[4] The Met also had Chemist Inspection Officers, who kept tabs on pharmacies, while the Home Office had scientists who were able to grade and categorise seized drugs. That being said, the regulation of pharmacies was not a priority and as time went on most faced fewer inspections.

The rapid implementation of Britain's drugs ban was remarkable. In the space of just five years, Britain went from gleefully allowing some of its most venerated institutions to flog drugs to soldiers, to almost entirely outlawing the consumption and sale of narcotics by its citizens. But powerful habits had already been formed and demand in a victorious Britain re-invigorated by the jazz age was high.

While dodgy chemists had previously been quite happy to supply drug addicts and their middlemen like Reggie De Veulle, the new punishments were now not worth the hassle — and most could not have kept up with demand even if they'd wanted to. Instead, a highly profitable and purely criminal market emerged in which people were willing to take great risks. Britain had invented its first drug dealers.

---

[1] The original legislation was drafted in consultation with Sir Vernon Kell, director of MO5(g), later to be renamed MI5. It would be nearly two decades before his agency would be called upon to investigate allegations of a vast drug trafficking plot (see Chapters 15 and 16).

[2] Meyrick herself was later jailed for fifteen months for bribing a Vice Squad officer, George Goddard, to the tune of nearly £20,000. She died in 1933 from the Spanish Flu.

[3] In 1922, Lau Ping Yau, whose wife Ada had died from tuberculosis in November 1920, was arrested alongside a number of other opium smokers. He was ultimately deported and described as "one of the principals in the opium traffic".

[4] This was the case in which George Goddard was jailed for taking tens of thousands of pounds in bribes from night club legend and vice queen Kate Meyrick. An internal investigation in 1931 led to disciplinary action being taken against forty three officers, with twenty seven of them being sacked.

# 2. SNOW QUEENS

**M**ay Roberts glanced over the back seat of the car as it zipped along Fleet Street. She was sure that the black taxi had been following them for at least the last mile as they drove from the West End back towards Limehouse. Now that she thought about it, the tail had first appeared in the East End at the very start of their evening.

May could see the driver, a squat man whose face, framed by his flat cap and the dark collar of his neck-high jacket, was etched in concentration. The two large gentlemen crammed into the back seat looked agitated and were urging the driver on. Coppers, May correctly assumed. The cab accelerated and tooted its horn. May slapped Albert on the shoulder and barked at him to put his foot down.

Albert, at the wheel, appeared as oblivious as ever. His head was always in the clouds. Probably it was the perpetual brain fog caused by long-term opium smoking, but perhaps also some grim memory from the war played on his mind — men rarely spoke of such things. In any case, it meant that Albert's mental awareness was on something of a time lag. But he could drive a car well enough, so for May he served a purpose. There was also the matter of his well-connected brother overseas.

The commandeered taxi managed to draw alongside them and May could now get a better look at the two passengers, a pair of handsome, well-built policemen in plain clothes, who motioned frantically for Albert to pull over. Albert seemed to freeze, considering for a moment what he should do.

In the next moment, the pursuers tried to make Albert's decision for him. Ordering the driver to speed up, the officers directed him to nudge in front of their target and slam on the brakes. Albert anticipated the maneuver and swerved around the taxi, continuing along Fleet Street. Unfortunately for Albert, the traffic at Ludgate Junction was unusually heavy and he had no choice but to come to a stop anyway, ending the short pursuit with no injuries and no damage done. He decamped from the car and legged it back to his home in Euston Square, where he was soon picked up. Albert Ellis, with his black curly hair, moustache and pince-nez glasses, cut a rather distinctive figure. When stopped in the street, he claimed he had been to the cinema with friends and was just returning home. Albert had no reasonable explanation as to why he was pouring with sweat and badly out of breath.

The date was December 29, 1922, and May Roberts and Albert Ellis had just become the first drug dealers to be arrested in Britain following a car chase.

SNOW QUEENS

May Roberts, aged thirty-one at the time, was charged with possession of opium. She gave her address as a squalid flat in Limehouse Causeway, giving rise to her subsequent nickname in the press — The White Queen of Limehouse. Ellis, thirty-five, was charged with supplying the drug. In addition to the twelve cakes of opium found in the car, worth about £100, police found a cloakroom ticket in his luggage which was used to retrieve a case left at London Bridge station. Inside the case were eight small wraps of cocaine, weighing in total five and a quarter pounds, although the powder was only 44.6 percent pure.

At Bow Street magistrates' court, the striking young woman argued that she had never actually been in possession of the drugs. They were, after all, found on the floor of the car. Ellis denied having any knowledge of either the opium in the car or the cocaine in the case. The *Pall Mall Gazette* reported how three Chinese men looked on from the back of the court as the "stylishly dressed" Roberts argued against the evidence presented by Detective Charles Owen, now back in full uniform.

Owen told how Roberts and Ellis had indeed been followed from the East End to the West End and halfway back again. The officers had watched as Roberts left her home at 6.10pm and walked towards a garage off the East India Dock Road. A car was waiting there and May climbed in. The officers quickly hailed a taxi and followed at a discrete distance. It was probably the first time any British copper had uttered the now cliched line, "Follow that car."

They watched as their target pulled up outside an address in Wellington Street, Westminster, from where the woman got out and walked to the Strand. It was at that point that a man appeared, placed a parcel on the floor of the car, exchanged a few words with the driver, Ellis, and then strolled towards a pub side-by-side with Roberts. When they came out again, Ellis drove them both to the Waldorf Hotel in Aldwych where the man got out. The car then made its fateful journey to Fleet Street.

Owen then described the dramatic arrests, admitting that his ploy to bring the chase to an end had initially failed, but insisting that Roberts had all but confessed to possession of the opium at the scene. "I am a police officer and suspect you of having prohibited drugs in your possession," Owen recalled his words in court. "What have you there in that parcel?"

"I don't know," Roberts replied. But after being told she would be taken to court, she allegedly added, "Don't do that, it is opium." She then admitted she was not authorised to have the drug. Further damning evidence was found in the form of £31 and 10s in notes in her bag and in a belt wrapped around her body.

Ellis also managed to incriminate himself. When charged at Bow Street, he replied "Not guilty," but then allegedly added, "I have been the mug, it was not my stuff. I had best get it over. Can I be dealt with here? I don't mind if it's a fine."

The hearing was adjourned for a week to allow the pair to formalise their defence cases and for the police to carry out further investigations. When the court reconvened, it heard that both individuals had Chinese connections. Ellis had been a Company-Quartermaster-Sergeant in the Chinese Labour Corps and was of previous good character. May Roberts, however, was more obviously suspect. She had ditched her husband back in her native Liverpool and moved in with a Chinese man, Wun Loo, in the East End. Roberts had long been suspected of drug trafficking by police in the northern city and was known to associate with opium smugglers. In fact, she was credited by the authorities with being a key underworld figure who had negotiated a peace deal between a number of the city's warring gangs after her first husband was killed.

Edmund O'Connor, the lawyer acting for Roberts, offered a bold defence by suggesting that a distinction should be drawn between opium being transited from the East End to the West End of London and vice versa, because the drug heading East would be destined for Chinese consumption. The substance was, he argued, "as necessary to the Chinese as tobacco to the British". The argument didn't wash. Roberts was sentenced to six months' imprisonment and fined £30, while Ellis was handed six months for each charge, to run concurrently, and fined £40.

Later, in an interview with the paper which coined her nickname, *Reynolds News*, Roberts gave a robust explanation of her fondness for Chinese men. "Whatever may be his faults the Chinaman has the power of fascinating a woman and of holding her in a way the White man cannot do," she reportedly said. "There is a subtle charm, a romance and a poetry about his lovemaking that makes the efforts of the average Westerner seem ridiculous. I have been told again and again not to have anything to do with Chinamen; that they have a degrading effect. I cannot see it." The paper described her as "absolutely fearless," handy with a pistol and able to "take care of herself in the roughest company".

# DOPE KINGS OF LONDON

The White Queen was back in the news again in November that year. A young, pretty and equally dangerous woman named Julia Kitt, twenty-eight, had also found herself before the magistrate. Like May Roberts, Julia was originally from Liverpool and was a good friend of the White Queen. So good in fact that when the latter was released from prison she went to live in Poplar with Julia, her Chinese husband Choy Ah Kitt, and their two children.

Choy Ah ran a shop, but he was also suspected of supplying opium and cocaine to revellers in the West End, using Julia as a courier who travelled by car just as May Roberts had done. At times, it was claimed, Julia had been in possession of as much as one pound of cocaine, but detectives had never managed to catch her with such a quantity. At the time of her arrest, Choy Ah Kitt was in Hamburg, meeting with the source of their supply. According to one July 1924 police report Mr Kitt, although not convicted, was a "cunning, crafty and persistent drug trafficker. He left his wife and two children about nine months ago and is at present acting as an agent for Choy Loy [a major trafficker] at Rotterdam".

The *Sunday Post* described Julia as "expensively dressed and owning a luxurious car". It said she was a "well-known figure in Limehouse. It is four years since she came there mysteriously, but to none would she ever relate the story of her downfall. Secretly she was ashamed of her position, but she had gone too far to draw back with safety". Julia had, the paper claimed, "abandoned herself to gaiety" after arriving in the capital, and it wasn't long before she met Choy Ah and agreed to marry him. It was then that she began her two-year involvement with the dope trade, being driven, like May

Roberts, back and forth to the West End to deliver drugs to its "notorious resorts".

The police delayed their decision to pounce for many weeks, because they wanted to uncover the source of her supply, which they increasingly began to believe was in Hamburg. "Julia Kitt is known to have made a great deal of money out of her drug trafficking," the report concluded. The *Empire News* gave Julia a nickname similar to May's moniker: "The Snow Queen of Limehouse," describing her as "the most successful drug-runner in the Metropolis". It added, "One minute, Julia was Mrs Kitt, the downtrodden wife of a Chinese, seeking relaxation or temporary forgetfulness in the bars of Chinatown; the next she was a beautiful, fashionably-dressed woman-about-town, sweeping gaily into club or dance hall...[Julia] invested in a fine-looking car of her own in which to 'run' the dope," and had an "ability to wear expensive clothes well" as well as to copy "society speech and manner".

Undercover police had been watching Julia for months, as she flitted between the dive bars and nightclubs of Soho and Leicester Square. One evening, a Detective Crisp waited as she left a pub on the West India Dock Road and clambered into a car. Detectives Dyer and Morris picked up the trail and followed Julia and her male companion as they went to two more boozers in Pennyfields and Limehouse Causeway. As they stepped out of the final premises, they were arrested.

Newspaper reports noted how Kitt had been dressed "expensively" on the night of her arrest, but when she appeared in the dock at Thames magistrates' court the following morning, she was decked out in "the oldest of clothes". It appeared to be a ploy for sympathy and perhaps an attempt to learn a lesson from the earlier court appearance of May Roberts.

The detectives had found 3.6 grains of cocaine in her handbag (a single grain is equal to less than one-tenth of a gram), although Julia claimed it was not there when the bag was taken from her. At her home, officers found boracic powder, a popular cutting agent. Like May Roberts, she too received six months' imprisonment for being in unauthorised possession of cocaine. "The West End has been troubled a great deal with this terrible traffic," the magistrate, JAR Cairns warned, "and I can promise that in this area no trouble will be spared to ensure that the traffic is not transferred from the West End to the East End".

The two East End dope queens made column inches largely because the women were suspected of selling what were then very significant quantities of drugs in the West End. But unknown to the public at the time the cases had an even greater significance.

Detectives continued to probe the associates of Roberts and Kitt for the next decade, and would uncover an international web of drug traffickers centered around two enigmatic and dangerous operators named Max Faber and Laurent Deleglise. For one dedicated police officer, the failure to bring them down would become one of his greatest regrets.

# 3. BIG MAXIE

Gazing out from the photograph with his big dark eyes, wide mouth, and luxurious black beard, Laurent Deleglise would undoubtedly have been a pleasing sight to some. But for Detective Inspector Walter Burmby the handsome Frenchman was an odious vision. It was not just that he was a nemesis, another name and mugshot in a growing dossier of dope peddlers he was desperate to bring to justice. Deleglise represented the much wider problem of the growing band of international drug traffickers who so often appeared to be just out of reach of the law.

Not much is known about Walter Herbert Burmby. Born in London in 1879, Burmby's father James had been a police officer and Walter duly joined the force himself in May 1904. He married his first wife, Edith, in 1908, but he was soon widowed. Burmby married again in 1918, to Rosa, the widow of a German man named Kampes. What happened next is not exactly clear, but Burmby certainly knew tragedy. Neither marriage bore children and his second wife also died young, in 1944.

In the meantime, Burmby became a detective sergeant and then a detective inspector based at New Scotland Yard, where he chiefly investigated drugs cases. His name first appeared in the Press after the arrest of the actress Cissie Loftus for possession of opium in November 1922, but he became most famous for bringing down the gangster Eddie Manning. Towards the end of his career, he was promoted to divisional inspector of D Division (covering Marylebone) at Scotland Yard in 1929, which warranted his mention in *The Times* as the officer who "for years [was] the special officer in charge of investigations in connexion with the drug traffic". He retired in June 1931 and died in 1960, aged eighty-one.

Burmby did not produce a memoir, which is a shame because he developed an encyclopedic knowledge of the world's most active international criminals. But his name and signature can be found across dozens of surviving reports on some of the globe's biggest drug traffickers of the 1920s.

The implementation of the Dangerous Drugs Act 1920 caused what is probably still the steepest law enforcement learning curve of all time. Almost overnight, the focus switched from dealing with wayward chemists and script doctors, to tracking a growing band of international adventurers with dozens of aliases who flitted between continents with ease, arranging drug shipments from one side of the Atlantic to the other. Unlike today, when most of the world's cocaine supply must be brokered at source in the growing countries, Colombia, Peru and Bolivia, and heroin in places like Turkey, Iran and Afghanistan, all the major drug deals took place in Western Europe, mainly in Germany, Switzerland, France and Holland, where factories continued to churn out medicinal products.

This meant the traffickers had a range of options for supply. They could buy legitimate, manufactured products and ship them abroad, often perfectly legally, with the crime only taking place in the importing country; negotiate a deal for raw materials and either ship them immediately or process them in their own illicit factories; or purchase either legitimate products and repackage them, or create counterfeit goods from scratch using raw materials.

Often, it could all be done through official channels with major suppliers, while sometimes deals were reached with corrupt employees. In many cases, the factories were not only fully complicit with the criminals but — particularly in the second half of the decade — the criminals ran their own factories as a front to legally import raw materials to Europe. This practice reached its zenith in the heyday of the Eliopoulos Cartel, as we shall see later.

In the early days, the Hoffman La Roche factory in Basel, for example, was happy to sell to smugglers and would even willingly package its goods under false labels if requested. Cocaine products made by CH Boehringer & Sohn of Hamburg, and CF Boehringer & Soehne of Mannheim, were frequently to be found among smugglers' loads. Boehringer also, perfectly legally, provided raw materials to factories in Holland which, again while legal, only existed to produce heroin for drug dealers.

Many seized opium products also came in branded packaging, although it wasn't always clear where they had been produced. There was the Lam Kee Hop brand, which came in tins marked with a chicken, or a chicken and an elephant (thirteen ounces of this type was once found in the personal baggage of the wife of the Chinese Consul in San Francisco). The Lo Fok Kee line was marked with a cock or an eagle, while there was also a Buddha brand with the name Ying. Another bootleg brand marked "CF Boehringer, Mannheim" with a peacock or skull and crossbones on the tin, presumably to differentiate it from the firm's legitimate goods, was seized in huge quantities in India, China and the Dutch East Indies.

There were, of course, thousands of smugglers and even more ways to hide the goods. The quantities involved were usually far smaller than are found today, so methods of transportation included soldering small tins of drugs inside larger tins filled with olive oil. Drugs could also come in via shoe heels, hidden inside rubber bags concealed under clothing, or in the hollow handles of umbrellas. Sometimes, the smugglers waited on ships and threw their goods overboard as they approached the dock, where they would be collected by waiting colleagues. Many of these techniques are still practiced today.

A report in a 1922 edition of the *Shields Daily News* sheds some light on the methods used to bring drugs into the country. One trick was apparently to hide cocaine and opium in the stems of artificial flowers landed at British ports — in one case opium was ironically secreted in the stems of artificial poppies. Drugs were also hidden in the hollowed-out middles of seasonal vegetables shipped from France and Italy.

The Germans, however, appeared to be the sneakiest of all the traffickers. In one case, a phial of snow was found inside a stuffed Dachshund on transit through the Rhineland. On another occasion, it was found that one in ten bottles in a consignment of ink contained carefully camouflaged cocaine hidden behind correctly printed labels. "Only the German mind could have sunk to the level," the article continued, "of using models of the Whitehall Cenotaph for smuggling dope into this country, but the French Customs authorities recently stopped a transit through French territory, a box of miniature cenotaphs that were found to be filled with cocaine." The growing list of illicit hiding places included German sausages, cheese, opera hats, briquettes and firelighters.

Huge quantities of drugs from Europe were also entering Egypt, China and India. One shifty character, said to hang around the docks in Rangoon, would collect small consignments smuggled in by sailors and hide them in the empty socket behind his eye patch. "These men (and women)," one newspaper article said at the time, "are the rank and file of the Dope-smuggling Hierarchy. Enormous numbers of them are held in slavery to those higher up, because they have become addicts and must peddle to earn their daily supply. The higher ranks in the hierarchy, though far more dangerous, are infinitely harder to catch."

Walter Burmby, along with Sir Malcolm Delevingne and MD Perrins at the Home Office, strived to do just that. But they struggled to keep up with the methods being employed. For example, in 1922 a man named Hertz, the head of Bayer's drug department, was suspected of personally trafficking cocaine from Germany to Britain and America, but it wasn't possible to bring a prosecution due to lack of evidence. And although it never became public knowledge, Walter Burmby at one point suspected the Glasgow-born professional boxer Walter 'Wally' Ross and his trainer father Robert Ross were secret drug dealers.

He believed they were travelling to France and Belgium "on the pretense of having boxing engagements to fulfil" when in fact they were bringing back cocaine to sell in the West End. The case never became public and was consigned to Burmby's files. It soon became obvious that the only hope of tackling the trade was through international cooperation.

Partly thanks to the global reach of the British Empire, this was easier than might be expected. In addition, the Metropolitan Police's Special Branch, a forerunner of the foreign intelligence arm MI6, already had officers based in major European cities such as Rotterdam and Antwerp. Alongside their core role of keeping tabs on anarchists, communists and subversives, they began to monitor drug traffickers and the growing legions of international adventurers, card sharps and other rogues who thrived between the wars.

An example of the quality of intelligence Special Branch was able to gather can be found in a report from the early 1920s, generated after the Belgian authorities furnished the British with a long list of convicted and suspected drug traffickers operating in the country. At the time, most of the names meant little and belonged to mostly small-time dealers rather than international operators. A separate list of card sharps and other rogues was also provided, because Special Branch wanted to know which of these criminals might be in Calcutta during an imminent visit by the Prince of Wales, later to be Edward VIII. There was obviously a real concern that the royal was a prime mark for swindlers.

One of the tricksters, Rudolf Stallman, was a German who famously posed as a baron to fleece gamblers at casinos, and who later worked as a French spy using the codename Rex. "My informant states that Rudolf Stallman is leaving Paris shortly for Persia and from there proceeding to Calcutta," read one September 1921 report sent to the Special Branch team. Another person of interest was the notorious Australian fraudster William Charles Warren, known as Bludger Bill. Other dodgy characters included a British man from Burnham-on-Crouch, in Essex, named Charles Henry Booth, who had been convicted of importing cocaine to Calcutta in 1913.

Booth was later linked to the case of Laurent Deleglise, which emerged thanks to Britain's best bet for tackling the international operators — Canada. This long-standing part of the British Empire, which joined the Commonwealth in 1931, was a key territory for the global traffickers. Drug laws were lax there and Montreal was a major passenger route to Europe. It was usually safer to bring drugs destined for New York into Montreal and then transport them over the border than to smuggle directly in the United States.

Britain's cooperation with Canada was therefore vital from a law enforcement point of view. The wider investigation into the drugs network involving May Roberts, Julia Kitt and Albert Ellis is a case in point.


One of the world's leading drug traffickers almost — but not quite — fell into Walter Burmby's lap. In December 1923,

Cortlandt Starnes, Commissioner of the Royal Canadian Mounted Police (RCMP) wrote to Sir Wyndham Childs, the Assistant Commissioner of the Met, asking for assistance in tracing a notorious and elusive criminal named Max Faber, a man Walter Burmby already suspected of supplying Roberts, Ellis and Kitt. The case was duly passed to the specialist drugs detective.

Max Faber was truly an international man of mystery who was obsessively tracked by Burmby, as well as by MD Perrins at the Home Office. Known by a variety of pseudonyms, including Sheba Maxie, Big Man, Big M and Big Maxie, Faber was born in Grodno, Poland, in July 1892. Described by the Canadians as being about five feet and three inches tall, with dark brown eyes a long "Semitic" nose, a round chin and dark brown hair, one report said he had "all the appearance of a Jew". More pertinent to the man's character, there was a scar on the left side of his forehead and another on his left hand, although the origins of these injuries were a mystery.

Faber lived, at least for a time, at 20 Demontigny Street, East Montreal. He also had a wife in the city who was installed in a property in Colonial Avenue, where he kept two ex-police dogs for protection. Faber was believed to have sailed to Britain en route to Hamburg on December 9, 1923, possibly in the company of another trafficker named Paul Stone, alias Paul Webster, alias Harry Jakes, alias Harry Stone, alias Charles Johnson, alias Paul Rupert, alias William Mack, alias JR Webster. Stone was a dangerous criminal with a long rap sheet to match his list of fake identities.

Born in Honolulu to American parents, records showed that Stone held a US passport when he visited Britain in 1920.

Described as sallow, with brown hair, Stone was more recognisable for his other physical traits — his right little finger was missing and he had two gold front teeth in his upper jaw, one on either side. Stone had several convictions for drug trafficking in Canada and had last served a prison term in Ontario, after escaping from a jail in Atlanta, before being released in November 1923. The prison warden believed Stone would travel to Germany to buy drugs as soon as he was free. Together, Faber and Stone were a formidable duo.

"Faber is a particularly important and elusive trafficker in drugs, whose methods of importation we are most anxious to discover," Starnes wrote. "He is the head of what is known as 'Maxie's Gang' in Montreal."

After a previous trip to Liverpool in 1922, the Canadians believed Faber had returned with drugs worth around $80,000, although the Liverpool police could find no trace of his supposed visit to the city. A more recent voyage had seen Faber return from Europe on the SS Melita. This time he had bought with him a "stage girl" described as a "clever dancer, speaking French, German and English," as well as several German export licenses. Faber had also apparently tried to recruit the purser of the Melita into his gang. The girl, it later transpired, dumped the gangster and went to New York, hoping to return to the stage. She had found Faber "disagreeable".

Cortlandt Starnes was desperate for more information on Maxie Faber and his associates. The Canadians believed Faber's method was to use stewards and crew based mainly on Cunard Line ships to transport shipments of between twenty-five and one hundred ounces at a time, often secreted in boxes of soap. But they were certain of little.

"Hitherto we have not known under what name he has travelled and he is said to have three passports," Starnes wrote. "And also while we suspect him to be a Russian Jew, we are not sure of his nationality." Starnes was able to provide a lurid description of Faber, which included such details as: "Hair, greasy black, long pompadour, greasy and falls over ears and face; high cheek bones; nose rather prominent; face appears rather transparent and flushed, especially on cheek bones; has bow legs. He usually dresses rather poorly, may have a fur hat (mink) and fur collar." A further description of Faber said he was "fairly well-built, loud voiced". And, Starnes added, Britain's police would have to work hard to catch him. "He is an exceptionally cunning scoundrel. In the drug traffic his part usually has been the handling of the money, leaving the passing of the poison to be performed by others."

All of this would have been of immense interest to Walter Burmby, who liked to keep track of his targets' personal associations and characteristics. But Starnes's report contained other revelations of even greater value. An informant for the Canadian police had unwittingly tied Max Faber to London's Dope Queens, May Roberts and Julia Kitt, by linking him to a fellow trafficker named David Ernest Ellis, also known as Harry Ellis, alias Lambert. David Ellis, it transpired, was the brother of Albert Ellis, and was known in the Montreal underworld as "The English Jew".

David Ellis was born in Hong Kong to British parents in February 1876. Just like his brother, he had a distinctive appearance — balding, with a dark complexion, a high forehead and pockmarked skin. David had one previous drugs conviction in Britain, dating back to 1915, when his wife Agnes had sent three cases stuffed with opium to the P&O shipping company, bound for Hong Kong. David was arrested under the Customs Act but was fined just £200.

The Canadians revealed how David Ellis had been working on a major drug deal in Hamburg with Maxie Faber when he heard of Albert's arrest alongside May Roberts. Their informant said David had raced to London to try and bail his brother out, but did not have the cash to do so. He then asked Faber to send half the stock they had accumulated in Hamburg to London and to sell the other half, in order to raise funds. Faber duly sent the drugs, but rather than help out the Ellis brothers he pocketed the cash and fled to Montreal. The double cross affected not only Ellis, but two London-based Chinese gangsters involved in the deal. This had apparently caused Faber to become persona non grata in certain parts of the East End. A further Canadian report in February 1924 said that "two Chinaman are waiting for Faber in London, England, to 'get him' for double-crossing them, and also fearing Ellis, he carries a gun".

This was a major intelligence coup for Burmby. He had overseen the original investigations into both May Roberts and Julia Kitt. Here was written confirmation from an independent force overseas that he had been right to believe the pair were two of London's most important drug traffickers. He was now confident that the cocaine found in the Roberts-Ellis case had been sent by David Ellis from Germany, David being the "mastermind" of the plot. However, contrary to the tale spun by the Canadian informant, the police in London did not believe that David had left Germany in a bid to bail his brother out, although Burmby felt it "quite possible" that Agnes had visited Albert in prison and communicated the situation to David (Albert's own wife, Ada, had long since obtained a separation order). Of course, all of this was in the past. But Starnes now gave Burmby something he might be able to act upon.

When David Ellis had left Europe with his brother in prison, he traveled to New York with twenty cans of opium, which he disposed of before heading to Montreal in a bid to get even with Faber. He also wanted to feel out Paul Stone about becoming his new agent in Montreal, now that Faber had unilaterally terminated their partnership. But by the time he reached the Canadian port city, Faber and Stone had already left on the SS Montclare, bound for Liverpool.[5] Burmby asked Special Branch to monitor the pair when their ship docked.

Max Faber did indeed arrive in Liverpool on December 15, 1923. There was no sign of his partner-in-crime, but then if Paul Stone had disguised his missing little finger with a glove and declined to bare his gold teeth, he might have been able to use one of his numerous identities to slip into the country.

Faber was followed by Special Branch officers as he made his way to London Euston by train and then when he took a taxi to the home of a Chinese man named Choy Loy, at 262 Burdett Road, Limehouse. Two days later, Faber left for Holland via Harwich. Neither Faber nor his four-foot black trunk was searched and he apparently had no idea he was being watched, although he did swap his bowler hat for a flat cap during the train journey to London. It was noted that in his Canadian passport, under the name Max Farber, the drug trafficker had a visa for Germany. He had told the immigration officer at Liverpool that he was a dye merchant and traveling to Germany on business.

Burmby and the drugs branch team at the Home Office now had evidence that Max Faber's interest in the British narcotics market had not ended with the arrests of May Roberts, Albert Ellis and Julia Kitt. In fact, the man Faber had lodged with in the East End, Choy Loy, was a known associate of Julia's erstwhile husband Choy Ah Kitt. The skillful observations by the Special Branch team (a Sgt Tansley wrote the reports) had exposed another tentacle of this international criminal network.

Choy Loy was born in Hong Kong in 1897 and settled in Limehouse in 1915. Five years later he began a series of international trips that led the authorities to believe he had set up a drug trafficking network. There was a six-month trip back to China in early 1920 and then a visit to Holland for only a matter of days. Loy visited Holland twice more in September and November. He visited China again in June 1923, returning to live with his Welsh-born wife, Violet Choy (formerly Milton), at 262 Burdett Road, an eight-bedroom property which he bought for £800. Further, frequent trips to Holland followed.

As well as working with Choy Ah Kitt, Choy Loy was closely associated with Lum Chong, the partner of May Roberts, and another man named Chan Nam, both of whom had left the country by the end of 1923 and were believed to be in Germany and Holland respectively.

# DOPE KINGS OF LONDON

Choy Loy described himself as a boarding house keeper, but the local police (K Division) were dismissive of this claim. Although well-educated and fluent in English, one report by Divisional Detective Inspector Ball, the head of the East End's CID, said, "When he first came here he was in poor circumstances and an associate of low class Chinese sailors and firemen. During the past four years however, he has become a fairly wealthy man, and there is no doubt he has obtained his money by trafficking in drugs and firearms."

Separately to the Faber investigation, MD Perrins at the Home Office knew that Special Branch was keeping tabs on members of Choy Loy's network in Holland, Germany and Belgium, including Choy Ah Kitt and Lum Chong (as we shall see, Choy Loy was by now thought to be a major global player). But in May 1924, Perrins got wind that K Division was set to pounce on the Burdett Road address, even though Walter Burmby was not keen on disrupting the network. Perrins feared the officers were not looking at the bigger picture. Loy might well have been a major player, but he was a link with an even bigger fish, Max Faber. If Loy was taken out, then Faber might have no reason to return to London, particularly after his disagreement with the other Chinese dealers.

Perrins wrote to Deputy Assistant Commissioner and head of the CID Sir Norman Kendal, filling him in on Faber's visit to London the previous December. Perrins also passed on Walter Burmby's doubts about striking prematurely. "It would be a calamity if he [Choy Loy] suspected anything at the present moment and we shall be much obliged if you will call your hounds off if they are on the scent," he wrote. "The

Hamburg police have butted in by arresting one of the gang and all their papers have been sent to London for safety!"

Perrin's missive went on to say that although he still owned the property, Choy Loy himself was now living in Margate, in Kent, where he was sending "frequent cablegrams" in code, much to the surprise of the postmaster. "We have been lucky to pick up the code and with further luck will shortly be able to hand the case over to you," Perrins wrote. "The case however is not sufficiently mature for even for 'discreet' enquiries."

Not only did Perrins' plea fall on death ears, but it seemed to fuel K Division's desire to take action and a warrant to search Burdett Road was obtained later that month. Perrins was at least allowed to come on the raid, and while no drugs were found Perrins was able to get his hands on Choy Loy's pocketbook, which detailed many of his contacts and meetings in London and Hamburg with "Big Man". Burmby and Perrins now had even more evidence on Max Faber.

The operation exposed tensions between the civilian Home Office oversight of the drugs issue and the police. One report of the raid mentioned acting on Perrins' "instructions". A handwritten note in the margins from a more senior officer asked for the passage to be deleted, adding that the officer had rather "discussed the matter with Mr Perrins". More importantly, just as Perrins had feared, the raid was the catalyst for Choy Loy fleeing the country altogether.

Meanwhile, the evidence within the pocketbook augmented details obtained from an unnamed Chinese informant in Hamburg some months previously. Its garbled text had read, "Maxtaber or Maxfabir or Big-Man is known as Gohman in Pennyfields, London, and he is [a] Jew, and he has a small shop in Hamburg and he is in partnership with Choy Loy. They both are in London now for supply any dangerous drugs to persons in London City from Holland and Hamburg by some cargo ship, and almost white crew on board cargo ship now, because the white crew are not much suspiciously, and if not in London it must be in the ports of England and Wales." The pocketbook confirmed the dates of Faber's time in the country, but there was no hard evidence against him.

Max Faber did return to Britain on at least one further occasion, in September 1924. Faber was recorded arriving at Folkestone, where his brown, crocodile leather Gladstone bag was searched to no avail. He was followed by Special Branch officers as he first made his way to Victoria station by train and then by taxi to Waterloo. Faber left the country in the early hours of the following morning from Southampton, aboard the SS Empress of France, bound for Montreal. Faber was described in a report by Walter Burmby as having a "black moustache (Charley Chaplin) slight side-boards, wearing black jacket, grey breeches, grey wolf stockings, black lace boots, tan leather overcoat with belt and a soft grey felt hat."

Faber had slipped the net, but the Canadians continued to ask the Metropolitan Police for assistance with stopping their most prolific drug smugglers.

Another long-term target was a man believed to be one of Max Faber's chief suppliers, the aforementioned Laurent Deleglise, or de L'Eglise, also known as Ernest Joules Grenout, a handsome Frenchman with a complete and utter disregard for the law.

# BIG MAXIE

Born near Rouen in 1891, Deleglise was the quintessential international scoundrel. He was first arrested in Louvier in 1909 as an accomplice to a robbery and sentenced to eight months in prison. Two years later, he was later arrested in Paris for forging coins. One of several surviving photographs of Deleglise was taken in Reading Gaol in November 1911, where he was serving a sentence for larceny, probably while operating as a card sharp. The photos showed him wearing a thick black beard and black hat. Deleglise was kicked out of the country the following year and as Walter Burmby noted, "This is the only occasion on which he came into our hands."

Deleglise was wanted by the German police as early as 1914. In a notice circulated to the police in Britain, they described him as a teacher of languages, of strong build with a "very long, long black beard, yellow eyes, straight forehead, large mouth, dimples in skin, dark healthy complexion." Said to be an "anarchist," Deleglise was also "fond of wearing officers' yellow leggings with yellow boots, [and] black and white striped English riding pants". Deleglise also had a criminal record for deserting the army (presumably in France) and was at one point arrested in Montreal for helping to arrange an abortion. His first drugs charge was in 1915 for illegally selling narcotics. Four years later, he tried to obtain an import license from Canada's Trade and Commerce department, but was arrested for bribery after sending a box of cigars containing a $100 bill to an official.

He was first convicted of illegally importing drugs in July 1920 and sentenced to pay a $1,500 fine. The drugs, worth $12,000, were confiscated. But Deleglise probably got away with far more. By the mid-1920s, the Canadians believed him to be "one of the largest international traffickers in narcotics in America" and estimated that he had made some $250,000 profit, around £3.1million in today's terms.

Deleglise had been naturalised in Montreal as a British subject in December 1917 and by March 1924 his career had seen him pick up police interest in Italy, Switzerland, France, England, Belgium and Canada and, most recently, New York. In that city, Deleglise was known as Ernest Grenout and he was wanted alongside his lover, Malvine Edwigge Buzzi, or Buzze, although the details of the charge were vague. A memo to London from the NYPD's narcotics division in March 1924, said Deleglise had recently been arrested for drug trafficking in Zurich, and described him as a "narcotic trafficker, counterfeiter and anarchist". At the time, the British authorities were reasonably certain that he had been spending time in a sanatorium in Skodsborg, Denmark.

The British interest in the case was as much about keeping Deleglise out of the country as bringing him to justice, and Sir Malcolm Delevingne made sure that all British consulates were told that although Deleglise might have a British passport, he was not to be allowed to travel to England again, after being spotted in London earlier in the year.

The cunning and charming Deleglise had established a sophisticated smuggling operation, making use of several corrupt officials on the Cunard and Thompson lines, none of whom knew about the others. In this way, the network could not be brought down by a single arrest.

Deleglise specialized in morphine, which he generally obtained on visits to England (at least in the early years of his trade), although he rarely, if ever, touched the drugs. Instead, he employed a middleman named Davis to take the drugs to sailors in measures of between five hundred and one thousand ounces.

One of these mules was the chief steward on the SS Saturnia, whose mother lived near Glasgow. Davis would await a wire from Deleglise advising him of the amount to be transported. The package would then be taken to the crewman's family home, where he would pick it up and store it in his baggage. Shortly before the ship docked in Montreal, the baggage would be moved to a pre-determined empty cabin. Once docked, the chief steward would invite the Customs man for a drink in his cabin. Another of Deleglise's agents would then board the ship and remove the drugs from the hiding place.

It was an ingenious system which ensured as little contact as possible between the conspirators. When family members were not available on the British side, other middlemen, including a butcher, were used.

Another of Deleglise's contacts in Britain was thought to be an Essex man named Charles Henry Booth, who had been convicted of trying to import cocaine to Calcutta in 1913. By 1921, he was back in his home county and apparently mailing packages of opium to Deleglise in Montreal. The drugs were later distributed to local suppliers, including Max Faber and Paul Stone. Drugs were also sent onwards to New York, mostly to Lucky Luciano's mob.

More than likely, the Customs man knew he was being intentionally distracted and might even have accepted a bribe. Other police officers and customs officials certainly did. According to an informant, on one occasion Deleglises'

Montreal bagman encountered a problem when a new officer on the gate began watching him closely. The bagman simply stepped into the Customs office, placed two tins 20lbs bags of morphine on the desk and smoked a cigarette. He emerged a few minutes later and the officer assumed he must have been cleared. In fact, the bagman had simply bribed the desk officer, probably for as little as $10, the going rate.

Some did not want cash bungs but were equally happy to turn a blind eye and accept drinks, meals or favours, such as men sent to do odd jobs around their private homes. One Customs officer in particular was known to steal some of the drugs for himself, which the smugglers could do nothing about. He managed to buy himself a smart three-story apartment house in the north of the town using the proceeds.

Deleglise also employed a wide network of smugglers who booked themselves onto ferries, had their baggage loaded but then failed to board the boat. The 'passenger' would then wire for his baggage from another town, hoping that Customs would not go to the effort of forcing open his trunk, or that an officer would accept a bribe. For example, Edward Ryan, from New York, and William F Reilly, from Boston, had both been found guilty of smuggling drugs into Canada from Europe aboard the Empress of France at Quebec in December 1920, both being fined $1,000 each. They were thought to be agents of Deleglise.

Another of Deleglise's dupes had been Dr Antoine Lortie, who in October 1922 sailed from Canada to Europe. Also on the SS Cornishman at the time was Montreal cattleman Maurice Genin, who got off at Liverpool and made his way separately to Paris, where he met Lortie and his wife,

Geraldine. It was believed that they were given drugs to smuggle back to Canada. Dr Lortie, of Montreal, had long been suspected of smuggling drugs on a large scale. He made several trips to Europe each year and was even suspected of roping his sister, Corrine, into the plot. She was found guilty of smuggling one thousand ounces and fined $500. Again, Deleglise was thought to be the mastermind.

One of the Frenchman's most successful smugglers, and a leading criminal in his own right, was George William Henri Joseph Howe, a Belgian who claimed to have a British father from Kent.

Born in Brussels in 1888, Howe had lived in Kent from the age of eleven and succeeded in using the claim about his father to obtain a Canadian passport while later living in Ottawa. But the British, under the direction of Sir Malcolm Delevingne, MD Perrins and Superintendant James McBrien, the head of Special Branch, were somewhat more forensic and succeeded in having his claims rejected, after finding Howe's father had in fact been born in France.

Howe was described as handsome, standing at five feet and seven inches, with a light brown complexion, grey eyes and red cheeks. One report described how he "walks quickly and bends or leans forward" but was usually "well dressed".

On one occasion, in 1920, Howe had sent relatively small amounts of cocaine and morphine into Quebec hidden inside statuettes he'd bought in Brussels. In total, there were fifty-one packages of one-eighth ounces of morphine, and five half ounces of cocaine. The packages were destined for a woman named Juliette Florentine, who ran a millinery store in Montreal. Miss Florentine also went under the name Madame

Howe. She was later convicted of importing goods without a license and sentenced to ten days in prison, with a $200 fine. In August 1922, police in Belgium seized a large quantity of drugs belonging to Howe, but the charges were dropped due to lack of evidence. Howe returned to Montreal where his baggage was thoroughly searched but, declaring that he been in Belgium studying chemistry and art, he was allowed to get on with his life.

In 1924, the Canadians obtained fresh information about Howe, using an undercover operative named "Agent Dufresne," although it is not clear whether this individual was an officer, a civilian volunteer, or a criminal informant. In any case, Howe had asked Dufresne to accompany him on a trip to Europe to purchase $3,000 of narcotics. Paul Stone, the erstwhile associate of Max Faber, had advanced Howe the money. Howe also told Dufresne that a man named Rossenblatt, "a heavy narcotic dealer of New York City", had given him another $2,000. The information was sent to Walter Burmby for his files.

Moving to Ostend in January 1926, Howe set up a delicatessen with his new lover, Catherine Dethier, who was described as "a woman of loose morals" who had "previously been in a brothel at Liege". Howe, who for years had posed as a pharmacist, did actually succeed in getting a job with the firm of Edgard Riou in Ostend the same year. No doubt the company became a useful source of supply.

Howe was still thought to be active as late as 1928, when Special Branch in Antwerp, under the watchful eye of Sgt John Probert, put him under observation after receiving information from the Canadian government that he was in town shipping drugs to North America. But Howe spent most of his time living at the Hotel du Cygne with Dethier. There was no evidence that he left the city for more than a few days, and certainly nothing to prove he had visited Canada.

The Canadians provided a raft of information on other drug suspects. There was Joseph Farley, a graduate druggist who had previously operated a firm called the Universal Drug Company in de Bleury Street, Montreal, but who later took to making frequent trips to Europe to stock up on illegal narcotics. There was also an extensive record on Keith Harrison Vaughan, a British citizen known by the aliases Kenneth Verity, Albert Perkins, Pierre Perrins and several other variations. The Canadians branded the slight and gawky Vaughan "one of the largest smugglers of narcotics on the American Continent". Despite his appearance, Vaughan was said to be a "dangerous man, [who] always carries a gun and uses it on the slightest provocation". He was said to be behind several major shipments to Montreal and New York from Switzerland during 1923, enabled by corrupt crew members.[6]

If Walter Burmby was in the habit of regularly reviewing his files, he would surely have been disappointed by some of the results between 1922-1928. Yes, his detectives had succeeded in putting away May Roberts, Albert Ellis and Julia Kitt, plus many other small-time drug dealers, as we shall see. But the big fish, the likes of Maxie Faber, Laurent Deleglise, Paul Stone and Choy Loy, remained out of reach. They appeared to be part of an interconnected organisation, perhaps the world's first drug cartel. But in a world without mobile phones, reliant on telegrams for communication and without the ability to instantly track individuals across the globe, smashing the gang proved to be too difficult.[7]

The cases of May Roberts, Albert Ellis and Julia Kitt were now inextricably linked to Max Faber, and by extension Laurent Deleglise. Roberts by her relationship with Lum Chong; Kitt by her marriage to Choy Ah Kitt; and Albert Ellis by his sibling David. All were associates of Faber, a beneficiary of Deleglise's ingenious smuggling schemes.

Yet MD Perrins and Walter Burmby would be left frustrated and the British public would never get to hear the full details of the sensational case of the Dope Queens with ties to an international drug trafficking network stretching all the way from Hamburg to Montreal, via the dark streets of Limehouse, Glasgow and Liverpool. The enigmatic Big Maxie and the handsome Deleglise had slipped through their fingers.

Slightly happier news (from Burmby's point of view) was received in April 1924. Paul Stone, also known as Harry Jakes, Paul Webster, and at least half a dozen other names, was dead. Stone had joined a gang of gunmen who ambushed a car carrying cash for the Banque d'Hochelaga in Montreal. The bandits killed the driver and escaped with $142,000, but Stone was later shot dead by police as they rounded up the gang members. Only a few months previously, Stone had allegedly chartered a private aircraft to fly drugs from Germany to England. He had arrived back in Canada shortly thereafter with a trunk full of opium. While the drugs were seized, Stone escaped, but his risky criminal lifestyle had caught up with him.

And there were plenty of other big fish yet to be caught. Indeed, by the time of Max Faber's final sighting in England, the dogged Inspector Walter Burmby was already several years into a long-running feud with a notorious villain much closer to home.

---

[5] With both drugs contacts vanished, Ellis unwittingly poured out his woes to a police informant in a bar, JJ McLaughlin's Joint, at 333 Berri Street, and discussed the entire sorry story (David Ellis had supposedly once lived at the property, where another informant's report had described him lying in bed "taking the cure", presumably from the Spanish Flu). It was then that Ellis revealed he also planned to go Hamburg to take part in a drug deal. He later sailed from New York on the SS Cleveland, possibly using his alias Lambert.

[6] Vaughan was an experienced smuggler who had first been arrested as far back as 1916 at the Hotel Berlin in New York City alongside a man named Louis Rosen, also known as Louis Roth, Louis Rothensky, Harry Jones or Jack Harrison. Keith and Jack went on the run, but a number of other men pleaded guilty, including Sam Cohen, alias Bully Harris, and George Wintner, or George Winters, and a Dr JB Twaddele of Boston. More recently, Vaughan had been behind shipments into New York estimated at some one hundred thousand ounces. Another of Vaughan's aliases, Pierre Perrins, was found among Laurent Deleglise's papers in Lausanne.

[7] Even with the best intentions and efforts, international cooperation did not always run smoothly, as evidenced by one note from MD Perrins to Colonel Sharman of the Canadian Narcotics Bureau. Referring to one trafficker, Perrins said Sharman's latest cable "was a bit of a crossword as it would not decode according to the code supplied by Anslinger [of the US narcotics bureau] which is arranged in four columns beginning front bottom third, down

second, up fourth, and down first; in names, A becomes Z and not B
as in your cable."

# 4. THE WORST MAN IN LONDON

**Y**ankee Frank was mean, muscular, scruffy and extremely unpleasant. Most people would cross the street to avoid him. But not Eddie Manning. In fact, Manning had spent the last half an hour furiously trying to confront him.

The stylish Jamaican's rage was somewhat out of character. Even though he would later earn the sobriquet 'The Worst Man in London,' he had few enemies. Manning was always immaculately dressed, with polished shoes, a walking cane and a bowler hat — which he would never fail to tip to a lady, a gesture usually accompanied by a polite greeting. On that particular day, July 11, 1920, the hat was a light gray with a dark band, while his well-cut Savile Row suit was navy blue.

Everyone knew that even though Manning was one of the most agreeable villains in the West End, he was not to be trifled with. Yet in the eyes of Frank Miller, Manning was nothing but a "black ponce," words the American spat towards his rival as he had strolled past one previous weekday afternoon.

Manning had found it easy to keep his temper under control on that occasion. But now Miller had crossed a line by assaulting one of his girls in a nearby café run by one of Manning's friends, Elizabeth Fox. She had overseen the establishment in Little Newport Street for around two decades, catering mostly for the West End's criminal underworld — namely its pimps, prostitutes and assorted lowlifes. Fox was known by the Press as Crime's Fairy Godmother and had taken a number of her cohort, Manning included, to the racing at Lingfield the previous day. Manning had come home £70 up, but the following afternoon Miller squared up to him in the café and demanded a share of his winnings.

"I have not a pound to give you," Manning replied, outraged at the American's temerity.

"You're a fucking thief," Yankee Frank shot back angrily. "I know how you're earning your living. You're a fucking shitpot."

That kind of abuse was like water off a duck's back to Eddie Manning, who felt no need to demonstrate his superior masculinity by engaging in a fistfight in his friend's café. The twenty-six-year-old Miller was a moron, a bottom-feeding, cigar-chewing pimp. Manning not only had more class, but also a burgeoning sideline in dope which he didn't want to be interrupted by the increasingly inquisitive local detectives. He sighed and turned away. Frank was all mouth and no trousers.

But an out-of-work actress named Molly O'Brien, a prostitute being pimped by Manning, had been watching the argument from a nearby table and couldn't help but giggle at Yankee Frank's humiliation. "And you're a bloody prostitute," Frank raged at her. Molly let out a huff of indignation.

"It's a pity you don't go and work for a living," she replied. "You're only a ponce."

Quick as a flash, Yankee Frank threw a coin at her head then flung his cigar in her face. Then he lurched forward and punched her in the eye. "If there wasn't so many people in here, I'd do something else to you," he snarled, before making a swift exit. Eddie Manning stopped to ask how she was, then followed Miller into the street.

Manning failed to catch up with his girl's assailant, but Molly, hardly a shrinking violet herself, also raced after him. She soon found Miller in the company of Charles Tunnick, aged twenty-one.

"What right to do you have to hit me?" Molly demanded. "I don't know you."

"What right?!" Frank laughed and looked around for dramatic effect. "You see your two eyes? I'll push them right in for you." Frank then grabbed Molly's thumbs and bent them back. She let out a yelp of pain.

"You can't bully me," Molly insisted, but without warning Frank then punched her in the stomach and stalked off towards Charring Cross Road, proving that he could do as he pleased. A third acquaintance, Robert Davies, aged thirty-nine, had ambled over during the argument and followed as Miller and Tunnick made their way towards Cambridge Circus and then turned down Shaftesbury Avenue, where they lingered outside the Palace Theatre.

Meanwhile, Eddie Manning was still looking for the thug. A restaurant manager, Morris Lucas, later described a pensive Manning approaching him in the doorway of his workplace in New Compton Street, asking, "Have you seen Frank?" Morris didn't know a Frank.

But a few minutes later, Miller, Tunnick and Davies saw Manning bowling towards them. According to some accounts, the trio rushed towards Manning. In the ensuing chaos, Manning ran around a passing bus and re-emerged on the other side with a revolver in his hand. He opened fire, hitting all three men in the legs. Yankee Frank, the foulest of the trio, was shot in both thighs at close range. It was a deliberate act of revenge on Manning's part. Manning threw his gloves and walking cane to the ground and ran up Greek Street, pursued by a passing film producer named Arthur Jones, who he quickly shook off.

PC John Thurston was on duty in Old Compton Street when he heard the shots. He raced to the scene and found Charles Tunnick standing but "bleeding profusely" outside the Palace Theatre on the corner of Greek Street, a bullet wound in his right thigh. Thurston probably saved his life by immediately applying a tourniquet. He then attended to Davies, who'd been hit in the lower left leg.

Miller was seemingly the worst hit, with his pair of bullet wounds, but in each instance the shots had passed clean through. Yankee Frank was able to hobble out of the hospital later that day, suffering only flesh wounds. The other men's injuries were more serious and they had to remain in hospital for treatment. In Davies' case, the wound had been close to the left knee and had caused a compound fracture of the tibia.

# THE WORST MAN IN LONDON

Manning made little effort to evade capture. The police found him in his flat in Margaret Street, close to Oxford Street, sitting by his bed and talking to a friend, Alexander Charles Philibert. When the police burst in to the room, the charming gangster calmly smiled and offered no resistance. "That's quite right guvnor," he reportedly said. "I shall give you no trouble. Miller is a blackmailer, it started in Fox's restaurant. He knew I had been to the racetrack and won some money. A few pounds. He came in and asked me for one, I refused."

Manning made no attempt to hide his disdain for the American. "He is a gorilla," Manning stated. "He ought to be out of the way. I am sorry for the others. I didn't intend to kill, I shot low and threw the revolver away." That last comment was a lie. In Manning's waistcoat pocket they found nine live .38 cartridges and under the bed a six-chamber Colt revolver, fully loaded. "I'm sorry I told you a lie about the gun," he added, feebly. "I didn't want to lose it." When he was formally charged at Vine Street police station, Manning answered, "All I have to say is that I did it in self-defence, not with intent to murder."

Manning's account of the row in Fox's restaurant was corroborated by Molly O'Brien, as well as a waitress, Mable Farr, and a housewife, Annie Faircloth. Mable added that Frank Miller had been in the company of another man, who she believed to be his brother, placing Tunnick at the scene of the original offence. The row, she said, had happened between 3.30pm and 4pm. The shooting had taken place about 4.10pm. In her statement, the restaurant owner, Elizabeth Fox, described Frank and his companion as "the brothers Miller".

71

# DOPE KINGS OF LONDON

It was fortunate for Manning that none of the three men's wounds had proved fateful, but the police were otherwise fairly unconcerned about the welfare of his victims. In fact, some of the officers involved in the case found themselves better disposed towards the well-spoken and courteous Jamaican than to the vulgar Americans. Yankee Frank, one officer later wrote, had spent the last eighteen months "doing no work but continuously residing with prostitutes...associating with Colonial criminals, blackmailers and bullies". Only the previous month, Miller had been acquitted at the Old Bailey of four charges relating to burglaries in Putney. Charles Tunnick had arrived in England in June 1920, apparently having deserted an American ship in France. He was said by police sources to be a "constant companion" of Frank Miller and therefore assumed also to be a criminal.

Robert Davies was a slightly different case. He was a well-known character in the West End, but not because of his villainy. A former boxer, Davies had served six weeks in prison for assault in 1906, after a street fight in which he had knocked out his opponent's eye. For the past sixteen years, Davies had worked at the National Sporting Club in Covent Garden and as a scene shifter at various West End theatres. Davies was the unluckiest of them all. Not only were his injuries decidedly more severe than those of Miller and Tunnick, but he had probably not deserved it.

During the argument in Fox's, Davies had been innocently enjoying a beer with his friend Charles Howard in The Cranbourne public house on Upper St Martin's Lane. The pair had stumbled on the second argument between Molly O'Brien and Frank Miller before joining the two brothers for a walk to another pub, The Cock. Charles Howard was fortunate — he had been walking about fifteen yards behind the trio when the shooting started. When he caught up to a bewildered Davies, by then on the ground, all he was told by his friend was that "a black man started shooting at us".

Davies told the police how he had seen Manning "with a revolver in his hand, standing in the middle of the road...He was firing indiscriminately. I heard several shots. As soon as I noticed him I tried to dodge behind a bus. Almost immediately I fell down and knew at once that I had been shot, as I felt a numb feeling in my left leg, just below the knee. He was a total stranger to me." Davies was able to describe his attacker, although not in much detail. "All I know is, he was a black man, very well dressed, wearing a bowler hat. Of this I am certain. He was slim, about five foot eight. I have not the slightest idea as to why he was shooting, and I do not think he shot at me in particular. I think I caught one of the stray shots."

Charles Tunnick's story was riddled with lies and racial slurs. He claimed to have been in England for just two weeks, after arriving from Holland hoping to rejoin his ship, the SS Orleans, in Tilbury, only to have found it had sailed for New York. He said he had only met Miller "five minutes previously" and he was a "total stranger to me". Nevertheless, he was walking along Shaftesbury Avenue with this 'stranger' when he spotted the well-dressed Manning and shouted, "Look out for that n*****, he has a revolver! He deliberately pointed the revolver at me and shot me in the right leg, just above the knee."

Tunnick seemed bemused as to why Manning would choose to attack him. "I said nothing, neither did I do anything to cause the n***** to shoot. I had never seen him before in my life. I could identify him amongst twenty thousand n*****. The only reason I can offer for him shooting at us was because I shouted, "Look out for that n*****."" In a later statement taken two days later, Tunnick did at least admit he had met Miller a week previously and had been lodging with him.

Yankee Frank, perhaps unsurprisingly, turned out to be an uncooperative witness. It was only after "considerable pressure" was put on him at Charring Cross Hospital that he finally relented and named Eddie Manning as his attacker. He had to be dragooned to Marlborough Street police court for Manning's first appearance but a week later, when he was due to be cross-examined, he said he was too ill to attend.

Tunnick too was a reluctant participant in the prosecution, but he was conveyed from hospital to the court by taxi. When it came time for the trial at the Old Bailey, neither brother could be found (the men denied being related, but police were satisfied "almost beyond doubt" that they were siblings).

Miller claimed in his brief statement that the row had started about two weeks prior to the shooting, when he called Manning a "black ponce" outside The Grapes public house in Seven Dials. Miller claimed Manning simply walked on and it wasn't until the shooting started that he saw him again. "There was a lot of shouting and the black man ran away...I cannot tell you any more than this," he said.

As far as the police were concerned, it was impossible to say for certain who was lying and who was telling the truth, because almost all of the witnesses were "loose and dissolute characters, associating with thieves and prostitutes," although the several witnesses to the row in Fox's café blew apart Miller's story about only seeing Manning once.

Manning pleaded guilty to a charge of grievous bodily harm, which was accepted by the prosecution, who dropped the attempted murder charge. Credit must go to Manning's lawyer, the famous Huntly Jenkins, who had previously defended Reggie De Veulle. Manning received a sentence of just sixteen months' hard labour, a sentence unthinkable by today's standards, not least because at the time Eddie Manning was already very well known to the police. Besides being one of the West End's most dapper and feared pimps, he was also one of the first of an entirely new breed of British criminal — the drug dealer.

Born Alfred Mullin in Kingston, Jamaica, in 1888, Manning's parents Benjamin Mullin and Cecilia Francesco were former slaves, who had both died by the mid-1920s — although none of this detail was known until much later in Manning's criminal career. Edgar, or Eddie, as he became known in Britain, had travelled across the Atlantic via America during the war. Apparently unable to take part in active service because of ill health (he later spoke of having had malaria in the past, but it is not clear if that was the source of his problems), Manning found a job working in the Dartford factory of arms manufacturer Vickers. He was forced to leave the role due to an unspecified illness and underwent an operation at Charring Cross Hospital in 1918.

# DOPE KINGS OF LONDON

Manning then joined a touring theatre company and played in a jazz band as a drummer. He must have been good, because the band became resident at the prestigious Ciro's nightclub, in Orange Street, near the National Gallery. At one point, the band was called the Ciro's Club C**n Orchestra, although the name, offensive even at the time, was later changed. Its Jamaican-born pianist and bandleader Dan Kildare would later achieve his own notoriety when, in the grip of alcohol and drug addiction, he walked into his wife's pub and shot both her and her sister dead, before turning the gun on himself. Despite Manning's apparent success with the band, there was clearly more money to be made from crime.

At the time of his arrest for the triple shooting, Manning was living with a prostitute, Doreen Taylor, also known as Peggy Manning. When police raided her rooms in Little Newport Street, off Leicester Square, they found two phials and eight small wraps of cocaine, which Doreen said belonged to Manning, who had been dealing the drug for three months. Officers also found his gun license at the premises. The paperwork had only been issued the previous month.

Detectives interviewed Doreen's landlady, Jean Straker, who said she had previously known Manning and had seen him rehearsing in a ground floor apartment with a jazz band. "I always found him very quiet and polite," she said. He had hired the room for his "wife" but admitted he would not be staying there. Instead, he asked, would she mind if another girl lived with Doreen/Peggy instead? Jean had no problem with it. Detectives also spoke to the landlady at Manning's own digs in Margaret Street, Celina Lemarchand. She said he was "always quiet and well behaved, but he used to drink a quantity of whiskey and frequently drank a bottle of whiskey a day." He would also habitually leave his revolver on the washstand.

Doreen told how she had met Manning after moving to London from St Albans. She had sparked up a conversation with Manning in St Martin's Lane and went back to his place, "where intimacy took place". After that, she moved in with her lover and they lived "as husband and wife" for several months. After speaking with a prostitute friend, Maisie Kitchener, Doreen decided she would also make money selling herself on the streets. This seemed to be fine with Manning, although she insisted he was not her pimp. Sometimes, she said, she would give Manning money, while on other occasions he would give money to her. Doreen was, however, happy to discuss the details of his drug dealing business.

"Manning has been selling cocaine to my knowledge for about three months," she revealed. "I don't know where he purchases it. Last Tuesday he brought two small bottles, which contained white powder, to my room. I said, 'What's that, cocaine?' He said, Yes'. Manning then cut up small pieces of paper and placed a small quantity of the cocaine in the papers, and folded them up. He told me he sold each packet for 5/- [five shillings, or a crown].[8] I also know that he has a man named Sydney who sells cocaine for him." Most likely, Doreen was one of several women also selling drugs on Manning's behalf, a method that would become his calling card.

Doreen had last seen Manning at 2.45pm on the day of the shooting, when he left for Fox's café, saying, "I shan't be long." While on the run, briefly, following the attack less than two hours later, he enlisted a white American friend to run a polite, handwritten note around to his lover. "My dear Peggy," it began, "this gentleman is a friend of mine and will speak to you confidentially. I am alright. Yours, Edgar."

Manning naturally returned to the West End after serving his time for the gun drama, but there was no chance of him living a quiet life. He was back in the newspapers again several months later after meeting a morphine and heroin addict named Eric Goodwin, who had picked up his habit after being gassed during the war. It became a heavy dependency. When the doctors stopped providing him with morphine, Goodwin, the son of a wealthy Liverpool tobacco merchant, convinced friends to smuggle drugs to him hidden inside chocolate boxes.

After the war, Goodwin became a mechanic, supplementing his income by stealing cars as well as repairing them. Manning was suspected of recruiting the ex-soldier to sell heroin for him in West End nightclubs. But one night in January 1922, while visiting Manning's new address in Hallam Street with a friend, Goodwin took an accidental overdose and died. As a result, Manning was placed under observation by Walter Burmby's drugs investigators.[9]

Manning was well aware of the extra police attention his activities were now attracting. He could spot a copper a mile off no matter how well they blended in with the West End street scene. As a result, Manning left the area and moved in with a Greek lover, Zenovia Iassonides, in Regents Park Road, Primrose Hill. There is no doubt that despite being a pimp, a drug dealer, a violent felon and a promiscuous lover, Eddie Manning was a serial romantic. No woman ever came forward to say he had mistreated her. In fact, Manning was generally well-liked and apparently admired by most of his female friends. He had a particular soft spot for the beautiful Zenovia, who may well have been the love of his life.

But although Manning was now living 'off-patch' and devoting much of his time to his new girlfriend, the move didn't do much to lower his profile. Zenovia was herself a notorious drug dealer who the police were desperate not just to lock up, but also to deport. She had previously run the Montmatre Café, in Church Street, Soho, with her husband, Alexandre.

He was aged forty-nine when he appeared at Marlborough Street police court in September 1922, following the arrest of his nephew, Leonidas, aged twenty. According to Detective Charles Owen, the younger man had been found with a phial of cocaine, scales and boracic powder, and had insisted he had been given it by his uncle. More cocaine was later found in the stuffing of an armchair in his flat. When officers searched his uncle's premises, they found six packets of cocaine hidden in a cigarette box concealed under a second-floor carpet. In a bedroom, they found a packet of cocaine on a dressing table, as well as a used syringe and cuttings about the recent convictions of two fellow drug dealers. Burmby later went back to the café with Owen, and the pair found another cigarette pack containing nine wraps of cocaine hidden under another piece of carpet.[10]

Leonidas was given six months' hard labour and recommended for deportation, while Alexandre managed to wangle a not guilty verdict by enlisting the family doctor to speak for him in court. The doctor told how his estranged wife, Zenovia, had been addicted to drugs and he suggested she might have been secreting her supplies around the house. Alexandre was discharged by the gullible magistrate.

Zenovia's decision to shack up with the younger man had left her husband incandescent with rage and provided Manning with another good reason to steer clear of the West End. But there is more than one way to skin a rabbit and the Greek may well have turned informant to exact his revenge. Manning and Zenovia rented two addresses in Regents Park Road, 33, where Zenovia lived, and 22, where Manning officially resided and from where he sold his drugs. He also used the premises as a shooting gallery for customers who wanted a safe place to get high (his landlady, a Mrs Mason, was also suspected of cocaine trafficking).

The local police received a promising tip from an anonymous caller about the address on April 12. "If you go to 22 Regents Park Road before midnight you will find Edgar Manning there with some cocaine," the caller said. "He is leaving there tomorrow. He has about 2lbs of it. The cocaine is in the ground floor front room." Given that the caller asked for no reward and left no name, we can only guess as to their motives, but it may well have been personal.

In any case, officers visited several days too late, on April 19. Manning told them they were free to search the house. When they found a packet of magnesia, he told them, "I take that for stomach troubles, you won't find any cocaine or opium here." Indeed, nothing illegal was found, and as the officers left Manning demanded their names, adding, "You'll hear further about this." Manning then fired off a letter loaded with chutzpah to the Metropolitan Police Commissioner, addressed "Honorable Sir" (sic):

# THE WORST MAN IN LONDON

I humbly beg your kind permission to grant me a personal interview at your earliest convenience, so as to allow me to lay my grievance before you, wherein Justice is concerned.

Sir- I humbly appeal to you, for I can no longer bear this torment, bullying and intimidating action from members of the CID department...My nerves are being badly strained, owing to the fact that I have been a victim of Malaria, an at times, not quite responsible for my actions. The fact is, I being by nature's desine black (sic), seems to make my persecution the more unbearable, it is now making my nerves a total wreck and also interferes with my dayle living (sic), also my place of abode.

The audience with the chief of police was not, of course, granted, and it left Walter Burmby, who was still pursuing Manning, furious and more determined than ever to bring him to justice.

It was Burmby who led another raid a few weeks later, this time aimed at both addresses. The police arrived first at 33 Regents Park Road. This time, an array of drugs and paraphernalia was recovered and Manning was arrested. Among the illicit goods found by detectives were fifteen morphine tablets, tucked inside Manning's jacket pocket ("I know nothing about it," was Manning's incredulous response), a bottle of cocaine, thirteen ounces of opium, an opium bowl containing recently smoked residue, a syringe case and needles and a pornographic book and photos. At number 22, they found a revolver, scales, a price list for drugs and a silver-topped walking stick with a hollowed middle, within which was an eighteen-inch-long glass tube, presumably for storing drugs. Manning was bang to rights.

He was brought to Marlborough Street police court, where he was represented by CV Hill, the barrister who also acted for Brilliant Chang, at an initial hearing, and then by Huntly Jenkins at his short trial a week later. The case was well covered by the Press, with Manning described in the *Evening News* as a "tall, respectfully dressed negro....said to be a Soho restaurant proprietor".

Huntly Jenkins argued that Manning should, to a certain extent, be pitied, in light of his long-term addiction to drugs. In contrast, Walter Burmby told the court of Manning's long criminal history. "I have known the prisoner for two years as a trafficker in drugs," he said, "and I have had quite a number of complaints from various persons as to the manner in which he has been selling drugs to them. He is regarded as an important trafficker in the West End of London."

The police thought the drugs had probably been smuggled through Customs at Tilbury, but they had no hard evidence against anyone else. Jenkins insisted his client was not a trafficker and the drugs were only for his own personal use.

"You can hardly expect me to believe that," the magistrate interrupted, "having regard to the amount found upon him." Manning was given six months' hard labour, which was then the maximum sentence allowed under the Dangerous Drugs Act.

A subsequent report written by Burmby for Chief Inspector Brown, illustrates the extent of the investigation into Manning. "Many hours of difficult observation have been kept by PCs Owen and Haines," he wrote, adding that "owing to the exceedingly cunning way in which he has carried on his nefarious traffic sufficient evidence could not be obtained until now". Burmby's operation had been interrupted by the previous week's raid, carried out by S Division, and as a result of which Manning "had the audacity to write a letter of complaint to the Commissioner that his 'business' was being interfered with and his 'nerves badly strained' and asked for an interview. I suggest that no notice be now taken of this letter."

Burmby was convinced that Manning had at least a dozen prostitutes working as dealers in the West End, and that he sourced his supply in the East End from smugglers. He lamented the fact that he had not been able to bring others to justice and then rattled off a list of further accusations that had not been brought before the court.

Firstly, he was convinced that Manning was at fault over the death of Eric Goodwin. He also said that in February 1922 he was approached by a Dr Gregory, of Russell Square, who said he had been treating a widow named Maud Davis, also known as Margaret Hasler, for cocaine addiction. Hasler, a dressmaker and prostitute, had later died at her lodgings in St Martin's Lane surrounded by drugs paraphernalia and an inquest found she had been injecting cocaine. The drugs, the doctor said, were supplied by Eddie Manning, although Hasler had not wanted to give evidence to the police. Burmby also mentioned another case, in which Manning had been arrested for buying a £60 diamond ring using a stolen cheque book. Burmby reasoned that there was now no point in pursuing it.

Finally, Burmby enclosed a handwritten letter from a man named Henry Walvish, who was serving eighteen months for burglary, identifying some of Manning's cronies, including a man nicknamed "Bigels". Burmby insisted his officers were already aware of Manning's co-conspirators and that they would be rounded up in due course. There was no need to speak to Walvish, he said.

Investigations certainly continued into Manning's Greek lover and her family. On July 26, 1922, Zenovia was sentenced to six months' hard labour for possessing cocaine. It was Detective Charles Owen who once again took the glory. Zenovia, aged twenty-nine, appeared at Malborough Street police court alongside her alleged customer, a young woman called Frances Benjamin, twenty-two. Zenovia had scuttled back to the café in Soho after Manning's imprisonment and Owen had put the place under observation. He watched as Benjamin popped in for just a few moments and then cornered her when she emerged. She admitted buying the small packet of cocaine found in her pocket for £1, from "Madame" who kept the drugs in her stockings. Owen later marched Benjamin back to the café alongside Walter Burmby and arrested Zenovia.

She came peacefully at first, although she offered Burmby a bribe on the way to the station. But while being searched by a matron, officers heard cries for help and rushed into the room to find Zenovia struggling with the woman. She had taken a packet of cocaine from her stocking and swallowed it, after her offer of a bribe of a gold watch was flatly refused.

In any case, the police had found more evidence back at the café. There was a bottle of cocaine hidden in a stocking as well as two packets in a tin on the mantelpiece and various slips of paper used for packaging up deals. Detectives also found a love letter from Eddie Manning and a newspaper clipping of his court case.

In court, Zenovia denied being in partnership with Manning and claimed to have only purchased cocaine for her personal use. Echoing the excuse made by her husband in his previous case, she insisted that the drugs were hidden around the house not through fear of arrest, but because she was an addict and had tried to hide it from her spouse.

The *Illustrated Police News* carried a typically florid report of the case, calling Frances Benjamin "blue-eyed, tall and fascinating," and describing how she placed her "white-gloved hands on the edge of the dock" as her lawyer made a convincing argument to spare her a prison sentence. Telling the magistrate that Benjamin was an addict who was often left to her own devices by a frequently absent husband, he said that she was determined to kick the habit and could go and live with her mother-in-law in Bow. The magistrate, the aptly named Mr D'Eyncourt, was having none of it.

"I understand that you are determined to give it up," he began, ("Yes I am," Benjamin mewed from the dock), "I am going to give you such a sentence as will fortify your resolution to carry it out. People who buy cocaine, they are the really responsible persons. If it was not for people like you, the traffickers would not exist." Benjamin was jailed, quite harshly, for three months.

Zenovia served her sentence and was later deported. Her estranged husband, Alexandre, also received the same sentence in March the following year after yet another drugs case. Zenovia and her nephew then moved to Paris.

# DOPE KINGS OF LONDON

When Manning was released from prison in November 1922, Zenovia wrote to him at his new address at 39 Lisson Street. Manning almost immediately applied for a passport to Paris, hoping to be reunited with his lover. Strangely, even though Burmby was now desperate to see Manning off the streets of London, the detective took an active role in having the application blocked, firing off a memo to Special Branch. Manning's application had been supported by a letter from Gordon Stretton, also known as William Gordon Masters, an internationally acclaimed band leader and Liverpool-born jazz pioneer who had played with Charlie Chaplin and was at that point based in Brussels, leading the Orchestre Syncopated Six in Paris. "He is not a person to be relied upon," Burmby wrote, adding that Stretton himself had unspecified criminal convictions.

As a result of the intervention, Manning was to remain in London, where Burmby kept a close eye on him. In June 1923, the officer applied for another warrant to search his home. "Manning is visited at his address by persons known to police as drug traffickers and addicts," Burmby wrote, "and I am informed and verily believe that Manning has in his possession or under his control concealed at the above premises quantities of drugs and documents contrary to the Dangerous Drugs Act 1920 and 1923."

The latter amendment was important because the maximum sentence allowed under the Act was now ten years in prison. Burmby was determined to put Manning away for a long stretch.

Eddie Manning had made another police raid all but inevitable by continuing to trade in drugs more or less openly.

# THE WORST MAN IN LONDON

Manning occupied the three rooms on the second floor of the Lisson Street property, renting under the name McManning. The top level was taken by Charles Ford, an engineer, and his wife Lilly. Manning made an immediate impression on his neighbors, albeit a bad one. On one occasion, he asked Charles whether he wanted to buy his revolver for a "fiver", showing him the gun in a shoebox. Ford declined. Manning also had visitors at "all hours of the day and night" many of them women, and Lilly noticed "peculiar smells" coming up the stairs. The noise was enough to prompt Charles to complain to the landlord.

Lilly was present when Burmby carried out his raid on June 18, 1923, and watched as his officers uncovered an opium pipe and several bottles of white powder, including some labelled boracic, some hidden inside a suet grater in the kitchen, and another packet hidden in the lavatory. Burmby also found a gun, a syringe and other drugs paraphernalia, including a piece of rubber tubing used for opium smoking. In the bedroom there was also a photo and letter from Zenovia, as well as an address for "man of colour" Gordon Stretton, who the police again noted in their report "had a criminal record".

A woman named Peggy Pearce, also known as Peggy Manning (the second), and a man named George Clements were also at the flat. Manning made no comment on the various discoveries, except to say, "I know nothing about them." Back at Crawford Street police station, where Manning was charged under the Dangerous Drugs Act for the second time in his life, he replied simply, "That will be a wrong charge altogether."

As a side note, police also found a £4 cheque drawn from the Bank of Australasia and made out to Manning from a Mr H Boan, based at Christ Church, Oxford. Inquiries were made by the police in Oxford, only to find that Boan had left the city for the summer, and was not expected back until October. Boan did, however, have an address in Green Street, Park Lane, and Oxford's constabulary advised that the Commissioner could be informed and the cheque returned.

The evidence may well be circumstantial, but at the time the Australian retail tycoon and politician Harry Boan was known to have an address in Park Lane. It is likely that the cheque was stolen rather than used to pay Manning for drugs. It had not been cashed and in fact had been returned by the bank stamped: "Signature differs".

Manning's court case was covered by the Press with levels of racism which are shocking today, even in their historical context. Under the headline "Evil negro caught," the *News of the World* endeavored to link Manning to the five years old Billie Carleton case, referring to him as the "notorious West Indian, familiar in high places and low haunts" adding that Manning was one of the "most dangerous and disreputable characters Scotland Yard have ever brought to book".

"This negro was money mad," the report said, "and he made it at the sacrifice of the souls of white women and white girls". Apparently plucked from nowhere, the paper claimed "poor Billie Carleton's fatal dose of 'dope' is stated to have originated from his seemingly inexhaustible store, and more than one woman has died since because of the ease with which they could get cocaine from this man or his associates." The article noted Manning's Jamaican origins, lamenting that,

# THE WORST MAN IN LONDON

"Unfortunately...if his story is to be believed, he is a British subject and therefore cannot be deported as an undesirable alien."

The paper did flesh out some hitherto unknown facts about Manning. It was claimed that he had been investigated by Det Insp Grosse of the Flying Squad as early as 1919, when he had a flat in Greek Street. At the time, Manning was allegedly being supplied by an Italian named Carlo Ivaldi, who was himself arrested in possession of thirteen packets of cocaine. Ivaldi, a film agent, had been sentenced to six months' hard labour in February 1921. He had been found by Det Insp Grosse with some seven thousand grains of cocaine, enough, the papers said at the time, "to dope half of London". He admitted trafficking the drug from Italy via Paris and was later deported.

Every night in Soho, Manning was, according to the article, "to be found around the nightclubs and doubtful cafes where the drug fiends congregated. He was the man directly responsible for the greater part of the cocaine supplied to that beautiful young actress, Miss Billie Carleton, who poisoned herself with an overdose of the stuff." The report also noted how the "immaculately dressed" Manning had shot the three men in Soho back in 1920, although the article claimed it was a "quarrel over a division of the profits of a cocaine deal". There was absolutely no evidence to support either claim.

As requested by Manning, his pal George Clements was asked to attend court as a character witness but was not, in the event, called to give evidence. It was the first drugs case on indictment since the 1923 amendment to the Act and allowed the judge to pass a sentence of three years penal servitude, a resounding victory for the detectives.

DOPE KINGS OF LONDON

"Without doubt", Burmby wrote in his report, "this man is a scoundrel of the lowest possible type and for years past has been earning his living by selling cocaine, etc, to prostitutes and others in the West End, and has had opium smoking parties at his flat. He has been exceedingly cunning and would never venture into the street with drugs in his possession." Burmby praised the actions and diligence of his officers, and also recommended that £5 be paid from the Informant's Fund to a man known as Thomas Harris, who "spent many hours assisting police to get sufficient evidence". The idea had been, all along, to catch Manning at home with drugs and they had at last succeeded.

Almost as soon as Manning was behind bars, Burmby turned his attention to having him deported, no doubt spurred on by the reaction to the case in the Press. "As there is some suspicion that this man is really an American citizen and not a British subject as he claims, I respectfully suggest that his photograph and fingerprints be sent to police at Kingston, and that they be asked to make enquiry to trace his birth," he wrote.

On September 18, 1923, Burmby again wrote to Chief Inspector Brown, reporting that police in Jamaica "have now informed us that no trace has been found respecting McManning, alias Manning. Manning is believed to have come to this country in 1914 from the United States of America." Burmby asked for a copy of his report to be sent to the Home Office "for consideration of Manning's position as an alien". A subsequent memo at the Home Office noted that despite the desire to get rid of Manning, it might not be possible because while there was no evidence of his Jamaican birth, there was also no evidence that he was American.

Apparently aware of what was going on behind the scenes, Manning spoke to the governor of Parkhurst prison, RH D'aeth, in October 1923. Manning stated that his real name was Alfred Mullin, his father was Benjamin and his mother named Cecilia Francesco. He believed he was born on February 23, 1888, and christened at a Roman Catholic church in Kingston, where he attended school for only a few years, leaving Jamaica aged 16. This was new information and Walter Burmby, to give him his due, passed it on to the Jamaican police, urging them to make fresh inquiries. He must have been sorely disappointed when, on December 27, the Deputy Inspector General of the Jamaica Constabulary wrote back to say Manning's statement "appears to be correct". They had located an "African woman" named Sarah Collins who, despite now being seventy-three years old, said she remembered the family. No trace could be found amongst the church records, but Sarah Collins' word appears to have been sufficient to prevent Manning being kicked out of Britain.

Eddie Manning was released under license in November 1925. He had evidently remained in touch with journalists because a piece appeared the next February under his byline in the *World's Pictoral News*. This was Manning's long-awaited opportunity to set out his case, supposedly in his own words. Titled "My Life as the Dope King of London," what followed was likely a blend of truth and fantasy, although by this time Manning had no real reason to lie.

He now claimed that he was sent to London in 1912 by his father to read for the Bar and to become a "member of the educated and official class". Yet he soon delved into London's clubland, meeting a woman called "Cocaine Daisy" as well as Billie Carleton. It was Manning, according to his own account, who introduced the tragic Freda Kempton to the Chinese dope dealer Brilliant Chang. He told how, among the Bohemian set, "dope had sapped away all their feelings of modesty and restraint".

On one occasion he had watched as a young girl writhed around naked, apparently in a state of ecstasy as the "rhythm of Africa's pulsing music — translated into American jazz tunes — did the rest". She eventually collapsed with a scream, as she "suddenly realised her nakedness". The event was, Manning said, "ordinary enough in the circle in which I moved. I have selected it to tell my readers because it is possible to recount without offence".

Manning went on to open Eddy's Bar, a Soho backstreet dive populated by villains. According to some later reports, Manning kept a vicious Alsatian to guard against further police raids, although Walter Burmby continued to target him. On the occasion of one raid Manning, who was said to run "hundreds" of hookers, told Burmby, "I'm sorry you came. I'm just going out for a walk, I'll come back later when you're through." A detective followed him into a nearby café, where he watched as Manning laughed, joked and twiddled his gold-topped cane. On another occasion, Burmby marched Manning to a police station where he was strip searched. Even the heels of his shoes were inspected, but there was no trace of drugs. Indeed, Manning was never convicted of drugs offences again.

He turned his hand mainly to pimping and other low-level crimes and was acquitted at the Old Bailey of receiving stolen goods in 1928. Manning struck up a relationship with a Russian prostitute named Dora Lippack and the pair were eventually arrested after being found in possession of items stolen from the car of Lady Diana Cooper. The evidence was overwhelming — Dora was wearing a pair of Lady Diana's stockings when found. She was deported after serving nine months. Manning was handed three years penal servitude, but would not make it out of prison alive. Speaking after the verdict, Det Sgt Powell said of Manning, "He could well be described as the worst man in London."

Like many male prisoners with health problems, Manning was sent to Parkhurst on the Isle of Wight, which at the time had some of the best hospital facilities in the country. But he quickly deteriorated and was found to be suffering from syphilis. He was treated by a Dr Maurice Ahern, who described Manning as a polite patient who was always full of gratitude. Manning's pleasant behaviour, despite his professional life of crime, stayed with him until the end. In return, Ahern allowed him to eat a diet practically of his own choosing, mainly eggs, soup and jelly. Manning died on February 8, 1931, with the cause of death given as acute myelitis, toxaemia and heart failure. Manning was buried nearby.

Even in 1955, long after Manning's death, he was still being talked about as the Worst Man in London. The famous ex-detective Robert Fabian, known as Fabian of the Yard, wrote in his autobiography, *London After Dark*, of the occasion in May 1921 when he first patrolled the streets of Soho alongside an older copper:

# DOPE KINGS OF LONDON

We walked down Lisle Street and my companion paused, drawing me into the shadows, as a tall, slim negro came out of a house. He was superbly well dressed — perhaps somewhat overdressed — in a tightly tailored black overcoat with velvet collar and homburg hat, and cigar in his big teeth. He glanced alertly up and down the street but did not see us. A white girl was with him — a pretty, delicate little creature, but rather disheveled and forlorn, I thought. 'Who is it?' I asked, when they were gone. The old policeman said solemnly: 'That son, was Eddie Manning — called Eddie the Villain. And take my advice son, if it means pinching that fellow, never go alone. If you get an urge to talk to him, don't. If he wants to give you a cigarette, refuse it. Never take a drink from him, never go to his place if you want information. Scrub him out of your life — he's the worst man in London.[11]

Did Eddie Manning deserve his nickname? Outside of the police and judiciary, there were few Londoners who had a bad word to say about him. Except, perhaps, for his long-suffering neighbours in Lisson Street. He never murdered anybody, although he showed during the triple shooting in 1920 that he was certainly capable of causing serious harm.

None of the scores of women who he allegedly pimped ever came forward to report mistreatment (that we know of) and in fact, the women who did commit their views to the record spoke well about him. There is the issue of Margaret Hasler, who died after supposedly being supplied cocaine, and Eric Goodwin, another overdose associated with Manning. But then again, both were long-standing addicts and would most likely have sourced drugs from elsewhere if Manning had not been around.

# THE WORST MAN IN LONDON

There seems to be no doubt that Eddie the Villain was a major West End drug dealer for at least part of his criminal career and was able to buy fancy clothes and finance at least one legitimate business in the form of his bar. Yet his various rented accommodations could never be described as luxurious and in fact remained relatively squalid throughout his life.

Manning was a talented musician who came to London to work or study, whichever version of his life story you choose to believe. It was only through his association with the vivacious West End nightlife that he recognised the profits that could be made supplying dope. But, as we shall see, Manning was really only a street-level operator, despite employing a team of sub-dealers to insulate himself from the law. And while Eddie Manning might have been known as the Worst Man in London, he was far from the only bad character to be selling drugs on the capital's streets.

Another dealer given a long sentence under the 1923 amendment to the Act was Jack Kelson, also known as Jack Delzim, a twenty-one-year-old from Trinidad arrested in August 1923. Kelson and a white companion had been followed by Det Sgt Roberts and Det Con Wakeling as they boarded a bus in Oxford Street and travelled to the Commercial Road in the East End, where they headed to a Chinese café in Limehouse Causeway. Sgt Roberts explained to the court how — after the duo spotted Kelson taking something out of his jacket pocket — he began to grapple with the suspect. Both men fell to the ground and Kelson put a white packet in his mouth.

At that point, Roberts said he "got him by the throat and tried to make him spit out what he had put into his mouth".

Kelson opened his jaw during the struggle and Roberts saw a packet and some white powder on his tongue. Another packet containing white powder fell out of Kelson's pocket and onto the floor. Kelson was, he said, "very violent and behaving like a mad man". Detective Wakeling, who had successfully arrested the other man, came to Roberts' aid.

Kelson had been investigated after he was overheard enticing women to try cocaine for 5s a packet, the same price charged by Manning. It was claimed that after they had become addicted, he would charge £5, although Kelson was suspected of dealing drugs on behalf of Chinese criminals based in the East End rather than Manning. Back at the station, the white suspect was released but Kelson was pressed for further information. According to his all-too-believable account, one officer told him, "Come on darkie, you coloured fellows know where the cocaine comes from. Tell me where you fellows get it and I will let you go."

Racism aside, it was a question still unsolved by the Eddie Manning case, not to mention the contemporary cases of May Roberts and Julia Kitt. How exactly did London's dope kings and queens get hold of their wares? Was there a criminal mastermind overseeing the whole of the capital's supply? As the detectives continued their fight against the dope traffic, they had only one name in mind — Brilliant Chang.

---

[8] Very approximately, worth about £10-12 in today's money.

[9] Detectives also requested Manning's file two months later, when the dancing instructress Freda Kempton died from a cocaine overdose. Manning was suspected of selling her the drug on previous occasions.

---

[10] The team of Walter Burmby and Charles Owen was not infallible. A 1923 case saw Owen and another officer, Detective Dixon, go undercover to purchase what they thought was opium from two immigrant coffee makers in Old Compton Street. After asking to buy the drug, Owen and Dixon were handed a "large cake of brown substance" which later turned out to be entirely legal hashish. The officers were reprimanded by the magistrate, who felt they had induced the sale from the two men, who otherwise would not have offered the 'opium'.

Scotland Yard insisted that because cannabis was often called opium in the home country of one of the men, Sudan, and that in any case cannabis was illegal there, they should press ahead with the prosecution. Charges were dropped against one man before trial, while the other was found not guilty. However, the police managed to spin the mess in their favour by giving off-the-record information to reporters. The case was reported under headlines such as "The New Dope Peril: Hashish to Come Under Dangerous Drugs Act" and two years later cannabis was indeed added to the list of controlled substances.

[11] Fabian may have been confused, or simply making the account up. After all, Manning was serving his sentence for the triple shooting in May 1921.

# 5. THE CLEVER DANCER

**F**reda Kempton was always in demand. Her job was to dance with the customers at Brett's Dance Hall, sometimes all night, for a small wage plus tips. As a 'dance instructress' the take-home pay was among the best in clubland at up to £80 a week, while the future prospects for the girls at Brett's could be even better. The daughters of the former owner, Kate Meyrick, had all married into the aristocracy, a policy Meyrick described as "Earls for my girls" (Mary to the 14th Earl of Kinnoull, Irene to the 6th Earl of Craven, and Dorothy to the 26th Baron de Clifford). Young women such as Freda could realistically hope to meet similarly well-connected members of high society, who might pluck them from obscurity to become their wives or kept mistresses.

# THE CLEVER DANCER

The most successful dancers, like Freda, were naturally also the most attractive, but even the prettiest young flower still had to combine charm, dancing ability and stamina if they wanted to become a top earner. And the key to staying up all night at Brett's was simple — cocaine.

Freda Kempton's story was typical of many of the West End's dancers, chorus girls and actresses. She was born in 1899 to a middle-class family affluent enough to employ servants in their Islington home. But her father, George, was a habitual drunk and ran away with another woman while on a trip to Canada in 1919.

Freda remained close to her mother, Jessie, but was determined to make her own way in the world. She yearned first for the stage and then, when it became apparent that she was not good enough, to meet a decent man who would make her his wife. Sadly, she ended up working at Brett's, after first finding work at the Palais de Danse, in Hammersmith, and then the Portman Rooms. At one point, in March 1921, she took up with a man named Harry Adams, who was one of the co-owners of the nearby New Court Club and Moody's, in Tottenham Court Road. She went to live with him before they broke up at Christmas of that year.

While Brett's attracted plenty of high rollers and would be considered tame by today's standards, for a world in which Victorian values still held great sway it was not a particularly salubrious establishment, with the same sort of reputation that a high-class strip club might garner today.

In May 1922, the new owner, Ernest Bosworth Barron, was summoned to Marlborough Street police court on charges of "drunkenness and disorder". The court heard from Mr Dimes, the prosecutor, about scandalous allegations made by an undercover police officer, Constable Banks. The copper, he said, had witnessed several "women of loose character" inside the club, many in a "drugged condition". On one occasion he saw "thirty men drunk". Another particularly egregious incident involved a gentleman pulling down the strap of a dancer's evening dress, which had "left her exposed".

A newspaper report described the scene as witnessed by the officer:

> He had seen some of the women soliciting inside Brett's club. The woman, he alleged, was drugged. He watched for five minutes. Her jaws were twitching and she occasionally went off in a dazed condition. There were over ninety in the hall where the act of disrobing he had described took place. Another constable stated that the dancing was of a suggestive character. On one occasion he noticed a man and a woman sitting on a settee behaving in an unseemly manner. Cross-examined, he agreed that the modern dances are very fantastic.

Barron was fined £100, the full penalty for allowing unlicensed dancing. Yet the story was merely a sleazy postscript to a tragic case that had gripped the nation much like the death of Billie Carleton four years earlier. The ever-vigilant Constable Banks, while working undercover, would certainly have noticed its tragic protagonist, Freda Kempton.

"Freda was a clever dancer," a friend later told a newspaper reporter. "Though personally I used to think her steps of an exaggerated type. Always full of energy, even at four or five in the morning she would still be dancing and showing very few signs of fatigue."

Freda had previously appeared in the newspapers herself when, in January 1922, she spoke at an inquest for her friend Audrey Knowles-Harrison, a twenty-four-year-old chorus girl who had killed herself by placing her head in a gas oven. Audrey's husband, Captain Knowles-Harrison, had been posted to India the previous year and Audrey had waived him off at Southampton. But she later wrote to him to say she was living with another man. Although the captain wrote back to forgive her, he never received a reply and later cut off his estranged wife's allowance. Freda recalled her friend a few weeks before her death, stumbling drunk into a club with three men, where she spent most of the evening crying in a corner.

A month after the inquest, Freda was feeling low herself, partly as a result of her friend's death but also because of the break-up of her relationship with Adams and another an unnamed man, thought to be a Brett's regular. Her mental state would not have been helped by her growing reliance on cocaine. And, while the occupation of 'dance instructress' was used as something of a euphemism, a police report at the time made no bones about it, stating that "there is no doubt that she has been...frequenting nightclubs and earning her living by prostitution".

Freda's close friend, Rose Heinberg, an eighteen-year-old girl who also went by the name of Jose Andre, later recalled how Freda suggested it would be "funny, if I, an important witness in Audrey Harrison's case, were to commit suicide". Rose also told how, when she stayed with Freda on one occasion, the dancer opened up her powder puff case to reveal thirteen packets of cocaine. In hindsight, it was a clear indication that Freda was dealing as well as using the drug.

At the time of her death, Freda was lodging above a furniture shop in Westbourne Grove, Notting Hill, owned by a woman named Sarah Heckel. At one point, Sarah asked Freda if she had ever taken cocaine. She said she'd tried it once, but would never do it again. Three weeks later, when Sarah's daughter Sadie caught her coming home at 6am with her jaw "twitching", Freda claimed she'd been drugged.

Another drug-fuelled late night and early morning adventure heralded Freda's demise. At this point in her career, Freda could genuinely claim to be a well-known West End personality. She was no Billie Carleton, star of the stage, but she was the most in-demand girl at Brett's and that meant her name was familiar to people across the club scene. It was gone three o'clock in the morning and Freda and Rose found themselves in the New Court Club, off Tottenham Court Road. It was there that a drinker named Micky pulled Freda aside and told her that a man named Billy wanted to meet her. Intrigued, the women left the club with Micky and headed to Billy's Chinese restaurant at 107 Regent Street.

According to Rose's later inquest evidence, Billy took an instant shine to Freda, keeping her glass topped up with port throughout the evening. Later on, she went outside with him and came back in with her mouth "twitching". Rose asked what was wrong and Freda insisted she had been drugged. "I know I have been drugged because a year ago when I used to take drugs my mouth used to twitch," she said. "I used to have to eat chewing gum to make people think I was eating sweets."

# THE CLEVER DANCER

This had been Freda's first introduction to Brilliant 'Billy' Chang.

# 6. THE LIMEHOUSE SPIDER

**T**he emergence of Brilliant Chang as a media sensation shocked the British public, while at the same time appearing to confirm some widely held prejudices. And just as in the case of Eddie Manning, issues of race and nationality figured highly in his Press coverage and treatment by the authorities.

In British minds of the early twentieth century, the Chinese were associated with three main enterprises, namely laundry, silk and opium. While the opium dens of the East End, Limehouse in particular, had been popular with certain sections of society since the 1860s, their prevalence was often exaggerated by accounts in both fiction, including in the burgeoning movie industry, and the frequently excitable Press. As a result, the small Chinese community, which had numbered only around five hundred and ninety in the 1891 census, was often on the receiving end of racism and discrimination. The irony that most Chinese dope smokers had only picked up the habit as a result of the British trade in the drug from India to China — leading to the nineteenth-century Opium Wars — was usually conveniently forgotten, particularly by the end of World War One.

From 1915, the author Thomas Burke penned several stories set in Limehouse and narrated by a Chinese character, Quong Lee. One such tale, entitled *The Chink and the Child*, followed a Chinese dope-smoking lowlife who beguiles his way into the heart of a forlorn and abused young white woman.[12]

An even more sensationalist account of the East End's Chinese contingent came in the author Sax Rohmer's 1919 novel *Dope*, which featured a Billie Carleton-esque protagonist named Rita Dresden, a cocaine-addicted actress who frequents Mayfair opium parties, embarks on seedy trips to Limehouse and to the home of a sinister one-eyed trafficker named Sin Sin Wa, whose wife facilitates the West End soirees. Rohmer always denied it was based on the Billie Carleton case, despite its obvious similarities and allusions to the Lau Pings.

Rohmer also created the dastardly Chinese supervillain Dr Fu Manchu, who probably did more to popularise the idea of the Yellow Peril than any other individual or event, real or fictional. Until Fu Manchu, the enduring caricature of the Chinese people was of a diminutive, somewhat feeble and deferential race. But Fu Manchu was an even more extraordinarily racist and xenophobic caricature, depicted as a mysterious figure who had a wicked hand in a wide variety of crimes, always as the puppet master, controlling assassins, criminals and femme fatales. The character appeared in ten novels between 1913 and the end of World War Two, as well as several comic strips and dramatizations.

When Brilliant Chang arrived on the scene, it appeared to the Press and public as though the mendacious Dr Fu Manchu had leapt from the fiction pages into the nightclubs, and courtrooms, of London. But the reality was that sophisticated Chinese criminals were already well-established across Europe and would continue to be major players in the dope game long after Brilliant Chang's heyday.

For example, in January 1925, a sergeant based in the Limehouse CID, Percy Janes, was on the case of Ah Kiu Tchai (alias Sei Sou). Tchai had arrived in London in 1918, registered as a seaman, and moved to Limehouse Causeway. He left for Holland after a few weeks and there was no record of him ever returning. Janes was also interested in Mun Won (alias Chan See and Wang Man), who had also arrived in 1918 before leaving for Holland.

Janes' investigations were prompted by Special Branch observations in Amsterdam, compiled in a December 1924 report. Ah Kiu Tchai was described as a restaurant owner and boarding house master, but also suspected of being a cocaine smuggler and an accessory to the murder of another Chinese gangster. In addition, he was suspected of being a member of the "Bo-On" and the "Three Fingers" Tongs. He was, wrote a sergeant based in the city, an "undesirable of the first order". Mun Won was regarded in similarly low terms.

Unfortunately, Sgt Janes was able to supply the officers in Holland with limited information, given the fact that they had spent only a short period living in London and Liverpool, and quite some time ago.

Another former denizen of the Far East was the Chinese criminal Won Tip, whose brushes with the law dated back to 1907. A violent bully who was arrested several times for causing grievous bodily harm, Tip made money from his fellow countrymen in Liverpool's Chinatown by processing opium. He also made a living preparing the drug for smugglers to ship to China. Chief Insp Harry Burgess, of Liverpool's City police, had recommended to the Home Office that Tip be deported in 1916, alongside several other Chinese involved in drug trafficking. But Tip hired an expensive lawyer to argue in the High Court that he had been born in Hong Kong and therefore could not be deported. Won Tip remained in Britain until 1925, when he moved to Antwerp to head up a network of dope and arms traffickers. There he came into contact with Special Branch officers and would routinely grass up his rivals sending drugs to Britain. It was not until 1929 that Belgian police managed to make a charge stick and he was locked up for just one month for smoking opium.

Percy Janes was able to supply more detailed reports on other characters now operating in the Dutch underworld. In December 1924, May Roberts, the White Queen of Limehouse, resurfaced in Rotterdam where she was briefly reunited with her lover Lum Chong, but she was swiftly deported as an "undesirable alien".

Choy Loy, the erstwhile business partner of Max Faber, was also in Holland. Loy had been deported to Belgium and his English visa cancelled. He tried to get back into England in November 1924, but was refused entry at Southampton. By then, the Met regarded him as a "boss cocaine and opium trafficker" with a restaurant and brothel in Hamburg known as "one of the notorious joints of that city". He vowed to return to Britain as a stowaway. Deceptively baby-faced and handsome, Loy's mugshot was copied and sent to all British ports. By this point, Loy was suspected not only of drug trafficking, but of being part of a major gun-running conspiracy, shipping German-made weapons to China in breach of the Treaty of Versailles.

Percy Janes compiled an extensive dossier on Choy Loy to help the Dutch and German police with their investigations. In addition to a long list of associates, including Julia and Choy Ah Kitt, Janes established that Loy spoke fluent English, possibly as a result of being born to a Chinese father and Venezuelan mother in South America. In fact, his English was so good that he had once been employed as an interpreter at the Old Bailey.

"The whole of our investigations here show that, although some of the arrangements might be made in this country, the actual purchasing and smuggling is done between Hamburg and Rotterdam, and thence direct to China," Janes wrote. "Choy Loy, who is now in a weak state of health, having recently undergone an operation for an internal abscess, is at present in Holland."

Before his failed attempt to re-enter Britain, Loy had in January 1924 sailed from Cherbourg in France for New York. The true purpose of his visit was not entirely clear, but from letters he sent to his wife back in East London, it appeared he was trying to broker a deal to sell guns to Chinese gangsters in the city, where there was an intense and bloody war between rival Tongs.

Describing a night out with friends at a restaurant, Loy wrote, "It happened that the former occupiers of this restaurant belong to a 'tong' and downstairs the landlord belong to a rival 'tong'". The letter has since been partially destroyed, but Loy went on to describe his fear, as the member of yet another tong, of being caught in the middle. He called New York's Chinese "a murderous lot" and "such brutes who got no pity for their enemies". Loy said that more than thirty people had already been killed and he was also fearful of new laws being made in Washington that could see him jailed for many years for arms trafficking, if caught.

"But it is too bad that very few ringleaders get killed," he added, "for these chaps deserve it while they enjoy life while the poor and innocent suffer...when they are in there they are so well protected by three or four detectives and about as much of their own gunmen....all the streets and the restaurants uptown are guarded by squads of police."

An underworld peace conference was later held in Chicago, but Loy was not confident of a resolution. "With money behind them they can well afford to pay for gunmen to kill....These chaps get a large some of money for each victim...Millions of dollars are thrown away already."

Some of the tongs in Britain were just as feared, although as ever, with the limited availability of firearms, not quite as violent.

# DOPE KINGS OF LONDON

One case that illustrated their ruthlessness had a tangential connection to Choy Loy, through his association with Lum Chong, the partner of May Roberts. This time, it was the Liverpool City Police who were able to supply considerable information on the drugs underworld in that city, at the request of Sir Malcolm Delevingne. In September 1923, Chief Inspector Harry Burgess wrote down what he knew of the Chinese trade in drugs:

> Chinese smugglers like anyone else engaged in the traffic experience the greatest difficulty in obtaining illicit drugs and their mean of supply are very limited owing to the extreme close surveillance which now exists, and undoubtedly what they do obtain, especially morphine and cocaine, they get from Continental countries. They do, however, procure a portion of the raw opium in Asiatic and African countries, for instance Asia Minor, Persia, the Red Sea or Egyptian ports, and cocaine I am told, by stewards who trade in the Canary Islands, can be purchased practically speaking without any restrictions there, and very cheap, but I have never known any cocaine to be brought into this port from the Canaries as there is no demand for it in this City.

Opium, he wrote, was the main drug being dealt by the Chinese in Liverpool, although he had been told that traffickers in Holland and Germany were smuggling cocaine elsewhere, again reiterating that there was, of course, no such demand on Merseyside.

On another occasion, Burgess was able to supply far more useful information about specific traffickers, namely Lum Chong and one of his business partners, William Hing, following a string of articles in *John Bull* about the Chung Yee tong, particularly one published in March 1923 titled "The Millionaire Dope King".

The article contained revelations about an unnamed former member who was "a person of affluence and importance in London, Cardiff and Liverpool. He holds a first-class season ticket to London and travels several times a week". The mystery man was described as wearing gold-rimmed glasses and carrying a gold-topped cane, to help him walk following a serious injury during a fight onboard a ship that left him "mutilated". The article went into lurid detail about his business methods and love life ("though he had a Chinese wife in Foo Chow, [he] keeps four white women in this country, two of them mothers of his children"). The article repeatedly called for the drugs baron to be deported.

Liverpool police believed the man referred to in the article was named Chan Chun Lee, and that the motive for publishing was far from the innocent campaigning journalism claimed by *John Bull*. Lee was a notorious figure in the Merseyside underworld. Born in Canton in 1886, Lee arrived in Cardiff in 1913, where he started out managing a boarding house for fellow sailors. He was later charged with running the premises as a gaming house. Lee escaped prosecution but was later found guilty of bribing four police constables and fined £100 at Liverpool Assizes. Lee then had a stroke of luck. His employer was suspected of trafficking in opium and deported. Lee inherited his businesses, which by now included a boarding house and tobacconist in Liverpool. He later expanded this portfolio by purchasing a restaurant.

Lee was a canny operator. His expanding property empire was frequently raided and opium found, but he had installed managers at most of his rented accommodation who would swear blind that Lee was not the true owner. By this method, he had a conviction for possession of opium quashed in 1920.

Lee had contracted syphilis in 1918, and used some of his new-found wealth to travel frequently to Harley Street for treatment, explaining the article's reference to first-class train journeys to the capital. At the time, Lee seemed to have a considerable amount of money, although by the time of the report he was "very hard up and very rarely leaves [the] city".

Lee had belonged to the Chung Yee tong in Liverpool, but was kicked out as a suspected police informant. He then joined the Sam Yep society, which as far as the police were concerned was a legitimate social organisation.

Harry Burgess wrote in his report, "The majority of the Chinese residents here bear the most dire hatred against Lee and would not hesitate to do anything to get rid of him, as they blame him for giving the information to the police that has led to the arrest of so many of their fellow countrymen during the past few years." Burgess added that a new society had been founded, called Chinese Masons, to mirror that of the Freemasons. Its true purpose, Burgess concluded, was to "devise a scheme to get rid of Chan Chun Lee".

One plot was to pay two men £150 to lure Lee to one of their laundries, then murder him and dispose of the body in quick lime inside a boiler. Alternatively, the conspirators planned to have Lee deported to China, where they "could very easily get him murdered". This they planned to do by planting opium in his pocket. It was believed that the *John Bull* article had been printed at their instigation and was written by a man named George Henry Kentwell, whose real name was Kum Tack Chow. The principal plotters included William Hing, believed to be the kingpin of Glasgow's opium scene, and his associate in the drug trade Lum Chong.

It's not known what happened to Chan, nor for that matter Hing or Chong. But the case shows that Brilliant Chang was far from the only highly successful Chinese criminal in the dope game, even if he did become the most notorious.

\*\*\*

There were various differing accounts of Brilliant Chang's early life and he made very little effort to set the record in stone, probably believing that ambiguity worked in his favour. Thought to have been born Chan Nan in Shanghai, or alternatively Canton, in around 1886, he insisted that "Brilliant" was a translation of his Chinese name, while "Billy" was a natural way to shorten it.

What is certain is that his father and uncle were both wealthy merchants and contractors to major British shipping firms and the Admiralty, with business interests both in Shanghai and Hong Kong. Chang was married as young as thirteen years old and his wife gave birth to at least three children.

There was some later press speculation, possibly plucked from a journalist's imagination, that the teenaged Chang developed a penchant for white women and took to trawling the areas of Hong Kong where Europeans were allowed to congregate, looking for sex. This led him to conversations with sailors and talk of London, where he was told the races could mix freely. Chang then set his heart on moving to England.

According to one report in the *World Pictoral News*, when Chang arrived in Limehouse he was "was amazed to find white girls, beautiful to his eyes, eating and drinking with men of the Orient. He knew that they would have been deported from China for doing the same thing". According to the article, Chang began to seduce women and would "shower them with gifts" before unceremoniously dumping them once he'd fulfilled his needs. Chang's sexual habits became expensive and so he took to drug dealing.

The true reason for Chang's descent into the underworld is probably more prosaic. The young man is known to have arrived in Britain in September 1914, registering himself with the authorities as a student. He had been sent by his father to study and then to oversee the British end of the family business. Yet according to later reports, just three years after arriving in Britain Chang had been suspected of drug trafficking, after police in Birmingham rounded up a gang and found paperwork suggesting he was the leader, although there was insufficient evidence to bring charges.

At some point, Chang moved to London permanently and opened an office in Leadenhall Street where he oversaw the family shipping business. He also started up one of London's first Chinese restaurants, at 107 Regent Street, and later a nightclub in Gerrard Street, years before it became known as Chinatown's high street. His involvement in drug trafficking, therefore, was not to meet the expenses accrued through his sexual excesses, but rather a natural sideways move for the young businessman. Simply put, Chang spotted the opportunity presented by the growing popularity of cocaine and his position as an importer, and decided to seize it.

One later report in *The Express* suggested Chang's private offices at the Regent Street restaurant had been used to host "secret parties of an indescribable kind" and he had also kept two flats in Piccadilly, where decadent gatherings were held. According to another report, the restaurant became the "rendezvous of Bohemians" and had "fascinated Londoners".

In other versions of the tale, Chang apparently met a man named Mr Enever (a convicted fraudster) and between them they concocted their criminal schemes. Subsequently, Chang made "scores of thousands of pounds" and much was sent home to China, to his wife and what the paper called his "three yellow children". Another article linked Chang to the notorious West End impresario, card sharp and fraudster Antoniani Dominico. On one occasion, it was said, Chang had lost his entire fortune in a game of cards with the Italian and had been forced to work for him as a barman. It took some years for him to recover his losses. Dominico was eventually deported in 1929.

Thanks to these various stories — none of them ever publicly confirmed by the man himself — Brilliant Chang became a myth in his own lifetime. The truth about his background and criminal exploits lay somewhere amid the salacious gossip, racism, rumour and misinformation (possibly some put around by Chang himself) that filled scores of column inches after the death of Freda Kempton. What is not in doubt is that Chang was closely connected to her demise.

# DOPE KINGS OF LONDON

Freda Kempton and Rose Heinberg returned to Brilliant Chang's restaurant together a few weeks after their initial drink and drugs session. This time it was merely a fleeting visit, because Freda asked Rose to wait outside and emerged a few minutes later with a small blue bottle of cocaine.

It was clear to Rose that Chang was providing Freda with the drug, but on what basis, whether to resell or for personal use, was not clear. In any case, the ongoing relationship between the dancer and the restaurant boss spelt the beginning of the end for Freda.

Like Billie Carleton's last night, Freda's final evening was raucous. She joined in with birthday celebrations for her landlord's daughter, Sadie, at the flat in Notting Hill, then headed out to Brett's at midnight. Later, she went with Rose and two male friends to the New Court Club for breakfast. When the men left, Freda tried to raise Chang on the telephone. Unable to locate him, the girls went to Kate Meyrick's latest venture, the Forty Three club in Gerrard Street. They guessed, correctly, that the charismatic Chang would be waiting there. They met, spoke briefly and drank, before heading back once again to Chang's restaurant, where they sipped whiskies until dawn. According to Rose, Chang gave Freda another blue bottle of cocaine. But the subsequent conversation was odd.

"Can you die while sniffing cocaine?" Freda asked him.

"No, the only way you can kill yourself is by putting cocaine in water," Chang replied, reassuringly.

As Freda and Rose headed home in a taxi, Freda startled her friend by saying she was going to kill herself by following

Chang's unwitting guidance. But it was not the first time Freda had made such a remark, and Rose let it pass.

When Freda arrived home she placed the bottle inside a pair of gloves, a familiar hiding place where she already had two other bottles stashed away. Freda's mother visited the next day and later described her daughter running, dancing and singing as she played "pick-a-back" with her young nephew, Ronnie.

Freda appeared in fine spirits and told her, "Goodbye mother, don't be fed up," when she left at 7pm. Journalists would later interpret the comment as a coded apology.

Freda went for an early evening nap and when she woke up asked Sarah Heckel for a glass of water. When Sadie arrived home about an hour later, she found Freda screaming in pain. She later went into convulsions and began foaming at the mouth, before dying at around 9pm.

Sadie claimed Freda had left a partial suicide note which read, "Mother, forgive me. The whole world was against me. I really meant no harm and-". Unfortunately, Sadie burnt the note, so its full contents could not be recorded at the inquest. Pages were also torn out of Freda's diary, although it could not be determined who had removed them, or for what purpose.

The newspapers carried startling reports of Freda's death the following day, calling it "another West End flat tragedy". Sarah told reporters how Freda had muttered, "Oh, let alone, I am fed up," before she collapsed on her shoulder, dying within half an hour. She added that the young woman was of "bright and happy disposition" but had become unhappy in the past fortnight.

# DOPE KINGS OF LONDON

The inquest at Paddington coroner's court opened a few days later, but had to be adjourned for further tests. Dr Bernard Spilsbury, who had also overseen the post mortem of Freda's friend Audrey Knowles-Harrison, said three bottles had been found which probably contained cocaine. He suspected the cause of death was cocaine poisoning, with the possibility that Freda could also have taken cyanide potassium. Further investigation was needed. Sarah told of giving Freda the glass of water and noticing later that it appeared "dirty and mucky". This too would need to be tested.

During the brief hearing, Freda's mother provided further evidence of her daughter's apparent depression, revealing how six months previously she had been injured after "falling through a glass skylight". The inquest also heard claims from Sadie that Freda said she had been drugged in the preceding weeks and that she had visited a Chinese restaurant. The scant but lurid details of the case helped to fuel growing public interest.

Before the inquest could be re-opened, an anonymous friend (possibly Rose Heinberg) sold her story to the *Sunday Post*, which published the account on March 12, 1922. The article, titled "Freda Kempton, as I knew her," described the dancer as "was one of the gayest little souls I ever knew" and a "reigning queen of various night clubs in London [who was] known by thousands of people, who will remember her for her real beauty and vivacious manner".

It was only in recent weeks, the article said, that Freda had become depressed as a result of Audrey Knowles-Harrison's suicide. "She was a beautiful girl, with dark, luscious eyes, an oval face, and her golden hair, which she wore bobbed, made her an attractive figure wherever she went," the article said. Until the age of seventeen, Freda had "lived a very quiet life" and only occasionally attended local dances where "the furore she created among the young fellows who crowded around her made her sigh for fresh worlds to conquer". The West End called out to her and, although she was not suited to the stage, she won the job of an assistant at a "high-class dancing academy" and began to settle into London society.

"Freda was practically without a friend in the West End when she entered upon her duties," the article continued. "She was just a little suburban girl, with very little experience of the gay life. She was dazzled by the dresses, the manner, and the gaiety of West End people. She took her position very seriously at first, devoting her time to teaching others their art, and when the dance was over went back to the quietude of her home, where she lived with her parents, her sister, and a brother, who was passionately devoted to her."

It was not long until Freda began to make friends and the "beauty, the grace, and the whimsical ways of this innocent little creature of eighteen attracted all who saw her, and in a short space of time Freda found that a great many people were making a big fuss of her". The article went on:

Then came the time when someone suggested a visit to a night club to have another little dance. Freda's eyes were opened to the staid character of the dancing places she had been in the habit of frequenting. At that time Freda's people were living in Kensington, and it was not long before she left her first appointment and took a situation at other dancing places in the West End, which was followed by invitations from the managers of night clubs who had found that Freda's presence was a magnet which attracted patrons to their places of amusement. An instructress at such places is so much sought after that she can command high fees, and Freda was now able to establish herself in a fashionable flat, to dress in a way which enhanced her reputation and made her an outstanding figure in the night haunts of London. She was like a child where pretty clothes were concerned, and was never so happy as when she was ordering a new or pretty frock. In some ways she was eccentric and prodigal in this respect, and always had a love for creating an impression. I have known her to leave a dance in the middle of it, drive to her dressmakers, change into a new and dazzling frock, and return to see the effect it would have on her admirers. With her dancing, too, Freda loved to create a sensation. She was very original in her expression of her art, and could always be picked out, even in a crowded ballroom, by the exaggeration of her steps. Whenever there was a big night at any of the dances Freda was always sure to supply the surprise of the evening. She used to take the central figure in the tableaux, and I well recall the pretty picture she made on one occasion when suddenly she appeared in a flower-decked trap drawn by a shaggy little Shetland pony. Tragedy had not yet come into Freda's life at this stage, and everyone was amused by the child-like glee of the pretty girl in the simple white frock and the sensation which she had made.

Scant reference was made in the article to Freda's hankering for illicit substances. But that angle was followed up the next week by reporter Olive Young, who took a tour of the West End in search of dope and dopers (accompanied, of course, by a male CID officer).

# THE LIMEHOUSE SPIDER

The trawl began at a well-heeled establishment, where "only the prettiest and most exclusive women are admitted to membership, and that conditional on their good behaviour. The average night club proprietor always starts with the best intentions in the world. Too well does he know that the police will only tolerate the place if it is well conducted, so at the beginning he carefully scrutinises everyone who comes into the club".

The place was packed with beautiful women and well-dressed men in evening suits, and was staffed by a "very deferential" doorman bedecked in a blue and gold uniform. The floor was "beautifully polished" and the walls "tastefully decorated in frieze". A black jazz band was playing on a stage (referred to in the article as a "n***** band"). Inside, the officer, apparently well-known to many of the workers and clientele, danced a fox-trot with a girl of nineteen:

> Her low-cut evening dress was a Parisian creation and must have cost thirty or forty guineas. When we were walking down the road half an hour later I asked my friend who she was. 'Oh,' he said, 'she used to be on the stage. Now she spends all her time in the night clubs, I hear she has been doing a bit of doping lately. There was a fellow who used to be very fond of her, and now, well, you can fill in the gap for yourself.' I knew. So many of the young girls who take to cocaine start the same way.

The rest of the tour of Soho, Piccadilly and Leicester Square hinted at danger and intrigue, although it produced little evidence of actual drug-taking. In fact, despite the officer speaking extensively of dopers, the pair could not actually find one, and instead the article went on to mention some "weird-looking" men including "three Indians, young fellows, who seemed to be medical students, half-a-dozen obvious foreigners" and a motley collection of others gathered in a "hole and corner affair in a basement".

In any case, the excitable reports in the *Sunday Post*, and in other papers, were just the build-up to the main event of Freda Kempton's inquest. At the re-opening, Rose Heinberg relayed the whole sorry story of Freda's meetings with Billy Chang and the events of her last night alive.

In total, Rose said, she and Freda had visited Chang's restaurant on four occasions. Rose denied being responsible for the missing pages from Freda's diary. She was also asked how she had learned of her friend's death and testified that her sister had received a call from a man named Basil Hennessey who was a customer at Brett's and formerly in the motor trade. According to Rose, Hennessey had said "Don't make any statement" or "Don't give any evidence". Hennessey, presumably, was the former man in Freda's life. He was legally represented at the inquest but not called to give evidence and little was made of him in the subsequent newspaper reports.

The same could not be said of Brilliant Chang, who was soon asked to step forward. He had no legal representation so the inquest had to be adjourned again, but the newspaper readers of Britain were now eager to hear from this mysterious Chinaman.

The next inquest date heard from John Webster, a senior Home Office analyst, who confirmed that a total of seven-and-a-half grains of cocaine had been found in Freda's stomach, kidneys and liver. Cocaine was also present in the glass tumbler and in the phials found by her bed. He estimated that Freda had taken at least ten grains. One grain, he said, would be enough to cause death. No other poison was found.

At last, with that deadly figure hanging over the court, Brilliant Chang was called to the stand. This would be Chang's formal entry into British criminal folklore, although behind the scenes detectives had already interviewed him and searched the restaurant, finding nothing.

The *Pall Mall Gazette* described how there was a "stir of heightened interest in the court when the coroner mentioned the name of Chang the Chinese".

At barely five feet tall, Chang compensated for his lack of physical presence with his charismatic demeanor and sharp dress sense. Decked out in a smart blue jacket with a luxurious fur collar, a "well-cut lounge suit", silk socks and grey suede shoes, Chang entered the stand.

His lawyer, CV Hill, raised a chuckle when he said the ancient Chinese method of taking an oath was by wringing the neck of a chicken.

"That, fortunately, is not the modern way," he added. "Nowadays I understand Chinese are sworn on the Testament."

Chang initially explained that he was a Confucian and that therefore a saucer should be broken as he did so, but in the end he relented and simply swore an oath. Chang was warned by the coroner, Mr HR Oswald, that anything he said could be used against him.

"I am going to say what is true," Chang insisted.

"You had better," replied Oswald.

Hill briefly cross-examined Rose, referring in the course of his questioning to his client as "Brilliant Chang."

The coroner interrupted, "Is that what you are going to call him Mr Hill?"

"Yes," he replied. "Brilliant Chang." There was a brief pause in the proceedings as an explanation was given as to why Chang had such an interesting first name.

The Chinaman went on to describe himself as a "general merchant" and said he was a contractor for the Admiralty, with an office in Leadenhall Street, in addition to the restaurant at 107 Regent Street. When questioned, he said that he had imported silks, tea and other goods, but never drugs, either intentionally or by accident.

"I have never done anything wrong in my life," he insisted.

Chang said he had met Freda Kempton at the New Court Club about five weeks before her death. She had arrived there with another girl, and went back with him to Regent Street. There were two men, Micky and Sammy, and she followed them alone, with Chang claiming Rose was not even there for the second part of the evening. Freda stayed at the restaurant for half-an-hour, leaving at about 6am. The coroner asked what Freda Kempton was doing there at that hour.

"She asked me for money. I gave her £5," Chang replied.

"Did you give her any bottles?" the coroner probed.

"No, sir."

Chang said he met Freda again a few days later at the New Court Club, where they drank port with two other men. Chang said she did not ask him for any drugs, powder or cocaine, only for money to pay for a taxi. Chang said she did come into his office, but only to ask about buying Chinese lamp shades.

The coroner again asked whether they spoke about drugs. "No," Chang replied. "She only asked me for the money to pay for a taxi cab."

Chang said he saw Freda again in her Notting Hill flat a few days later. She had phoned him several times asking for money. On that occasion her landlady, presumably either Sarah or Sadie, had called to say Freda was ill and needed money to pay for expensive medication. Chang said he had been told that Freda was "doping".

"Who told you that?" The coroner asked.

"The landlady," Chang replied.

"Did she mention the word cocaine?"

"No."

Chang said that he left £6 with the landlady and that evening Freda phoned to thank him, adding that she was much better and was going to the New Court Club that night. "The money had cured her," the coroner joked, to some general amusement in the courtroom.

About two weeks before she died, Freda visited the restaurant again and Chang gave her £1. "Didn't she ask you for something to take?" The coroner asked.

"No."

"Have you ever heard of cocaine?"

"I have never had it."

"Have you ever heard of it?"

"I have heard somebody say cocaine, but I have never seen it. I have seen people smoke opium."

Chang denied ever having possessed cocaine and emphatically replied "no sir" when asked if he had supplied the dancer. "Freda Kempton never asked for cocaine, nor did I give her any," he once again insisted. Chang said he was sad to hear of Freda's death the day after she died, but he had still gone dancing at the Forty Three club that night.

The jury found Freda Kempton committed suicide by taking cocaine during a state of temporary insanity and that the drug was supplied by person or persons unknown. "In my opinion," the coroner said, "whichever way you decide, whether you believe Miss Heinberg or Chang, there is not sufficient evidence on which to find a verdict of manslaughter against Chang."

It was reported after the verdict that "some of the girls [who had been in court] rushed to Chang, patted his back, and one, more daring than the rest, fondled the Chinaman's black, smooth hair and passed her fingers slowly through it".

Brilliant Chang's legend rapidly grew on the back of his sensational court appearance. Another report, in the *Daily Express*, recalled his dramatic entrance to a nightclub a few weeks previously:

> A dance had just finished and the little tables were crowded. Suddenly the curtain covering the door was pushed aside and 'Brilliant' Chang stood at the entrance. He paused a moment, silhouetted against the dark curtains, while his eyes searched the room. A murmur ran around the tables, 'There's the rich young Chink!' Half a dozen girls rose to greet him. Nodding slightly, he advanced and spoke to one of them. The others, shrugging their shoulders, sat down again.

A few weeks earlier, in the immediate wake of Freda's death, the same newspaper had run another report on the West End club scene, describing an unlicensed dance hall on a seedy backstreet where a Chinese man, probably Chang, had appeared at the top of the stairs in a similarly debonair manner:

> He was not the 'Chink' of popular fiction, a cringing yellow man hiding his clasped hands in the wide embroidered sleeves of his embroidered gown. This man's evening clothes had been made up not far from Savile Row. His long, thin hands were manicured, his manners were too perfect to be described as good. The picture he made as he stood there framed against the dark stairway, smiling around the room with that fixed Oriental smile which seems devoid of warmth and humanity, was so typical of the novelist's ideas of dopedom that he seemed like a vision conjured up by the surroundings. 'Everything's going strong!' he laughed, as he stepped down. A young girl ran up to him, held her arms out, he clasped her closely to him and they danced. Not only did he dance in perfect style, but he also reveled in an atmosphere of general approbation.

The coroner later wrote of the "grilling" he had given Chang under cross-examination, claiming that "largely as a result of the questions I made him answer, police attention was directed to the drug traffic of which he was subsequently found guilty. Had I not been able to cross question this man his filthy trade might never have come to light." The reality, however, was that the Press was at least equally as responsible for focusing police attention on Chang, if not more so.

The widespread publicity in the wake of the Freda Kempton case gave the Metropolitan Police a problem. It was clear to the public that Brilliant Chang was a man who deserved some measure of justice, yet there was really no evidence to proceed with any charges. Meanwhile, the newspapers continued to produce reports about London's mysterious "Chinese dope king," although for fear of libel they could not always explicitly link Chang's name to their stories.

For example, after the inquest, the *Evening News* ran a story about West End drug dealing, in which a Fu Manchu-like criminal mastermind controlled a vast network of "porters, cloakroom attendants, railway officials, milliners, coffee-house proprietors and, of course, women victims who recruited other women into drug slavery". The *Express* ran a similar story the same day, entitled "Cocaine Girls in the West End."

Another writer, in the *Illustrated Sunday Herald*, noted how the nightclub "exists for the purpose of trading in drink and drugs; and the more important of the two is the trade in drugs. One only has to go to any night club and see the Chinese and South Americans, and aliens of all degrees of colour, to see that the best brains of every country's roguery are attending to these things." Just as in the early war years, the press and by extension the public, was gripped by fear of a drugs epidemic directed by foreigners, Brilliant Chang in particular.[13]

A few weeks after the Freda Kempton inquest, Brilliant Chang was in the news again. This time, it was a man named Henry Cadogan Best who found himself up at Marlborough police court for assaulting a man named John Nelson Miles inside Chang's restaurant.

Miles had been sent to the restaurant by a group of solicitors to take charge as the new manager, but found Chang, Best and two other men in an upstairs office. It wasn't clear exactly why Miles should be the new manager if Chang was the owner, but the arrangements may well have been more complicated than the available records demonstrate. Chang may also have been in the process of selling his stake in the business, hence the confusion. In any case, an argument began because Best, who had one Chinese and one English parent, was branded a "half-caste" by Miles, who then approached "in a threatening manner".

"So I gave him one with my left," Best said. "And he went down like a log of wood." The comment provoked much laughter within the public gallery. Best added that he was "of Eastern and Western extraction and I have been educated in a comparatively gentlemanly manner".

For his part, the victim John Miles said Henry Best was "a personal friend of the proprietor, Mr Brilliant Chang, and I have full power of attorney to run the place". He tried to suggest the assault was "an echo of the Freda Kempton case," but was impatiently closed down by the magistrate.

"I don't want any echoes," he said. "Please keep to the facts."

Best was ultimately fined £4 with £1 costs. Brilliant Chang himself had no involvement in the case, but it was not the last time his associates would be brought before the courts.

---

12 The film based on the story, Broken Blossoms, or The Yellow Man and the Girl, which premiered in New York in 1919, was well-received and softened the Chinese protagonist to mitigate against the national concern over the so-called Yellow Peril.

13 It was during this new moral panic that the film Cocaine, made by director and Alfred Hitchcock's mentor Jack Graham-Cutts, was

released, becoming the subject of a major censorship row. The plot, essentially, was a retelling of the Billie Carleton/Freda Kempton narrative with a Chinese bad guy.

# 7. DOWNFALL

The police felt they had little choice but to keep the pressure on Brilliant Chang. They placed the Regent Street restaurant under observation and monitored one man in particular, Ah Sing, who lived above the shop with seven other Chinese men.

Officers saw him in a doorway in Warwick Street, where he showed a woman something wrapped in brown paper. "I will get you £5 of the real stuff tomorrow," he was overheard telling her. The next day, the officers watched the pair in Swallow Street, then observed as Sing went into the restaurant and emerged to cross Regent Street a short time later, at which point he was arrested. They found two packets of opium and one of cocaine on Sing.

Another man, Lo Li Foo, aged twenty, was also arrested as he left the restaurant. He "became violent" according to police, and was taken to the station, where a small amount of cocaine was found in a silver matchbox. Foo's room in a nearby flat in Seven Dials was decked out as an opium den, with five blankets and pillows on the floor, a saucer full of ashes and an opium pipe. It was discovered that the cocaine was diluted with boracic, an antiseptic powder.

In both cases, detectives had used two undercover informants, Gertrude Lewis and Mabel Smith ("both dressmakers out of employment") to gather their evidence.

The men were convicted in August 1922 and given six months' hard labour for drugs possession. Three other men were also convicted as part of the operation. One of them was named Sin Fong, aged fifty-two, who was arrested after offering a packet of cocaine to a woman in Glasshouse Street, saying, "You want £5 worth?" He said he had obtained it from Chang's restaurant, leading to the arrest of another chef, Lon Chenk, aged thirty-seven, and a cook, Yong Yau, thirty-nine, both believed by police to be working under Sin Fong.

The police were extremely pleased with their efforts, even though Brilliant Chang had not been snared. "These convictions are most satisfactory and will undoubtedly have a deterrent effect," one detective wrote in his report. "The proprietor of the Chinese restaurant in Regent Street has sold his business and the den of depravity [Foo's flat] where opium and drugs were freely used, has been closed. Mabel and Gertrude were each given £3 from the informants' fund.

The following February, when the convicted men were deported from Liverpool Street station en route to a cargo ship waiting in Harwich, the newspapers reported the scene, describing the men as "cocaine fiends" being "sent back to their own country". The men were seen off at the station by "a dozen flashly dressed English girls and women, not one of whom was more than thirty". The girls handed the men cigarettes and chocolate for their voyage and "some of the girls even kissed the men just before the train left the station". Three of the women "were so overcome at the departure of their Oriental friends that they became hysterical and it was with difficulty that they were induced to leave the station".

For the police, it was a good result. But there was still no hard evidence linking Brilliant Chang himself to drug dealing. The closest they came was an unsigned note, scrawled in black ink on a scrap of paper and stamped August 10, 1922, which read, "A consistent supply of cocaine can always be obtained by Nancy O'Murray from Brilliant Chang who is hidden in a Jermyn Street doorway when she arrives in a taxi. A big deal was carried through at Brett's last evening."

It must have appeared obvious that Chang was at the head of a drug trafficking network. Not only did he have the means to import narcotics disguised among legitimate goods, but a drug dealing ring had been operating out of his restaurant. It was most likely with the latter point in mind that Chang decided to quit the restaurant game.

He opened up the Palm Court Club in Gerrard Street, not far from Kate Meyrick's joint. But with constant attention from the police, Chang lasted just six months and 'retired' to a poky second-floor flat above a new Chinese restaurant he opened in Limehouse Causeway.

Despite the downmarket address, Chang continued to live in some opulence. A later report in *The Express* described it as an "astounding apartment, a nest of Oriental luxury". The walls were papered in blue and silver, "with silver dragons rampant" while the bed was "a great divan of luxury". The floors were covered in a carpet which "silenced the softest tread".

On one occasion, when police officers burst into the flat, they found Chang in his luxurious bed with two West End chorus girls. Bizarrely, they also found a stack of handwritten letters Chang used to seduce young women. Nobody could fault Brilliant Chang for his chutzpah:

Dear Unknown One — Please do not regard this as a liberty that I write to you, as I am really unable to resist the temptation after having seen you so many times. I should extremely like to know you better, and should be glad if you would do me the honour of meeting me one evening where we could have a little dinner and a quiet chat together. I do hope you will consent to this, as it will give me great pleasure, and in any case do not be cross with me for having written to you. Yours hopefully, Chang. PS, if you reply, please address it to me at the Shanghai Restaurant, Limehouse Causeway, E14.

Brilliant Chang was finally brought down thanks to a young female drug addict and failed actress named Violet Payne, also known as Mary Deval or Ruby Duval. Payne had been arrested for shoplifting in May 1923 and quickly spilled the beans on her source of supply for both cocaine and heroin, a Lisson Grove chemist run by a couple called James and Mary Burnby. As a result of her evidence, Mary Burnby was jailed for six months and James Burnby for two months. Violet needed a new supplier. Unfortunately for him, she chose Chang.

# DOWNFALL

In March 1924, officers watched as Violet walked out of Chang's Shanghai Restaurant arm-in-arm with a man named Edward Bolton. The pair headed into the Commercial Tavern pub in Pennyfields, and after Bolton left alone he was seized by two officers. Bolton told the coppers Payne had offered to sell him dope but he'd decided to call it a night. He explained that Violet had approached him in another pub, the Oporto Tavern in Poplar, and asked him to go for coffee in the Chinese restaurant, where she disappeared out the back before coming back with a small amount of dope.

As Violet herself left the pub, she was seen hiding two packets on her person, one up her sleeve and the other up her skirt. She was grabbed by the watching officers, PC Gerald Pond and PC Herbert Gray, both on probation for the CID. Back at Limehouse police station, Payne became violent, threw herself to the floor and shoved one of the packets in her mouth, swallowing its contents. The other packet was found and, when it was later tested, it was found to contain cocaine. According to the officers' account, Violet insisted that Chang had sold her the drugs.

Chang's flat above the restaurant was subsequently raided, although the suspect had to be fetched from the restaurant to obligingly let the officers in. "I heard a young woman was asking for me tonight," Chang told Sgt Percy Janes. "But I did not see her. If I had any cocaine I should not hide it here as I know the police have been after me since poor Freda Kempton's case. You can search everywhere, you won't find any here."

But when Janes found a small packet of cocaine hidden behind a loose board in a kitchen cupboard, Chang replied, "I did not know that was there. It must have been left by the people who were here before me." When Chang was shown a copy of Violet Payne's statement, which had been taken at 4am, he replied angrily, "There's a bloody cow."

Chang and Payne were taken to the police court the next morning where Chang asked for an adjournment to consult his solicitor. Janes later wrote that he "had reason to believe" Chang's defence would be funded by the Chee Kong tong.

When the case reached the Old Bailey, where Chang once again cut an impressive figure in his familiar fur-lined coat, Violet told how the deal had been done. She explained that she had met Chang in his restaurant and asked for cocaine. The pair left separately and a hand appeared over a wall clutching a packet, for which she exchanged £1. She also admitted to sleeping with Chang on a previous occasion in return for drugs. As the *Sunday Post* had it, "Brilliant Chang, dope fiend and uncrowned king of the underworld from the dark alleys of Limehouse to the brightly lit nightclubs of London, has at last been run to earth."

The article described his courtroom performance in glowing terms, but suggested hubris had been his downfall. Chang insisted that he was not a drug dealer, was out of work and only had £50 left in the world, £15 of which he had borrowed. While Chang managed to pick apart Violet's story and his fluent English allowed him to understand and answer questions clearly, he was "too glib in his answers, too explanatory about 'snow' and acquaintance with white women to convince a British jury of his innocence". When asked whether he believed the police had planted the evidence, Chang took a diplomatic approach. "Perhaps it was left there by the previous tenant," he replied. Too clever by far, the journalist reckoned. Chang's standing with the jury was probably damaged further by the Recorder of London, Sir Ernest Wild, who at one point blurted out the surely prejudicial demand, "Why don't you speak the truth?!"

A more committed lawyer would, no doubt, have found grounds to appeal.

The entire case was steeped in racial prejudice. When PC Janes gave evidence he made it clear that Chang had a penchant for "white women". He would never deal directly with a stranger, Janes said, but would only supply those who came to him through other women he had previously made a "dupe" or "corrupted". As the detective described it, "He used of late to sit in the Chinese restaurants of Limehouse and clients would come to him. His motor car would take him on mysterious journeys to the West and to the suburbs." None of these women, until Violet, had so far found the courage to testify against him, Janes insisted.

Chang's alleged drug trafficking was further linked with the plight of the West End's cocaine-addled young women. "There is no doubt that Chang supplied Freda Kempton with the cocaine which caused her death," the detective told the court. "This man would sell drugs to a white girl only if she gave herself to him as well as paying him," he added.

And in reference to the secret hiding place where the cocaine was allegedly found, the detective added, "This man has carried on the traffic with real Oriental craft and cunning." Janes pointed out that, although Chang claimed the drug had been left there by previous occupants, he had previously searched the same spot in Chang's presence and found nothing there. Chang was found guilty by the jurors in a matter of minutes, so quickly in fact that he did not have time to leave the dock between them retiring to the jury room and reaching their verdict.

For the purposes of sentencing, Janes gave a detailed description of Chang's alleged methods of importation and his wider criminal network although, tellingly, no actual evidence was produced. Chang, he said, had sold five types of dope, not just the "white snow" of cocaine, but also heroin, morphine, opium and hashish. His supplies came from Chinese and other foreign sailors, and he also had a network of agents in Paris, Brussels, Berlin and Antwerp, as well as in China. One of these agents from Paris was said to be a woman who sewed the drugs into her young daughter's dress to smuggle them past Customs.

None of this had anything to do with the charge for which Chang had just stood trial, but despite the drugs found in his flat having a wholesale value of just two pence Chang, now aged thirty-seven, was sentenced to fourteen months' imprisonment, with deportation ordered to take place later. In sentencing Chang, Sir Ernest made the following observations, "It is you and men like you who are corrupting the womanhood of this country. Girls must be protected from this soul-destroying drug and society must be purged."

All three officers involved in Payne and Chang's arrests were given commendations. A handwritten note from the Assistant Chief Constable on a report of the trial described it as a "splendid case which attained an unusual amount of publicity in the press. The officers are deserving of the highest praise and I recommend that they are granted a reward."

# DOWNFALL

The Press naturally had a field day with the case. New details and allegations emerged about Chang both in court and from detectives speaking off-the-record who wanted to ensure their victory was given acres of newsprint. *The Express* told how "the yellow king of the dope runners" and "leader of organised Oriental vice" had at last been brought to justice. Chang had, the paper said, taken "the sentence completely unperturbed. He was the unemotional yellow man, his narrow slit eyes blank, his face a mask."

*The Sunday Post* unarguably obtained the scoop of the week, securing an exclusive interview with Freda Kempton's grieving mother, Jessie. While powerful, her testimony about meeting Chang in the wake of her daughter's death was delivered in decidedly purple prose. "Sooner or later," she was quoted as saying, "I knew that the fingers of the law would close around Brilliant Chang."

Jessie described going to confront Chang in the days after her daughter's death. On being shown into the opulent Regent Street restaurant, she could scarcely believe that a man of such obvious wealth and taste would denigrate himself by dipping his fingers into the drug trade. Chang's male secretary, she said, possibly referring to the punchy Mr Best, was a "very handsome foreigner" who initially claimed Chang had gone out. But when Mrs Kempton refused to leave, Chang reluctantly emerged in his dressing gown. "I stood face to face with this perplexing Chinaman...A diminutive Chinaman with a huge head and black, beady eyes, that stood out from a parchment-like skin, he advanced to meet me and holding out a thin, bony hand he exclaimed in pigeon English — 'Ah, so you are poor Freda's mother. Me velly, velly solly she meet with sad accident.'"

Jessie said she came away from the meeting convinced that Brilliant Chang was a "deeply wronged man," but of course she insisted that she had been blinded by Chang's "Oriental cunning" and knowledge of the affection between him and her daughter. To the delight of readers, Jessie went on to make several revelations about their relationship, previously unheard at the inquest.

She believed Chang would have married her daughter, if Freda had consented to marrying a Chinese man. Freda had Chang wrapped around her little finger, Jessie claimed. According to her version of events, Freda could call the restaurant at any time of day or night, and a chauffeur-driven limousine would be sent to any address to ferry her around the West End.

Yet Chang also cast a spell on Freda in return. He was, Jessie said, a "man in whose hands young girls were like clay in the hands of the potter. In a soft purring voice and with subtle flattery, he could talk any girl round and turn her head. When he came into the nightclubs faultlessly dressed in evening clothes over which he usually wore a fur-lined coat the girls would flock around him, vying with one another to obtain his favours".

Jessie believed that at least one of Freda's friends was wracked with jealousy, while on Chang's part he always courted his girls with caution. He would not be seen in the street with them, and instead would have taxis ferry them to his various apartments while he followed behind in his own car. Jessie told of one occasion when her daughter arrived with Chang at "one of the dirtiest quarters of Chinatown". She was led through several "mean-looking rooms" only to emerge into "one of the most beautifully decorated chambers she had ever seen. The room was hung with rich curtains and there were myriads of lamps and Oriental ornaments".

Chang himself lived in one of the "most magnificently-decorated flats in Park Lane," which he "very rarely" left during the daytime. But at night he could always be found prowling the night clubs and dance halls of the West End, searching for conquests and customers.

Just how much of Jessie's story was true and how much was fantasy either imparted to her by Freda or attributed to her by the newspaper, is impossible to say. But the basic details ring true. Chang had amassed significant wealth and did indeed appear to be admired by many young women.

Brilliant Chang was deported from the Albert Docks in April 1925. It was reported that as he prepared to board the vessel, where his uncle had ensured he would travel in a first-class stateroom, a young friend of the tragic Freda Kempton rushed forward and yelled, "Come back soon, Chang."

There is much mystery surrounding what happened to Chang from that point on, but his name remained in the headlines for some time. In US newspaper reports of the case, he was dubbed "The Limehouse Spider", a clear nod to Dr Fu Manchu.

In February 1925, five years after the Dangerous Drugs Act had come into force, Scotland Yard declared the war on dope all but over. As of Valentine's Day, there had been no drugs cases at Marlborough Street police in court in more than a year, compared with one or two cases every week in the preceding years. Much of this was put down to the elimination of Brilliant Chang, who was widely credited with being behind much of the trade in "snow". As an article in *The People* put it:

> The gratifying fact is that the cocaine trade is looking around in vain for new customers. The rise of the nightclubs presented an easy hunting ground for the touts and harpies of Chang's international dope concern, but their decline has killed that lucrative market. Cocaine finds its way into the West End; it can only be obtained by those known by the agents to be addicts; there is now no touting. Even in the worst nightclubs, the old question 'Would you like some snow?' is never heard.

The article added an ominous rider, "The traffickers will, sooner or later, attempt to creep back via the underworld, but the police stranglehold will not be relaxed."

The following January, Brilliant Chang was reported to be back on the continent, running another restaurant in Berlin under an alias. He was now head of a new drug trafficking network with tentacles all over Europe, taking in Paris, Antwerp and Amsterdam. His network was feeding a resurgent club scene in the West End and the mere presence of drugs in nightclubs, according to *The People*, was therefore evidence of Chang's involvement.

Other reports had variously suggested that Chang had escaped from the deportation boat at Marseille; or that he was directing his empire from Zurich; or Antwerp; or that he was arrested in Paris and on the run with a young lover, a report which was probably correct. In 1929, it was reported that Chang was wanted by the German police over the drugs death of cabaret singer Minna Spermel, and the addiction and subsequent mental deterioration of an actress, Marie Orska.

Other reports handed Brilliant Chang an even more ignominious end. Chang was said to be blind, poverty-stricken and insane back home in China. It was later reported that Chang had invented the story himself and used a double to complete the fraud.

Chang was, in a way, partially rehabilitated in a 1928 *People* article titled, "The Passing of Brilliant Chang". This time Chang was portrayed as an opportunistic businessman who had cashed in on the cocaine boom and only continued to give Freda Kempton the drug because he was in love with her and could not refuse her demands. When he was forced to live in Limehouse, the local Chinese looked down on him and he took up with Violet Payne, determined to leave the drug trade behind. But she was an addict and would leave packets hidden around the house. Meanwhile a new drug trafficker, Ah Ket, persuaded Chang to work for him as a street dealer. The two developments combined to bring him down. Again, there is no way to determine how much was truth and how much fantasy.

It is still impossible to fully assess Brilliant Chang's true role in the interwar drugs underworld. Brilliant Chang remains an enigma, despite his enduring position as the world's first celebrity drug dealer. There can be no doubt that he was involved in supplying cocaine — the sheer volume of testimony against him speaks to that. But was Brilliant Chang a "dope king" or a glorified street dealer?

There appears to have been no objective investigation into Chang's business or finances. Much of his wealth no doubt came from his family background. His restaurant and club also provided legitimate funds. There was no real evidence that Chang was wholesaling to other dealers or operating an international crime gang, therefore he was likely selling drugs hand-to-hand and employing dealers to sell for him, similar to Eddie Manning but on a much grander scale. In addition to the Chinese operating out of the restaurant, the names of Jack Kelson, May Roberts and Julia Kitt were also linked to Chang's network.

It is also possible that the real heads of the network were Chang's own father and uncle back home in China, a scenario that was apparently never explored. Interestingly, police files on Max Faber show that MD Perrins at the Home Office thought it "probable" there was a link between Chang and the aforementioned Choy Loy, because Loy had sent newspaper clippings of the Chang case to friends in Hong Kong.

As a footnote, Chang may well have left behind an heir. In May 1924, a woman named Lily Brentano, known as "Limehouse Lil," was given six months' hard labour for cocaine dealing. It was an unusual case because no drugs were actually found on her person. Lil had been seen getting off a bus in Holborn with a Chinese baby in her arms, shortly before she was arrested for offering to supply the drug to two women. Lil told the magistrate that she had been living in the East End with "Bill Chang". When she was handed her sentence, Lil shouted, "Fancy! Six months for nothing!"

\*\*\*

# DOWNFALL

Brilliant Chang had not been the only drugs kingpin to fall in the first half of the Roaring Twenties. In fact, the authorities had achieved a string of successful prosecutions against wealthy criminals.

One of the most high profile cases was that of Howard Montague Fogden Humphrey, a City of London businessman who was, on the surface, worlds away from the likes of Chang. As far as his family knew, he left his home in Brighton each day and headed to work at his office in Basinghall Street, where he owned a cutlery manufacturer. But his most profitable venture was procuring huge quantities of cocaine and morphine for the Tong Say Company to ship to China.

In March 1923, Humphrey was described in court as controlling a "powerful, secret and wealthy organisation for dealing in cocaine and morphine". He had been caught after Customs officers boarded a steamer off Hong Kong and arrested a Japanese passenger with four cases of furniture. The upholstery was sliced open to reveal 2,400 ounces of morphine and 2,500 ounces of cocaine. A receipt for £7,280 was signed by the Englishman, while other signed documents related to further shipments, with a suggested profit of nearly £80,000.

Humphrey claimed the drugs had never entered British territory and he was merely an intermediary for licensed manufacturers in France and illicit dealers in China. But in damning letters read to the court, Humphrey had bragged of his connections and demonstrated his criminality. "I would like to say that I have a perfect organisation," he wrote. "I have many friends amongst Customs etc, and I understand the business very thoroughly, in fact I do not believe that there is anyone who has a better control."

The case also exposed major British corruption. His customers preferred British-made morphine so be bought, when possible, from T Whiffen in London. To get around the issue of export controls, the president of the British chamber of commerce in Paris, John Laurier, ordered the drugs and had them officially imported into France. They were then sold back to Humphrey, who had them shipped to the firm of Bubeck and Dolder, where they were collected by smugglers. T Whiffen must surely have been suspicious of the orders, but failed to take any action because they accounted for more than forty percent of their annual sales. Humphrey was fined £200 and jailed for six months. Sir Malcolm Delevingne ensured T Whiffen lost its license to produce narcotics.

A similar character found himself up at the Old Bailey in December 1923. The Ludgate Hill-based shipping magnate Yasukichi "Sess" Miyagawa was aged thirty-five when he was found guilty of procuring 500lbs of morphine and shipping it to his home country of Japan. The drugs, valued at £9,000, had been uncovered in the port of Marseille. They were destined not just for Japanese consumption, but for onward shipment to China, India and elsewhere, possibly even back into Britain, after being 'laundered' by legitimate companies. More morphine was found at his premises. "The authorities are of the opinion," said the prosecutor HD Roome, "that the defendant before you is the largest trafficker in drugs who has ever been brought to justice".

The unassuming, bespectacled Miyagawa's network included manufacturing and shipping firms in Switzerland and

Germany, chief among them Bubeck and Dolder, and CH Boehringer. Both companies were fully aware of the illicit nature of his trade. On one occasion, Boehringer helpfully labelled a £37,500 shipment of heroin as aspirin, while Bubeck and Dolder included a handful of blank invoices in case he needed to make amendments to get the load past Customs.

Miyagawa had on one occasion sent to Japan, in one single consignment, enough morphine to serve the needs of London's hospitals for one thousand years. One shipment alone was worth nearly £40,000. Despite his battered bowler hat and tatty suit, Miyagawa had reportedly become a millionaire thanks to the drugs trade, and was frequently to be found among the more salubrious nightspots of the West End. As a result of his arrest, the court heard, police in Hamburg had also rounded up a large number of suspects. "Behind this man is a very powerful and wealthy organisation for dealing in these drugs," Roome added. Miyagawa was jailed for three years, with nine months' hard labour. He was also recommended for deportation.

Delevingne sent an angry missive to the German government, claiming that Boehringer was "up to the eyes in the illicit traffic" and pointing out that the British had previously closed down T Whiffen for doing the same thing. Boehringer, he believed, had been reaping the profits as a result. The Germans took no action.

Back in the East End, several high-profile Chinese dope dealers arrived on the scene after Brilliant Chang, although by the end of the decade most had been removed from Britain. A man said to be Chang's protégé, Ah Wong, was taken down soon after his mentor. Wong was busted after police watched

147

him approach a woman in Dean Street and ask, "Do you want some snow?" The dealer, who had been in the country since 1917 and had fathered four children with a Devonshire woman, was jailed for six months and recommended for deportation.

A black man named William Alan Porter tried to capitalise on the absence of both Chang and Eddie Manning by stepping up from street hoodlum to drugs kingpin. He purchased six ounces of morphine and was sat in a Chinese restaurant in Pennyfields with an Irish crony named John Mason when police burst in and arrested them in January 1925. Porter tried to convince Mason to take the blame, using the carrot and stick approach. He offered the younger man £200 and also threatened to "jump on him in the dock if he get ten years for it". Porter got twelve months' hard labour, while Mason got six.

As early as May 1925, *The People* speculated that there was a new "dope gaffer" running "snow" in the West End, and it was likely a black man or woman, although the latter was thought "unlikely as women are apt to talk too much, whatever their organising capabilities". The paper all but ruled out Chinese criminals, suggesting none would dare move now that their "leader" had been removed from the country. As the paper noted, "The heads of the dope traffic are foreigners almost to a man, the only Englishmen who are engaged in the work are dupes men who are down on their luck. The sooner the foreign traffickers are rounded up and deported the better for our young womanhood — for women are the chief victims. They are the worst example of the alien menace in our midst."

# DOWNFALL

The following month, the paper continued the theme, asking, "Is the new dope king a black man?" The report went on to describe the case of James Rich, supposedly a new breed of criminal taking the place of the "furtive-eyed Chinese" who previously ran the dope game from Limehouse.

Now, the traffic was being controlled from the "black man's colony" of Seven Dials and the Tottenham Court Road, all since the deportation of Chang, the "Prince of Dope Dealers" (forgetting, of course, that Eddie Manning had long been held as the 'king' of the area). Many of these men, the paper said, described themselves as jazz musicians, although at least one always carried a saxophone case despite not being able to play a note.

James Rich hailed from Carolina, USA, and arrived in Britain in 1910, where he sought theatre work. The newspaper said he had the "impertinence to describe himself as a stage manager" while in fact he was a "baggage handler with a third-rate touring revue". Another job had seen him standing outside a cigarette kiosk in Wembley, dressed as a Turkish soldier. In any case, Rich found himself up before the court after he was arrested coming out of a venue known as the "Black Man's Café" in Seven Dials.

Two undercover officers had been tracking Rich and another man as they meandered around the West End. The officers saw nothing untoward for days, until they eventually spotted Rich handing over a small packet to a couple in Shaftesbury Avenue. Unlike Brilliant Chang, James Rich did accuse the police of planting the evidence, but he was disbelieved by the jury. He was given six months' hard labour and recommended for deportation. Rich created an air of mystery by refusing to say anything about his life between 1910 and 1918, hinting that he had previously gone under another name and worked for an underworld boss.

The authorities did know where Rich had been *since* 1918: he had received various prison sentences for indecency, keeping a gaming house and grievous bodily harm, having bashed a man over the head with a hammer the previous year in a row about dope. Like Chang, he kept a coterie of female admirers, but when he begged them to come to court as character witnesses, none obliged. Rich was given six months' hard labour.

Meanwhile, the "Black Man's Café" remained a hotbed of criminal activity, although not every plotter within its notorious walls was black or foreign. In fact, as the watching detectives of C Division would soon learn, the dope traffic was not a game played only by immigrants and the down-at-heel, as some of the newspapers would have it. Even a scion of one of Britain's most famous families had been enticed by the profits that could be made from cocaine.

# 8. BUSTED!

Londoners ventured inside Jim Kitten's café at their own risk, but regular Soho-dwellers adored the room's loud, boisterous atmosphere and edgy clientele. Nicknamed the Black Man's Café and located in Great White Lion Street, Seven Dials, street-walkers from nearby Covent Garden — sometimes teenage girls as young as fifteen — would spend their earnings on tea, coffee, cakes and hard liquor, while the men, most of them black and virtually excluded from the West End's other nightspots (unless employed as band members), drank, smoked and gambled at card tables. Some of them, not coincidentally, were also the girls' pimps. It was not unheard of for a whispered conversation to suddenly erupt into a brawl, or even for one of the participants to end up with a knife in his back.

# DOPE KINGS OF LONDON

Jim had taken over the café in 1921 with his eighteen-year-old bride Emily, probably with the genuine intention of running an entirely respectable establishment. But by March 18, 1926, when recreational drug use in the West End was still at the tail end of its boom, the restaurant's reputation was such that it had become the perfect place to stage an illicit business meeting.

That night the place was full of its typical vim and vigour. But still, the observer could quite clearly hear the conversation taking place between the three men who had shuffled inside moments earlier and taken the table to his left. One of the men was white, immediately making the group stand out.

"Have you got any stuff?" the white man asked his companions. The two black men looked at each other for a moment and then the largest of the two, a nightclub doorman named Mohamed Ali, replied confidently, "Yes."

Ali had been trying to find a buyer for a rather large consignment of cocaine for weeks, so this out-of-the-blue approach was a fantastic stroke of luck. Ali produced a small tin and handed it to the potential buyer, who dipped a finger inside and put the resulting residue on his fingertip to his tongue.

"How much?" he asked, obviously satisfied.

"For you, £25 an ounce."

"How much could you get tonight?"

"One pound within five minutes," came the response.

Without so much as ordering a drink, Ali got up from the table and made his exit, leaving the other two men to make small talk for a few minutes. As promised, he returned after a few minutes, this time with a strapping, six feet tall white companion who, despite his burly figure, appeared of a nervous disposition.

"I have sixteen ounces on me," the newcomer declared in a whisper, which was not quite low enough to escape the ears of the man listening in. "That's £25 per ounce, £400 in total."

"Can I see it?" the prospective buyer asked.

"Not here, but I can show you in two minutes. Do you know Stacey Street? Meet me there."

At that point, Detective Constable Charles Mann, who had listened to the entire conversation, got up from his seat to slip out just ahead of the conspirators. He would be seeing them again very soon.

Minutes later, the young officer settled into his hiding place inside a Stacey Street garage, alongside Detective Inspector William Bradley, the man who had instigated the entire undercover operation after taking charge of Vine Street CID. Detective Constable Robert McBean — who had watched and followed Mohamed Ali from Jim Kitten's café to his meeting point with the mystery white man and back again - walked in behind him. The fourth and arguably most important member of the undercover team, Sgt James Coleman, was outside in the street, posing as the buyer. So far, the operation had unfolded brilliantly.

In the days before the invention of wiretaps, mobile phones and long lens cameras, an undercover sting was the best and only way to make a major drugs bust. The Met had used two of the country's first female police officers, Violet Butcher and Lillian Dawes, to tackle the West End trade inside pubs during the 1916 uproar over cocaine being sold to servicemen. The same tactic had netted a string of low-level street dealers during the second cocaine panic in the wake of Freda Kempton's 1922 overdose.

One of the more interesting and unusual cases had unfolded at Westminster police court in April of that year. Its protagonist was an Indian named Sitaram Sampatro Gaikwar, a twenty-seven-year-old nephew of the Maharaj of Baroda who had been educated at Rugby and Cambridge. Until the previous summer, Gaikwar had received a £5,000 annual allowance, which was suddenly reduced to just £50-per-month, for reasons never made clear to the investigating officers. In any case, to maintain his lavish lifestyle, and a young, pretty girlfriend named Nancy Seymour Mackay, from Leytonstone, Gaikwar began to pawn jewellery. He also started to make frequent, mysterious trips to Europe, bringing back cocaine to sell. Gaikwar was betrayed by an informant named CJ Holmes and the long-established team of Walter Burmby, Charles Owen and DC Haines went to work.

Owen posed as a bent chemist and met Gaikwar at Victoria Station, where the Indian said he could get two pounds of "the pure stuff" for £750-£770, or £25-£30 an ounce. The 'deal' was done in the back of a taxi as it drove along the Embankment, with DC Haines acting as the chemist's assistant. Owen tasted the cocaine on his tongue and handed over a bundle of fake banknotes. When he revealed that he was a police officer, Gaikwar blurted out, "Oh what rotten luck."

Gaikwar insisted in court that he had been induced by the officers to fetch the cocaine and had only done so because he felt sorry for the "hard up" pair. The drugs had been obtained from a "Jew friend" in Paris who Gaikwar said he dared not name in court. "He would take his revenge," Gaikwar insisted. He denied offering the drug but admitted possession and was sentenced to six months' hard labour, with a £200 fine or an extra three months' hard labour for the offer to supply. Some newspapers had over-excitedly dubbed Gaikwar a "cocaine king".

Walter Burmby seemed to have some grudging respect for the man, writing in his report, "He maintained an indifferent attitude and declined to give any information about drug trafficking. His only regret is that it transpired in the case that he was the nephew of the Gaikwar of Baroda." Burmby added in another memo that Gaikwar intended to "take his punishment like a man. He looked upon his capture as an unlucky incident in his career".

Inspector Bradley had tasked his men with watching Jim Kitten's café in the hope of achieving a similarly high-profile result. He described the joint disdainfully as a "resort of coloured men and white women of low repute" and he was certain it would provide his officers with a chance to catch drug dealers red-handed. Mann soon recruited an informant named Claude Williams, who tipped him off about dealers operating in Charring Cross Road. Mann and McBean had headed to the spot where, just as their mole had predicted, they saw Mohamed Ali talking about cocaine with another black man. Sgt Coleman, acting as a dope fiend, had ambled over and sparked up a conversation. The trio then dipped into Jim

Kitten's café, where Mann was already waiting to listen in on the conversation.

Now the officers were about to harvest the fruits of their labour. They watched as Ali and the other black man flanked their tall, white companion and approached Coleman. They listened as he once again re-reiterated his price, adding that if Coleman could afford it, then he would be able to supply more cocaine in the future.

With that, Coleman reached for his wallet and then raised his hat, a pre-arranged signal to his watching colleagues. The hiding detectives pounced. In the ensuing bundle, the other black man managed to run off. But Mann seized Ali, while Coleman and McBean struggled with the white seller, later described by Bradley as a "powerfully built man". Eventually, both were overpowered with the help of a nearby garage attendant and arrested on suspicion of unlawfully possessing cocaine.

The seller had been true to his word. A 2lb tin containing one pound of cocaine was found in his overcoat pocket. Ali possessed a single, small packet, the sample. Detectives also found a telegram in the white man's pocket. Dated a few days previously and addressed to, "Butler, Domhotel, Coeln", it read: "AM Saturday morning, Cologne, have difficulties for small quantity finally promised Tuesday." The 2lb tin was marked, "Cadbury, Bourneville, England."

As the case unfolded, it would go on to have all the makings of a major society scandal, but few details would make it into the newspapers of the day.

# ILLUSTRATIONS

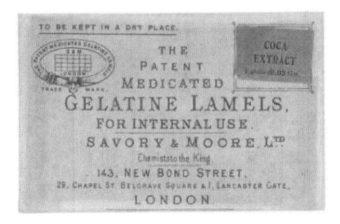

'A useful present for friends at the front'- the cocaine and opium-infused gelatin lamels that helped to herald Britain's war time drugs regulations.

Her identitiy is a mystery, but this photo of a 1920s woman simply labelled 'Dope Queen' was found in the collection of a former detective. It likely depicts either May Roberts or Julia Kitt. '

Top left: Max Faber. Top right: Choy Loy. Bottom left: Mun Won. Bottom right: Ah Kiu Tchai.

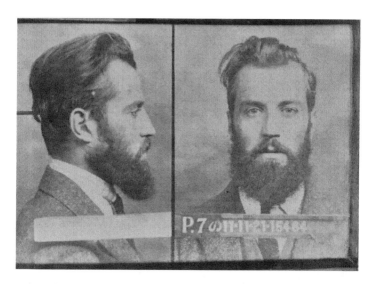

The many faces of Laurent
Deleglise.

Top: Deleglise's lover Malvine Buzze, or Buzzi. Below: The dangerous Keith Harrison Vaughan.

Deleglise's dupes. Above: The Lorties. Below: Ed Ryan.

ILLUSTRATIONS

The original Dope King. Eddie Manning was a talented jazz drummer who turned to pimping and later drug dealing. His criminal career became the defining case of Detective Walter Burmby's career.

163

Brilliant Chang dressed in his trademark fur-lined coat outside the coroner's court.

The tragic Freda Kempton.

Top left: Arnold Butler posing for a portrait in 1897.

Top right: Arnold with a young Richard at a family wedding.

Below left: A Cadbury's chocolate tin, similar to ones used by Richard to store cocaine.

Thomas Wentworth Russell, better known as Russell Pasha. One of the Godfathers of the international drug laws, Russell made sure criminal factories were squeezed out of Europe and then Turkey.

# DOPE KINGS OF LONDON

Top left: The camel hair trick.

Middle: A smuggling trunk owned by a member of the Vienna gang.

Below: The waterside factory in Kuskandjuk, Turkey

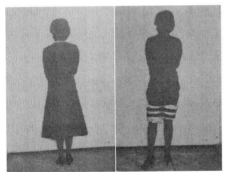

Top: Three female drug traffickers in Egypt. Middle: A smuggler caught in the same country. Below: How drugs were hidden in toilet seats.

Top left: August Del Gracio. Top right: Eli Abuisak. Bottom left: Jean Voyatzis. Bottom right: David Gourevidis.

# ILLUSTRATIONS

Top: Paul Carbone, alias
Venture. Below: Seya Moses.

William Angus Drogo Montagu, Ninth Duke of Manchester, and his wife, Helena Zimmerman, Duchess of Manchester.

Bottom left: The duke in his later years.

Herbert Johannes Stahl, better known as Johannes Steel. Enemy of the Nazis, Soviet spy and suspected arms and drugs trafficker.

Left: George Hatherill of the Yard in his later years.

Below: Sailor Jack James Johns.

# ILLUSTRATIONS

The drugs found on the SS Beaverford in Bob
Adams' cabin.

# 9. THE BLACK SHEEP

As he sat forlornly in one of Vine Street police station's dingy Victorian cells, Richard Cadbury Butler had plenty of time to consider his plight. At twenty-seven years old, he had already been married and divorced once, squandered a small fortune, and now he was almost certainly facing a stretch in prison. It shouldn't have been like this for a privileged Englishman of his background and breeding.

Cadbury Butler was born in April 1898, the son of Arnold Butler, a magistrate and social reformer, and Edith Cadbury, daughter of the late Richard Barrow Cadbury, the second son of the chocolate company's founder John Cadbury.

In less than a century, the Cadbury clan had become one of Britain's most celebrated entrepreneurial families. John, a Quaker, had started off selling tea, coffee and hot chocolate from a cart in Bull Street, Birmingham, in 1824. He soon moved into production and formed the Cadbury Brothers company with his brother Benjamin. Their chocolate bars hit the market in the late 1840s and in 1854 they became the official chocolatiers to Queen Victoria, receiving a Royal Warrant. Richard Barrow Cadbury and his brother George took over in 1861, turning what was then a failing business into a profitable one, by shifting primarily into chocolate and improving the quality. They were one of the first chocolate companies to exploit St Valentine's Day by selling boxes in the shape of a heart and also pioneered the Easter egg. At the turn of the century, Cadbury's was selling chocolate bars on the mass market, introducing the iconic Dairy Milk bar in 1905. The following year, it introduced the dark chocolate Bourneville line.

When Richard's daughter Edith married then-Sunday school teacher Arnold in 1897 they went to live in Edith's old family home in Wheeley Road, Birmingham. The marriage settlement provided Arnold with a guaranteed £5,000-a-year income from the family trust, worth about £300,000 today. After Arnold's death, the annual allowance would go to Edith, and when both were dead it would be split between their four children, Richard, Arnold William, Elizabeth Edith and Christine Winifred. The trust also allowed each child to draw money, with their parents' consent, up to one third of their projected legacy.

The vast income generated from the trust meant Arnold could indulge a variety of social interests. As well as becoming a Justice of the Peace for the city of Birmingham in 1909, he was president of the Birmingham and District Social Services League, chairman of the Borstal Committee, the local RSPCA and president of the Birmingham Police Institute.

Arnold was a somewhat unusual man. He collected moths and insects and proudly showed them off to journalists who visited his office-cum-museum. He also had several mottoes inscribed on the wall in cardboard, including one that read: "A man's reach should be beyond his grasp, or else what's a Heaven for?" He was a dreamer, and instilled some of his personality in Richard.

Arnold's cases in the magistrates' court regularly made the papers. On one occasion in 1925 he sentenced a labourer, Richard Horne, fifty-four, to one month in prison for being drunk and disorderly. Horne had told the JP, "I went to your Sunday School for a year and eight months, Mr Butler."

"Then you left, then you got drunk, then you got into trouble, and now you are here," Arnold had replied waspishly.

Richard Barrow Cadbury had died in 1899, aged 63, on an ill-fated trip to the Middle East. Edith and Arnold had accompanied their elders. They visited Cairo, the Pyramids and the Sphinx, but Richard Snr became ill with 'Nile throat' and died of diphtheria in Jerusalem on March 18. Arnold and Edith returned home, but soon found the old man's young namesake had developed his own health problems. Aged six, young Dickie began to suffer from a condition known as St

# THE BLACK SHEEP

Vitus' Dance, or Sydenham's chorea, a disorder that causes rapid jerking of the face, hands and feet, and which is often brought on by rheumatic fever. It's impossible to know for sure, but he may have picked up the original illness in Egypt. A Cadbury family history skirts over the nature of the boy's ailment, but describes him as being "seriously ill" following Arnold and Edith's return to Birmingham.

Richard initially went to school at the Leighton Park Friends School in Reading, but on the advice of doctors he was packed off to Tasmania aged seventeen, where it was hoped the agreeable climate would cure his "nerves".

On the outbreak of war, Richard asked to join up and was accepted into the 3rd/4th Northumberland's Royal Field Artillery, and enlisted upon a ship as a gunner. He later obtained a commission and was stationed at Luton. Richard was then drafted to Ireland, where he was put in charge of a battery and fought against the rebels. He was later asked to join the Royal Flying Corps, the forerunner to the Royal Air Force, which he did in late 1916.

Richard attained the rank of captain, but while flying at Richmond in 1918 his plane caught fire and plummeted into a field. It was a horrific accident. Richard suffered a fractured skull, broke his jaw in nine places and suffered several other injuries. Richard was picked up believed dead and taken to the mortuary, where he lay on the slab for several hours. But a doctor making his final rounds eventually detected signs of shallow breathing and gave him oxygen, bringing him around.

It was a miracle recovery, although at no little cost to Richard's health and wellbeing. He remained in hospital for five months, where doctors pieced his jaw back together with silver and ivory. Almost all of his teeth had to be replaced. The accident affected his nerves even further and Richard received a discharge from the Army on a pension of £42 per year. And that was when his problems really began.

During his Army career, Richard had enjoyed an illicit affair with a Leeds-born actress, Mary "Queenie" Hall, who was also the wife of a non-commissioned officer in another regiment, Edmond Hill, a sergeant in the Royal Army Service Corps transport section. Following the end of the war, she got a divorce and moved in with Richard. The lovebirds married ("very much against the wishes of myself and my wife," Arnold Butler later said) at Brighton in November, 1920. In fact, the Butler family's animosity towards Queenie was such that none of Richard's relatives attended the wedding. Queenie's father, George Hall, had been a lowly timekeeper on the London and North Western Railway and the family was deemed to be well below the station of the Cadbury Butler clan.

Despite this snobbish disapproval of the union, Arnold Butler nevertheless set Richard up with a £3,500 loan to start a motor company in Brighton, a sum roughly equivalent to about £215,000 today. At around the same time, Richard also inherited £1,250 from his grandmother, which he used to buy a nearby chicken farm. George Hall had been invalided out of the railway after suffering a serious leg injury and Richard moved his in-laws there to run the farm.

But Richard's car business flopped, partly thanks to prolonged industrial action taken by a moulder's union. Even though Arnold paid off his son's £1,500 overdraft with Brighton Bank in 1920, it wasn't enough to save the farm.

# THE BLACK SHEEP

Richard sold the property and moved with his wife to a flat in Maida Vale, west London. Arnold paid the rent for twelve months and set his son up with a £5-a-week allowance. Richard tried to turn his hand to acting, but got no further than occasional work as a film extra. He did, however, become a regular fixture on the West End club scene.

One of his regular haunts was the legendary Rector's Nightclub, in Tottenham Court Road, a leading London nightspot and a favourite of aristocrats, peers and celebrities, including Douglas Fairbanks, where the cabaret shows and dancing went on until the early hours. Richard was one of around seven hundred paid-up members. The club, while decidedly higher class, was similar to Brett's in that it employed young, beautiful, 'dancing instructresses'.

The club ran into trouble in 1924, after licensing inspectors found that the basement nature of the venue constituted a fire hazard. A court hearing described how one officer had paid £2 to spend the evening with one of the women, who suggested breakfast at 3am and then ordered up coffee and cherry brandies at 4am. None of the individuals who gave statements in connection with the case ever alluded to Richard using drugs, but he certainly moved in circles where they were prevalent.[14]

With little money coming in, but plenty going out, the passion between Richard and Queenie soon fizzled out. Queenie packed her bags the following year, complaining bitterly that Richard did not have enough money to provide her with the lifestyle to which she aspired.

Typical of the one-time actress, her walkout was carefully stage managed. While working as a waitress at the Corner

House tea shop in Coventry Street, she became acquainted with a much older Belgian businessman named Leon Cornelis, a man already in his sixties. Queenie told him she was married but that "my husband was unable to keep me" and so Cornelis began to top-up her income with regular cheques of up to £20. Perhaps politely glossing over the true extent of the relationship, later police reports said the pair "became friendly". For her part, Queenie claimed that Richard had become "acquainted with several women in the West End" and she decided to leave him on that basis. In any case, Queenie moved in with Cornelis at his rooms in the Russell Hotel, in Russell Square.

Cornelis seemed to have plenty of ready cash. During the war, he had owned a wholesale chemist and druggist business based in Antwerp and Hamburg. Now, he was in London running a similar operation shipping chemicals between Germany and the US, as well as running two other firms, the Continental Fur Company and the Bell Battery Company, which supplied batteries mainly for use in the increasingly popular wireless radios.

Cornelis gave Queenie a job at the fur company and she began to accompany him on his frequent trips to Europe, ostensibly as his "business manager".

Richard would later describe Cornelis as a man who "spent money lavishly", while he continued to earn just £8 per week. He tried to win Queenie back on several occasions, but each time his pleas were flatly turned down. Despite his much younger years, Richard was no match financially for Cornelis and he had few future prospects — at least until his parents died.

# THE BLACK SHEEP

Queenie was now being kept at an agreeable standard by Cornelis. She had a flat in upmarket Gordon Mansions, Fitzrovia, near Tottenham Court Road, her own car and, crucially, spending money. Cornelis also paid for another house, at Park Villas, Watford Road, Sudbury, where he installed Queenie's parents. Cornelis stayed there himself from time to time, and would in fact die there after a short illness in November, 1925.

But before that, Queenie tried to obtain a divorce so that she could marry the ageing tycoon, perhaps sensing that the combination of his advancing years and apparent wealth could set her up for life. Richard clung desperately to their married status. Yet somewhat unexpectedly, he remained on good terms with both Queenie and Cornelis, and the trio became friends, frequently dining together. She would buy him gifts, including a gold cigarette case, watches and walking sticks. Richard eventually agreed to a divorce, with his father paying all the costs. Unknown to Arnold Butler, who assumed his son to be the adulterer, Cornelis was named as the third party.

In addition to his womanising, Richard might have been bisexual. In a later statement to police, Arnold said that while his son had "several female acquaintances" he also had a "particular friend" called Victor Smith. Richard, he explained, had bought a small plot of land on Canvey Island in Essex and built a bungalow there. He and Victor would often spend weekends together and on one occasion Victor was arrested and convicted of indecent exposure. Arnold gave no further details of the case and Richard didn't elaborate in his statements.

Regardless of the messiness to be found in Richard's private life, his ongoing platonic relationship with Queenie did afford him what he believed was a golden opportunity to set himself up in a new business.

In the summer of 1923, Queenie suggested to her former husband that he invest and become a partner in Cornelis' new venture, a company that would import pharmaceutical goods from Germany to Britain. It was to be called, rather unimaginatively, the Pharmaceutical Supply Company. It would bring in "anatomical specimens" as well as various medicines and medical equipment such as microscopes, operating knives and stethoscopes. Queenie assured Richard that Cornelis would train him up in the world of business. He would be like an apprentice, but an apprentice who could earn an extraordinary amount of money during the learning process.

Enticed by the offer, both Richard and Arnold Butler met with Cornelis, who gave them as a reference the solicitor Oscar Seligman, of the firm Cohn, Seligman and Bax. He was, at the time, also a director of one of Cornelis's firms, the Bell Battery Company. Arnold was extremely impressed with both Cornelis and Seligman. The JP asked the lawyer whether he would advise him to put up the £3,000 for which Cornelis was asking.

"Put in all you can," Seligman enthused. "I wish I had £10,000 to put in as well. Your son is very fortunate to have such an offer. You need not have any fear as Cornelis is the greatest business genius I have met for many a year." Armold was also swayed by Queenie, who at this point still had not given Arnold the impression that she and Cornelis were an item, and he believed that "no immoral relationship existed between them".

# THE BLACK SHEEP

Cornelis and Seligman both said they were putting £2,000 each into the business. With Butler Snr happy he instructed the family trust to make it so and Richard was handed £3,000 to start the new venture. The company was formed on August 28, 1923. Both Seligman and Richard were named as directors, receiving £100 per annum for their services. Seligman, Butler and Cornelis also each held one third of the three hundred ordinary shares. Despite the promises made by Cornelis and Seligman, one hundred percent of the capital was put up by the Butlers.

Very little official business was carried out. A sum of £1,000 was immediately paid to Cornelis to travel abroad. He resumed his frequent trips to Europe and obtained some surgical instruments, but according to the books only about £100 worth of goods were sold back in Britain. The rest of the cash was drawn by Richard as rent for offices in Hatfield Street, salary and expenses for himself and staff — a typist, a German naturalised American "expert" called Louis Krumm, and a packer in the basement called Lippman. Both were friends of Cornelis who Richard was supposed to learn from. Arnold was impressed when he visited the office and marveled at the goods on display. But it was all window dressing. Amazingly, the alarm bells didn't start to ring even after the company encountered a spate of legal problems.

Firstly, Krumm disappeared with the books and later re-emerged in Germany where he was convicted of drug trafficking. Then Lippman also suddenly returned to his homeland, never to be heard from again. Leon Cornelis was himself arrested in Germany, supposedly on suspicion of fraud concerning the buying of surgical instruments. Although he was swiftly released, it was unsurprising when the business collapsed eighteen months later.

At the end of 1924, Leon Cornelis met with Arnold Butler and told him that due to "trade depression" and the unfavorable exchange rate with Germany he had been forced to close his battery and fur businesses. Cornelis said he had also fallen out with Oscar Seligman, and was accusing the lawyer of stealing £6,000 from him. When Arnold later asked Richard why Cornelis had not pressed charges, Richard couldn't give him an answer. In any case, Cornelis proposed to return all the "stock" from the pharmaceutical company to Germany and merge anything that could be salvaged from his affairs into a new venture, Lorraine and Co.

For this, Butler Snr agreed to invest £500, made up of £400 for the business and £100 to clear one of his son's personal bills. It was, he felt, his "only hope" of clawing back some of the £3,000 he had so far lost. Cornelis vowed to invest £250 of his own money, but never did. The company again employed Queenie, and opened an office in Charterhouse Square. But this new venture would quickly become Richard's worst blunder to date.

Cornelis almost immediately resumed his trips to Germany, funded by a new account at Barclays and sometimes accompanied by Richard. On one of those trips, Richard wrote to his father from Bonn, boasting of their "very successful" business in batteries, how they were turning over thousands of pounds and how he intended to buy his father a Rolls Royce to thank him for his unwavering faith. And, of course, he would pay back all the money he had borrowed. But once again, the truth was that Lorraine and Co did virtually no real business.

# THE BLACK SHEEP

As the police later wrote, "No doubt these two firms only existed as a means for Cornelis to obtain money through the medium of Butler Jnr, who had no conception whatever of business matters. He doubtless believed that Cornelis was sincere in his representations about making the business a success and also was influenced to a very great extent by his divorced wife."

Richard himself gave a description of the meetings taking place in Germany. In the summer of 1925, he went to Cologne for a three-day trip with Cornelis to meet his long-time associate Karl Murhard, of the Hugo Bursch company of Bonn, supposedly to discuss the purchase of batteries.

The first meeting took place in a café and was a cosy affair, at least for Cornelis and Murhard. The entire conversation was conducted in German, leaving Richard clueless about the nature of the discussions. Even worse, the following day the Teutonic pair took off for Bonn and left Richard twiddling his thumbs in Cologne. When Cornelis returned, he told Richard that business was good and re-iterated that Murhard was an old, trusted friend. In fact, he revealed, Murhard was the very man who had set him up in the chemical business in Antwerp all those years ago.

A few weeks later Richard and Cornelis visited Murhard again. This time, Richard claimed, Cornelis revealed the true purpose of their trips. Their negotiations were really about the purchase of cocaine, a product that could see them recoup their previous business losses. Cornelis said a kilo could be purchased for £100 and go on to make up to £500. "That is the position of affairs now," Cornelis said. "It is either to go broke or to recover our losses by this means."

DOPE KINGS OF LONDON

Richard was furious at being kept in the dark, by his partner but nevertheless a down payment of 1,000 marks, or £50, was subsequently made through Lorraine and Co's bank account to Karl Murhard. Cornelis and Richard visited Germany again in late October 1925, planning to make it back to Britain with a package of cocaine. But Murhard said he had been unable to source the drug. The pair returned downbeat and empty-handed on November 1.

To make matters worse Cornelis, who suffered from asthma, had struggled with his breathing throughout the trip. Now he was back in London, his condition rapidly deteriorated, and he took to his bed at the Palm Villas address. Ironically, one of the legitimate enterprises Cornelis had dealt in was an asthma cure, employing Queenie's father to post products out to customers who ordered it through newspaper adverts. But there was no cure for Cornelis. He died at home, attended to by his lover, her ex-husband and his former in-laws, six days after returning from Germany. The funeral was an equally bizarre affair. Both Arnold and Richard Butler attended, as did Queenie and two of Cornelis' brothers, who revealed that their late sibling also had a wife living in Belgium.

At first, Arnold was baffled by Queenie's overwrought display of grief for the man he had believed was simply her employer. Slowly, as the ceremony went on, the truth dawned on him: the old man and his much younger daughter-in-law had been lovers. "What am I to do now Leon has gone?" she wailed at the graveside. Cornelis had died practically a pauper.

More pressingly, thought Richard, what am I to do? The Butlers had invested thousands into Cornelis and he had left them with nothing. His death sent Richard into an internal

188

panic, although on the surface he remained calm. After some discussion with his father, he declared that he could carry on the battery business without his erstwhile mentor.

But he did ask his father to clear a £325 debt accrued by Cornelis because, he claimed, the old man had borrowed £200 from a Piccadilly moneylender secured on furniture owned by Queenie. The interest had sent the debt rocketing by more than half the original amount and Richard wanted to make sure Queenie got her property back. In fact, Richard used the cash to repay the original £200 and allowed the moneylenders to sell the furniture to cover the interest, pocketing the difference.

He also asked for more cash to inject into the business, a sum of £1,000. But this time the trustees were reluctant to agree a figure and said they were unhappy with Richard's management of the previous business. They told Arnold that his son "was not fit to carry on the business and looked as if he ought to go into a hospital".

Eventually, it was agreed that Barclays would grant a £500 overdraft, supposedly for an order of talcum powder to be shipped from Germany to Cuba. It was also agreed that the family trust would wire money to make a down payment on a shipment of batteries once a telegram had been received from Germany confirming the deal. Richard later obtained a £240 cheque after sending the family lawyer a simple telegraph: "Two hundred forty two pounds business good. Dick." He later claimed to have bought four thousand batteries in Germany, offloading half in Belgium, although there was no paperwork to support this claim.

Throughout these dealings, Richard never once produced any documentary evidence that he was involved in a legitimate business. Arnold later told police that he had simply never doubted his son's word, so therefore never pressed for receipts or invoices. In total, Arnold later said, he had given his son £9,500, of which at least £4,500 had been lost since he met Cornelis. Even worse was that Richard had pawned most of his belongings and even when his father sent him money to retrieve them, he simply pawned them again. Arnold would occasionally peruse the company accounts, but saw very little business being done and most of the activity was in withdrawals. So what had really been going on?

Before he died, Cornelis confided in Richard that he had asked Karl Murhard to communicate via telegrams addressed to Queenie's father George Hall at his home in Sudbury, when the shipment was ready. There was no reason, he said, that Richard should not complete the deal without him.

When a telegram arrived confirming the availability of "batteries" Butler travelled to Germany. Once again, the deal hit a snag. Murhard now required a £100 cheque as a deposit, plus cash to complete the deal. Richard was then forced to return to England in order to withdraw £200, which he then took back to Germany hoping to pay off what Murhard had said would be the remaining balance on the consignment. This time, Murhard did at least produce three tins containing white powder, which he said amounted to one kilo of cocaine. But it turned out to be cut with strychnine and Richard refused to take delivery. It wasn't until January 1926 that the deal was back on.

# THE BLACK SHEEP

Murhard had sent another telegram, prompting Butler to travel yet again to Cologne. The pair met in a cafe where Murhard handed over one kilo of cocaine, split between envelopes each containing one hundred grams. Murhard said the price was £150 and that he would wire when the rest was ready. Butler took the cocaine back to his hotel room, where he transferred the powder into a waterproof body belt. He then returned to London via Ostend and Dover, with the drugs concealed under his shirt. The time was right, he felt, to try and recoup some, if not all, of the money by selling what he already had. But as ever in the life of Richard Cadbury Butler, the task was easier said than done.

Before he died, Cornelis had told Richard the name of a middleman in London who could arrange the onward sale of the drugs, but Richard was unable to find him. The only other person who he thought might be able to help was another Belgian, who he knew only by sight and who was living with a French woman on Shaftesbury Avenue. She was a fixture in the West End's nightclubs and would probably be able to sell it on. But Richard couldn't find the pair, even though he searched "night after night". Instead, he resolved to do the business himself. "I thought that if other persons could get rid of cocaine, I could do the same," he later said. Richard approached Mohamed Ali, a man he knew by sight from various clubs, and asked him to find a buyer.

In the meantime, Karl Murhard wired to say that he could source more cocaine, but that the quantities would have to be greater, such as in batches of four or five kilos, and therefore he would require more money. Richard withdrew more cash and went to Germany to pay Murhard £150. Once again, he returned to England empty-handed. So far, Murhard had induced at least £450 from Richard, but given him cocaine worth just £150.

On his return, Ali told Richard that he'd found a potential buyer for the original consignment. This was more than likely the police informant Claude Williams, who had seemed to know exactly where Ali would be when he spoke to the detectives monitoring Jim Kitten's Cafe.

But before Richard could handle the deal, he would have to handle his father. On March 18, 1926, Arnold Butler travelled down to London to see his son. On a stroll around Trafalgar Square, Richard insisted that business was good, and nodded his head as the older man once again implored him to have nothing more to do with his scheming ex-wife. The pair parted company at 2.30pm, with Arnold heading back to his hotel for an early night, ready to catch the 9.10am train from Euston the following day. Richard made his way to Covent Garden and later to the doomed meeting in Stacey Street.

No sooner had Arnold Butler arrived home on March 19 than he received a startling telegram from George Hall. "Come at once — serious trouble, urgent," it said. Arnold replied, saying, "Cannot come, do not understand, wire more particulars. George Hall instead got on the phone and blurted out something about Richard's arrest and sentence for selling "jewellery". Arnold rushed back to London on the midnight train.

Later that morning, as he slumped wearily into a chair in the Euston Hotel's restaurant, he picked up a copy of the *Daily*

*Herald* and learnt the truth from a report about the case at Marlborough Street police court — Richard had been dealing in cocaine.

---

[14] Rector's also had a tenuous link to the Eddie Manning case. The American jazz musician Sidney Bechet had played there on a visit to London and had later enjoyed drinking in The Bell on Little Titchfield Street. The pub was owned by the wife of the Ciro's Band leader Daniel Kildare, who shot and killed her and her sister, as well as a barmaid, in June 1920.

# 10. LAW AND DISORDER

**A**rnold Butler JP read the article over and over again with a growing sense of horror and disbelief. "A tin containing a little less than a pound of cocaine, worth about £400, at a rate of £25 per ounce asked for it, was mentioned by the police in evidence at Marlborough-street Police Court yesterday," the short newspaper report said.

It described his son simply as Richard Butler — no mention of the proud and renowned name Cadbury — and said he was a "dealer in electrical appliances". His friend Mohamed Ali was described as a "colored man" and "ship's fireman". It also listed Richard's address as the one he had given to the court — the flat in Maida Vale where he had once lived with Queenie.

The police had found a very precise 15.5 ounces of "pure cocaine" in the tin, while a sample packet containing "two grains" was found on Ali. Unbeknown to Arnold, the second man in the case was quickly becoming a mere footnote for the investigating officers. Ali was a nightclub doorman originally from Somaliland, who said he had served in the East African Rifles from 1914, although the police doubted the veracity of this claim. In any case, after finding nothing more than a small tube of morphine tablets at Ali's address in Tottenham Court Road, they figured that Richard was the main player in the plot.

Both Richard and Ali immediately pleaded guilty to possession of cocaine and were therefore sentenced to four months' hard labour. It was remarkable that Richard was spared the six month term usually given to drug dealers. His sentence was nothing compared with the three years dished out to Eddie Manning, or the fourteen months plus deportation given to Brilliant Chang, even though Richard had been found in possession of a much greater quantity of cocaine.

Inspector Bradley was most displeased with the swift action taken by the magistrate and he complained bitterly that the court case had come at a "premature stage of the investigation". "The sentence of these men," he wrote, "nullified detailed enquiries being made respecting them." And that might well have been the end of the story, if only Richard Cadbury Butler's father had remained at home in Birmingham. But Arnold's dash to London would blow the case wide open, with unintended consequences for the older man.

After reading the article, Arnold went to visit George Hall. From there, the pair went to check out his son's real address, a flat in upmarket Bayswater, West London. Arnold knew the address because he still paid the rent.

There he found a large leather trunk and forced the lock. Inside were three more one-pound Cadbury chocolate tins and another, smaller tin, each containing a white powder. The powder was later weighed and found to be 14.68 ounces of "pure cocaine". Including the drugs on Richard's person, the cocaine found added up to just under one kilo. There were also letters from various women, as well as photographs and a banjolele. The discovery of the musical instrument was nearly as surprising to Arnold as the drugs.

Arnold asked Hall to package up the documents and have them sent up to his Birmingham office. He then gathered up the tins and headed to the court where his son had been jailed the previous day. Marching into the well of the court, Arnold Butler grandly informed the chief clerk that he was himself a Justice of the Peace and that he wanted to hand over a further quantity of cocaine found in connection with his son's case. His reason for doing so soon became clear. Arnold Butler immediately asked for the cocaine to be sold legally so that the money he had loaned Richard, which he now realised had not been for batteries, could be returned to him.

The clerk summoned Inspector Bradley. Thanking him for his honesty and candour, the officer wasted little time in going to inspect the Bayswater address himself, where he found little more of interest, except for nine empty, airtight one pound tins, eleven smaller tins, and one square tin. There was also a telegram from Germany dated March 7. It read: "Expect you soonest possible to arrange matters. Batteries still available. Can only work at your arrival, wire." Richard's passport, also found at the address, showed he had travelled to Germany on March 9, arriving back on March 17. Other seized items included a set of "very accurate" pharmaceutical scales and six weights.

Arnold Butler gave a brief statement to Bradley, promising to forward any documents or information of relevance. He then followed up the plea he had made in court with a letter to Scotland Yard, written that afternoon, explaining, "As all this was purchased by MY OWN MONEY I sent to my son to purchase batteries with, I think I am entitled to ask that the proceeds of the drug when disposed of into legal channels, shall be returned to me, as it amounts to nearly £1,400."

On his way back to the hotel, Arnold called in to see friends at the Home Office, both to disclose details of the affair and to inform them of his son's injuries sustained during the war, in the hope that the information would be passed to the prison governor. It wasn't until March 26 that Arnold was able to visit his fallen son in Wormwood Scrubs.

The prison visit would have been utterly humiliating for a man of Arnold Butler's social standing. Never in a thousand lifetimes would this proud pillar of the community have imagined walking through the iron doors of the Scrubs to visit his own son, and for such a base offence as selling cocaine. It was also on his mind that he too was a victim of sorts. Arnold was in no doubt that it was his money that Richard had used to make the purchase.

The meeting was an unhappy reunion. Arnold asked about the source of the cocaine, but Richard was reluctant to speak about anything in detail. Eventually, under pressure, he gave up the details and Arnold wrote them down in his notebook, "Carl Murhard, Hugo Busch, Bonn, Germany."

"There is a lot of money in it," Richard pleaded. "I only looked at it from a point of view of making a lot of money quickly, but I should have thought of the moral side."

Arnold said he would write to Murhard for the return of the £300 which Richard had handed over but received nothing in return. He also agreed to let Queenie have £25, which she had unsuccessfully tried to withdraw from Lorraine and Co's now frozen bank account. Good to his word, the JP penned a letter on March 29, informing Murhard of his son's arrest but also, unwisely, threatening to turn him in if the money owed was not sent back.

"I am writing as a magistrate," he warned, "and as his father, to give you the opportunity of returning to me...the £300." Arnold enclosed an envelope for the purpose, and promised to reply with a receipt, adding as a further warning that Richard had given him the serial numbers of the £5 notes that had made up the transaction.

"Unless this is done I am handing over to our English police at Scotland Yard the whole of the correspondence, along with your name and address, for them to take up with the police in Bonn. I do not in any way wish to offer threats, but you see the position." He added, "I do NOT intend giving your address or name, to the police if the money is returned, as it is not my business. I know they are endeavoring to find out, I am only concerned about my money given to my son for another purpose." Arnold gave Murhard a deadline of April 6.

Arnold penned another letter on the same day, this time to "the chief of police" at Scotland Yard, regarding an official interview request. The idea of his name getting out in connection with the case evidently made Arnold extremely anxious. "Someone rang me up this evening re my seeing him in London, or his coming to Birmingham," he wrote.

> It was finally suggested that your representative should come down and see me at my office, New Street, Birmingham, on Wednesday next...I have since thought that as I am so well known in this city, and that up to now, I am glad to know that Richard Butler has not been linked up to me as my son, that whoever comes shall not mention my name to the police in this city. Every one of them know me and I am glad to know respect me. If there is any possibility of my name being mentioned [to the local police] I would rather come up to you in London...I hope you can appreciate my position as fathers cannot be responsible for their son's actions when they get married and are 28 years of age.

As a result of the letter, Arnold was summoned back to Vine Street for a further interview with Inspector Bradley, who evidently felt some sympathy for the man. Arnold arrived on March 31, and told Bradley that after examining the ledgers from the Bayswater flat, he had found evidence that Cornelis had made large sums of money from cocaine dealing during the war. He later had to admit that he "had no actual proof" and had merely surmised from viewing what he said were "vague entries" in the company books.

Arnold also disclosed that his son had met Cornelis and Seligman in 1923, and all three had travelled extensively to Germany, he believed becoming acquainted with a "several cocaine traffickers". Again, Arnold had no actual evidence of this and Seligman later gave a statement denying any involvement in or knowledge of drugs. Nevertheless, Bradley later wrote in a report that "this clearly proves that [Cadbury] Butler was quite aware of the nature of the drugs with which he was dealing".

Bradley asked Arnold whether he knew the name and address of the source of the cocaine. Arnold lied and said he did not, but then Bradley told him the force had already written to the police in Bonn, as a result of the telegrams found both on Richard's person and at his flat. At that point, perhaps realising that his letter to Murhard would soon come to light, Arnold admitted that he did in fact have the name and address of the supplier and had already written to him. Bradley made a note of this suspicious u-turn in his report.

Murhard finally wrote back to Arnold on April 10, claiming to have been "ill in bed" for the last week and unable to reply. He said he was "truly sorry that such a mischance has befallen your son" but he was in a bind himself. While he wanted to return the money, he said, the cash had already been passed to his supplier. Therefore, Murhard reasoned, he would need time to get the money back, if it was still possible to do so.

"Unfortunately, I am not myself in a position to undertake this return out of my own means. I am 65 years of age and have experienced heavy losses through the war and its consequences," he reasoned. Murhard further blamed his plight, conveniently, on the now-expired Leon Cornelis. The German signed off, promising to do what he could to return the money and imploring Arnold to "refrain from any steps which must bring a criminal prosecution in their train, and lead to the ruin of myself and my family without doing any good at all to yourself".

Arnold wrote back on April 13, this time making another thinly veiled threat. "I want to help you all I can," he insisted, "but I want you to realise that until that £300 is returned to me, you are in danger of arrest. Unfortunately, Scotland Yard know that you owe the money, and what steps they have taken I do not know. I [did] not inform them of anything detrimental to your interests, but you will see that when the money is returned, they have nothing against you, so for your own interest get it and send it to me as soon as possible." Arnold heard nothing back from Murhard. But copies of both letters fell into the hands of Scotland Yard, thanks to their interception by the police in Bonn.

"This case gets more and more interesting and difficult," Bradley wrote in a report dated April 26. He went on:

> Arnold Butler's letter of the 29th of March, a copy of which has been sent to us by the German police, is really a demand for money with menaces but I do not think that a jury would find absence of 'reasonable and probable cause'. The letter shows however that he has, or had, in his possession a considerable amount of correspondence beyond that which he has disclosed to us, and it clear that we shall have to see him and get all correspondence that he has got out of him....It may be possible before seeing Butler to obtain a search warrant under Sect 1 sub sec 1 of the Dangerous Drugs Act 1923 and if so such a warrant should be to search both his office and his house. It looks as if we shall have little difficulty in recommending to the Home Office that this gentleman's name should be removed from the list of Justices of the Peace for the City of Birmingham.

On the very same day, Arnold wrote once again to Scotland Yard with a simple and to-the-point request: "I shall be glad to know if the drug has been sold yet, and when I may expect a cheque in settlement. Thanking you, yours faithfully, Arnold Butler." There is no record of the force's reaction, but his latest missive would have done nothing to alleviate the suspicions now hanging over Arnold Butler.

The police obtained their search warrants. On April 29, Chief Inspector Alfred Collins and a Sgt Clark travelled up to Birmingham to search Arnold Butler's office and residence in Moseley. Collins explained to a somewhat startled Butler that he had in his possession a translated version of his March 29 letter to Murhard. Its contents revealed, he explained, that Arnold had knowledge which he had not disclosed to police, therefore drawing him deeper into the case.

Arnold was adamant that he had no prior knowledge of his son's involvement in cocaine trafficking, and he was more than happy to let the officers rifle through his papers and possessions. While nothing of any note was found, the officers did take possession of accounting books belonging to the Pharmaceutical Supply Company and Lorraine and Co, both of which Arnold had salvaged from his son's lodgings.

The next day, Arnold made a detailed statement. He insisted that he had "no intention to willfully conceal anything from the police" and had only mentioned not handing over Murhard's address in his letter as a "bluff" in order to get the money back. "As a Justice of the Peace," he blustered, "I knew it was my duty to inform the authorities and was at the time making preparations to examine the books and correspondence sent in the cases [from the Bayswater address] to collect such material as they required, and which I intended sending to them. I had not opened all the cases at this time. At the time of writing this letter I did not realise the seriousness of the nature of the offence."

When asked why he had made a point of letting Murhard know he was a magistrate, Arnold explained that he only wished to create "an impression on the mind of a foreigner, as I knew through living on the continent that a magistrate is regarded as one possessing great power. On reading this letter I now realise that I have acted very, very foolishly and I express regret for having done so and offer my sincere apologies to the authorities. I should never have written a letter of this description to an Englishman." He agreed that it was "improper" but said "at the time I believed that the man Karl Murhard was the cause of the downfall of my boy and the loss of thousands of pounds. In my distressed state of mind I did not think out as I should have done under normal conditions".

Arnold was also asked to explain why, in his previous interview with Bradley, he had made no mention of the potentially incriminating letters, or his discussions with his imprisoned son, until the officer informed him that discussions had already taken place with police in Bonn.

Why hadn't he told him what he knew of Murhard? It was simple. Arnold felt "honour bound" not to disclose Murhard's address because he had said in the letter that he had not done so, however he felt that by the end of the conversation he was no longer "honour bound" and had been "released from my promise", on account of the police in Germany already being involved, and that as a JP he could "honourably" give up all the information.

"After posting the letter to Murhard," he said, "I regretted that I had made such a promise, which I felt honour bound to abide by till such time as I could obtain the return of the money before being able to act, as I fully intended doing, as a Justice of the Peace, later on." If anything, Arnold reasoned, his problem was that he was just too honourable.

While Arnold re-iterated that he had no prior knowledge of his son's involvement in cocaine, he had since come to believe that Ricgard and Cornelis had been involved together for some time. He also revealed that he had sent a list of questions to his son in Wormwood Scrubs, which he produced for the officers. One of the questions was in fact a demand for a statement making clear that the money Richard had obtained from Arnold was provided in good faith.

Richard duly obliged, writing: "I hereby state that all monies given to me by my father was meant for the purchase of wireless batteries and talc and nothing else." Other questions included the legal value of the cocaine (about £50 per ounce) and whether there was any more of the drug presently unaccounted for (no). Arnold had ended the questionnaire with these words: "Please answer all these questions carefully and thoughtfully, as they are of vital importance, if the matter is to be cleared up before you are discharged. If there is anything else we should know, please state it all NOW."

Throughout his statement, Arnold's pain at the fate that had befallen his son was clear. Frequently referring to him as "my boy" it had obviously brought shame on the family. "Since my boy's conviction I have, as far as possible, paid up all his debts and redeemed many things from pawnbrokers totaling over £200. Upon his release it is my intention of sending him abroad," he said.

Arnold once again reiterated that he had possessed no prior knowledge of the cocaine deals and had had "full confidence" in everything Richard told him about the businesses. "I now realise that the whole family have been grossly deceived by him," he said. "I now believe that my son and Cornelis have for some time past been engaged in drug traffic and that my boy has been the tool for Cornelis and that the money advanced by me has been used by both for illicit purposes."

Chief Insp Collins concluded his report of the Birmingham raid with scathing criticism for father and son. "The prisoner had no conception whatever of business matters and as a result of my interview with Mr Butler Snr I formed the opinion that he had had very little experience in the ways of the world beyond that of his own social circle," he wrote. "He appears to have taken everything for granted and had great faith in the representations put forward by Cornelis that he was going to make his son a successful business man."

On May 3, 1926, about five weeks into his sentence, Richard Cadbury Butler agreed to give a full and detailed statement to police. "My father knew absolutely nothing about my dealings in cocaine," he said. "I deceived him and obtained monies from him by representing I was dealing in batteries. The cocaine business was a secret between Cornelis and myself, I realise now that Cornelis has had the greater portions of the monies which I have obtained from my father for these so-called businesses."

Queenie also came in to give a statement, claiming to have known little about Cornelis' business interests. She said he was "extremely secretive" although she observed that his financial position became worse as their relationship continued.

Meanwhile, the police in Germany had been investigating Murhard. His premises for Busche and Co, in Munsterplatz, and his home address in Niebuhrstrasse were both raided, although no cocaine was found. He admitted supplying Butler with the cocaine and named his source as a Munich-based apothecary, Wilhelm Schiefer, although he denied ever dealing in cocaine before or since, despite his association with Cornelis going back nearly twenty years.

Another German national named Lang and two Austrians, named Biemann and Brancker, were later named as the ultimate source. The men were punished under German law, all except for Brancker, who shot himself.

The Cadbury-Butler affair was a tale with few winners. That being said, officers Mann, Coleman, McBean and Bradley were given commendations, while the heroic garage attendant who helped to wrestle the drug dealer to the ground, Reginald Smith, was sent a thank you letter. The informant who first pointed out the spot where Mohamed Ali was touting for buyers, Claude Williams, was paid £20 from the Informants Fund.

Richard Cadbury Butler was released from prison and later remarried. Again, the woman was a wife of a serviceman and for the second time Richard was named as the co-respondent in the divorce papers. He remained the black sheep of the family and his name, war record and troubles with the law have since been airbrushed from the family history. When, in 1931, more than one hundred members of the Cadbury family, including Arnold, Edith and their other three children, gathered for a photograph at Bourneville for the firm's official centenary celebrations, Richard was noticeable by his absence.

His obituary was carried in the *Birmingham Daily Post* in October 1957. It said only that he was a grandson of the social reformer Richard Cadbury and that he had died in Jersey. "He left Birmingham many years ago to devote himself to horticulture in the Channel Islands," it added. A copy of his Will shows that he married again, this time to a woman named Joan Neison, leaving everything to her. The full story of his involvement with cocaine and the sullying of the Cadbury-Butler names, never did make the newspapers.

On May 21, 1926, Arnold Butler received a distressing communication on House of Lords headed notepaper, a letter signed by RL Overbury, the Secretary of Commissions, on behalf of the Lord Chancellor:

I am directed by the Lord Chancellor to inform you that his attention has been called to proceedings which have been taken against your son, Richard Cadbury Butler, for illegal dealing in cocaine, and particularly to letters which you wrote dated the 29th of March and the 13th April 1926 to Carl Muhard, Hugo Bursch, Bonn, Germany, from which it appears that when you became aware of the person from whom your son had obtained cocaine, you did not communicate the address to the police authorities but offered to suppress it in consideration of a money payment. The Lord Chancellor also notices that in your letters you made improper use of the fact that you are a Justice of the Peace, so repeating the offence of which a complaint has already been made to his Lordship, and about which he has recently written to you. In these circumstances the Lord Chancellor is of the opinion that it is undesirable that your name should remain on the commission of the peace, and he directs me to ask you to resign within a week from the date of this letter, failing which his Lordship will direct your name to be removed from the commission of the peace.

The nature of the previous offence mentioned in the letter was never brought to light. But Arnold took no time in desperately trying to salvage his position. Firing off a letter on headed notepaper from his private office in Birmingham's New Street, to Chief Insp Collins, Butler begged for help. "Can you not help me in this matter," he wrote, "as [the Lord Chancellor] certainly has not got the true statements about my writing to Carl Murhard, re the cocaine. It is hard lines if I have to suffer this ignominy when I feel it is not deserved. Is it possible for you through the Home Office to have the matter put straight for me? The matter is urgent as you will see."

Two days later, on May 25, Collins sent a memo to his superintendent, asking him to reply with a blunt message. "I beg to suggest that the letter be at once returned to Mr Arnold Butler and that he be informed that any communication relating to this matter should be addressed to the Lord Chancellor," he wrote.

No record exists of any direct plea Arnold may have made to the Lord Chancellor. But he must have sweet-talked his way out of trouble somehow, because he continued to dispense justice as a magistrate and carried on in his various public roles for a number of years after successfully suppressing the scandal.

Finally, on Christmas Eve 1932, Arnold Butler JP was forced to resign over what he said was a "technicality". He told the *Birmingham Gazette*, "For many years I have received many letters from successive Lord Chancellors pointing out that my social work clashes with the rulings of magestraterial procedure. The Lord Chancellor regretfully suggested that I should give up on or either of these interests, and I have decided that my social work must come first and I should resign from the bench. There is nothing wrong, the whole affair hinges on a technicality."

Arnold went on to explain that the "specific instance" involved the wife of a prisoner, who he had spoken with in connection with penal reform. "I think the Lord Chancellor is right and I think I am right. If the two works clash it is better to give up one and carry on with the other." There may well have been no direct link to the cocaine affair. After all, the two Lord Chancellors concerned were different men from two different political parties. But perhaps secret knowledge of the 1926 drugs case informed the decision.

It is also worth mentioning Jim Kitten, the owner of the café under police observation at the time of Richard Cadbury Butler's arrest. His venue's deservedly dire reputation did nothing to stop him from suing the publisher Odhams Press over an April 1926 article in *John Bull*, which described it as a "terrible negro haunt" and Jim as an "unsavoury-looking person" who is "cunning and disreputable [and] has no respect whatever for law and order". The article said of the café, "Day and night alike, crimes and robberies, murderous assaults and blackmail coups are planned here by black desperadoes, who assemble in force and who often carry with them revolvers and other dangerous weapons."

Jim took furious exception to the racist descriptions of himself and his customers, and the language used during the High Court proceedings was not much better. During the trial, Justice Horace Avory baulked at the suggestion that white girls were seen there sitting on black men's knees. When Jim's lawyer suggested the same thing happens at "respectable dances for white people" the judge remarked, "I don't know where learned counsel derives his experiences from".

Irrelevantly, a member of the jury asked whether it would be possible to close the café down. But regardless of the clear racial prejudice in the case, the core allegations were most serious. Jim denied knowing a string of criminal characters, including counterfeiters, pimps and prostitutes and, while one customer had stabbed a man, he admitted, the attack itself had not technically taken place on the premises. He also admitted once being fined £15 for allowing gambling. But one customer spoke up for Jim. Jazz musician Frank Kennedy said it "was the only place I could go without being sneered at and insulted".

During the case, Jim was also asked whether any "black drug carriers" had been arrested at the café. He replied no, although officers named at least two people arrested with drugs, one with opium and another with £4,000 worth of cocaine. Only in a few newspaper reports was the man named: Richard Cadbury Butler. No further details of the case were published.

In the end, Jim rightly lost the case and was ordered to pay costs. Despite the *John Bull* article and the court case being saturated with the racial prejudices of the day, there was no doubt that the café was a den of iniquity, a meeting place for criminals and a source of drug dealing in the West End.

One further footnote from the case illustrates just how unaccustomed the police were to dealing with the fallout from the new anti-drugs legislation. Even by the following year, the officers were still dealing with admin. A note written on August 29, 1927, from an officer at Scotland Yard's evidence store to MD Perrins at the Home Office, wondered just what to do with the cocaine.

"We wrote many months ago asking for directions as to the disposal of dangerous drugs which have accumulated in prisoners' property store and have had no reply," the missive said. "Perhaps you will look the matter up. We used to deal with Whiffen and we want to know the name of the new authorised firm or firms. I think you said that we should have to sell the heroin and cocaine to different people."

There is no record of a reply nor, for that matter, is there any suggestion that Arnold Butler JP ever got his money back.

# 11. DEATH IN A HOTEL ROOM

**W**ilhelm Kofler was happy to be pushed around, so long as it meant a modest slice of the profits and the chance to move up, or at least keep his head above water, in New York's hectic and bloody underworld. The Austrian was a yes man, a professional pawn. He would transport the cash one way, carry the dope the other, and ask no questions. Even when he was ambushed and subjected to a savage beating and robbery, the dutiful middleman simply bandaged his head and traipsed back to the hotel room to explain why and how he had lost the drugs. Wilhelm Kofler was not destined to live a long life.

Kofler had been tasked with collecting a shipment of heroin smuggled into New York City by a Peruvian diplomat named Carlos Fernandez Bacula, who was equipped not only with total indifference to the law and ethics, but crucially a diplomatic passport. Bacula had smuggled something in the region of one-and-a-half tons of heroin during his criminal career, skillfully shipping dope into Miami, Montreal and other North American ports, acting on behalf of a major Athens-based cartel. In August 1928, Bacula made his final, ill-fated trip for the gang.

Arriving in New York via Vienna with one hundred and fifty kilos of heroin stashed among his belongings, Bacula was greeted at his hotel by Kofler. The pair had never met before and Bacula was wary. Kofler was also acting for the same cartel, as a liaison with the mobster August 'Little Augie' Del Gracio, a long-time associate of mafia boss Charles 'Lucky' Luciano.

Acting with caution, Bacula agreed to hand over just fifty kilos of the drug in the first instance. If all went well, then he would relinquish the rest the following day. It appeared to be an inspired move on Bacula's part, because less than one hour later Kofler reappeared at the hotel, his head wrapped in bandages. The Austrian had been robbed, although he wasn't sure whether a corrupt police outfit or a rival gang had been responsible.

Given the fact that Kofler had returned to the hotel after his beating, Bacula was quite convinced that whoever was behind the attack would know all about him and the rest of the consignment. He tried to think of a way out of the mess, but unfortunately Kofler was his only contact in the city. Bacula's options were limited. He could either leave with or without the drugs and take his chances with the cartel, or wait at the hotel for Kofler's assailants to inevitably track him down. Before he could make a final decision, the Peruvian received an unexpected visit from the flamboyant gangster and close ally of Arnold Rothstein, Jack 'Legs' Diamond.

Diamond assured Bacula that Kofler was not to blame for the robbery, and that he would flex his underworld muscles and see to it that the drugs were returned. Diamond left and, lo and behold, returned a short time later with thirty kilos of heroin. The haul was twenty kilos short, he admitted, but it was the best that he could do.

Bacula would have been a fool not to smell a rat. But by now, he didn't give a damn what happened to the heroin. He released the full shipment to Kofler, with Diamond acting as guarantor. Bacula's illicit luggage was duly moved to Kofler's suite at the Central Hotel on Broadway. The following day, Kofler's body was found inside the room with both wrists slashed wide open. The one hundred and thirty kilos of heroin were gone. It had been an elaborate double cross. Del Gracio, Luciano, Rothstein and Diamond were all part of the same outfit.

Bacula cut his losses and fled back to Europe to relay the news to the head of the syndicate, a man so powerful in the drugs underworld that it would take the efforts of at least three police forces to bring him down. His name was Elias Eliopoulos.

***

# DEATH IN A HOTEL ROOM

For most of the first war on drugs, Western Europe was the global traffickers' power base, although that began to change with the unravelling of the Eliopoulos Cartel.

The reason was simple. It was in countries such as France, Switzerland, Austria and Germany that narcotics could be legally manufactured, ostensibly for medical use, but purchased by criminals. And as the worldwide popularity of the drugs grew, fewer questions than ever were being asked.

Part of the problem was that there still major inconsistencies in the way drug laws were enforced. For example, an international certification system under the auspices of the League of Nations was introduced in 1925, which meant the importing country had to issue a certificate to the exporter stating the goods were only for medicinal or scientific use.

But the Dutch government did not issue the certificates unless they were specifically required by the exporting country. As a result, tons of opium was legally shipped to Rotterdam where it was processed in factories and shipped out as heroin under the guise of medicines, perfumes or talcum powder. Some of the supplies came from the German company CF Boehringer. In 1928, the Dutch police began to tackle this trade and found sixty kilos of heroin on a steamer sailing from Antwerp.

Sometimes, this corporate irresponsibility extended to other sectors. For example, one memo written by Sir Austen Chamberlain, half-brother of future prime minister Neville, while based in the Berlin Embassy in July 1928, set out in black and white how German companies were turning a blind eye to dodgy practices. Responding to an enquiry from Cairo about a

215

trafficker named Gornegradsky, Chamberlain listed the German companies the dope peddler had been in correspondence with. They included: Vogel & Halke, Hamburg (which made scales and weighing machines); Braun (chemists); and Eugen Schuing, Stuttgart (corset manufacturers). Gornegradsky, it appeared, had been on a shopping trip for industrial sized quantities of drugs, weighing scales and clothing for his mules.

France had a more acute problem — by the late 1920s the traffickers themselves were running the factories. At one end of the scale were men like Paul Carbone, the gangster and pimp, who operated low-cost opium processing plants.[15] At the other were facilities with more surface legitimacy. They included the Societe Industrielle de Chemie Organique, known as "Sico" (the director was one G Devineau); the Roessler factory in Mulhouse, on the Swiss border; and the Comptoir Central des Alcaloids (this time, a Belgian named Paul Mechelaere was in charge). Although the business sounded above board, the same man had been arrested in 1926 trying to smuggle morphine through Southampton concealed in a shipment of Vaseline.

These factories were legally allowed to produce narcotics, but were working almost entirely to supply the black market. The system worked because French law allowed authorised couriers or brokers to purchase drugs directly from the factories. The brokers had no legal responsibility for their ultimate use — that was down to the end customers. So long as they obtained an export certificate from French Customs, the authorities didn't much care what happened next. They even signed off on shipments which they could see were concealed within other goods and which were obviously destined to be smuggled into other territories.

The law was altered in 1929 to make the brokers responsible for the export, but as long as the goods never showed up back on the illicit market inside France there was little likelihood of them falling foul of the law. At the time, there were three hundred and twenty five licensed brokers, many of whom were shady characters, some even operating under known aliases.

Investigators later found out the names of several underworld figures who helped the drugs make it to New York, including Broadway impresarios the Newman brothers, Charles, George and Harry, a trafficker named Louis Lyon and the aforementioned August Del Gracio. Lyon faced his own problems when, in 1930, New York police seized a shipment of one hundred kilos of heroin shipped by his firm, Lyon and Co, from Paris.

By far the biggest beneficiary of this corrupt system was Elias Eliopoulos, known as Elie. A Greek national born in Piraeus in February 1893, supposedly to an affluent merchant family, Elie based himself in Paris, where he lived a fine life.

Described as pale with dark hair and a medium build, and standing at five feet and nine inches, Elie was sometimes likened to the silent movie star Conrad Veidt, famous for his depiction of bad guys, particularly his 1928 title character in The Man Who Laughs, an inspiration for Batman's nemesis The Joker.

Elie certainly had much to smile about. The well-connected businessman was often to be seen promenading through the city with a gold-topped cane, or being driven to the fanciest nightspots and cafes in a luxurious chauffeur-driven car, usually with a young, glamourous woman on his arm.

When in London, Elie would stay at the Imperial Hotel in Russell Square and describe himself as a banker. Very few people outside of Scotland Yard and the Home Office knew his real business, his connections to New York's underworld, or his Anglo-Saxon alias, Eric Elliott.

Elie's brother George, born August 1895, was also a frequent visitor to Britain. Said to be a snappy dresser and of a reserved nature, George was described as arrogant and an obsessive bridge player. He had spent eleven years working as a clerk at the Bank of Athens in London before joining his brother's cartel. George was married to Florence and the couple had a daughter, Kitty, who they sent to school in England and who lodged at an address in Madeley Road in Ealing.[16]

Florence was a glamorous, petite woman who was aged thirty two when she was followed by Special Branch after arriving on a visit to Britain in November 1932. She was described by officers as, "Slim build, pale face, wearing tortoiseshell spectacles: Dress — black Persian lamb coat with roll collar to match, black close-fitting hat, black dress with red wide collar, black shoes and stockings." Florence also wore a rectangular diamond brooch at her throat, about the size of a domino. It was established that Florence's son from a previous marriage, Tony Denaxes, then aged seventeen, also lived at the Ealing address.

Elie's youngest brother, Anasthasios, or Nassos, was born in June 1897. He also described himself as a banker and split his time between Athens and Paris. Like Elie and George, Nassos had good connections in London, and it was while living in Britain that he completed the purchase of the steamship Anthemis.

The Eliopoulos Cartel system was both brilliantly simple and complex. Elie didn't just buy and ship drugs. He brokered deals, took commissions, and received and sent numerous payments for services rendered. Profits were huge. At one point, Elie was buying morphine and heroin in Europe for £40 a kilo and selling in China, by that point the biggest illicit drugs market in the world, for £70. According to their records, the Eliopoulos brothers received some £250,000 during just the first eight months of 1931. Today, the same amount would be worth nearly £16 million. As a result of the Wall Street crash and the consequent fall in sterling, the brothers were said to have lost as much as twenty-four million drachmas in the Far East. But the loss barely affected their privileged lifestyles.

Almost inevitably, their success attracted police attention. Elie had been able to operate beyond the reach of the law in France largely because he paid a ten thousand francs per month bribe to Inspector Martin of the Paris police, who oversaw the national drugs issue. Martin was the French equivalent of the Met's Walter Burmby and the Home Office's Delevingne and Perrins rolled into one. He agreed to protect Elie as long as the drugs were not sold in his country.

On one occasion, when the United States tried to extradite a notorious trafficker named Jacob Polakiewitz, Elie told Martin, "That's my best customer!" Polakiewitz was duly left alone by the French police.[17] The partnership with Martin only came to an end when Louis Lyon, jealous of Elie's success, grassed him up to the French CID, the Surete. Partly as a result, Lyon, who was by then working with Paul Carbone, continued to be a major supplier to American gangs until his eventual arrest in 1938.

It was in part thanks to Nassos that the brothers further came to the attention of French police in April 1931. Nassos had accused his Parisian flatmate, a Russian-born Greek named David Gourevidis, of robbery and attempted blackmail. The case went nowhere, but Gourevidis, evidently feeling aggrieved, spilled the beans on the brothers' drug trafficking operation, claiming the turnover for the gang's Far East operations alone ran into the hundreds of thousands.

His decision to become a turncoat may well have been because he was himself under suspicion of drug trafficking (one of his brothers, Jacob, would go on to be convicted in China). It was also the case that unlike many other characters caught up in the Eliopoulos case, Gourevidis was less of an employee and more of an associate and independent trafficker. On one occasion, Gourevidis had kept hold of the commission on a drug deal brokered by Elie. Elie called him a "despicable, double-crossing thieving Jew", although they continued to work together. Besides his brother, David had criminal connections across the world, including a brother-in-law in New York. As a result of his testimony, the US Treasury Department's Federal Bureau of Narcotics took an interest in the group.

Investigators found that another Greek named Jean Voyatzis, then living in the Chinese port city of Tianjin, was making regular payments, often for several thousand pounds at a time, to Elie through a London bank. Voyatzis, aged fifty-two, was a former clerk for a cotton broker in Egypt, a job he had previously held down for twenty five years. But he had decided to start up as a 'coffee importer' in Tianjin and suddenly became extremely wealthy.

Investigators found that Voyatzis had corrupted dozens of officials in the city's French section. He was allowed to stroll into the Customs warehouse at night, retrieve drugs from their hiding places and cart them off with his nephew Dimos. The drugs were then taken to the Hotel Bourgeois where they were divided amongst local dealers. It was later found that the drugs had been manufactured in Istanbul. This was because, by June 1930, the French factory system had been overhauled.

The reforms were largely thanks to the intervention of the Egypt-based British policeman and anti-drugs campaigner Russell Pasha, who had publicly shamed France during an impassioned speech at the League of Nations in Geneva. The factories used by Elie and the cartel were ordered to wind up and the corrupt brokering system was abolished. However, many of the dodgy manufacturers, including Carbone, Lyon, Devineau and Mechelaere, simply moved their operations to Istanbul, then known as Constantinople.

Turkey, aside from already being a mass producer of opium products, had not signed the International Opium Convention of 1925, which had created the system of import and export regulations. To add to Turkey's allure for criminals, the internal laws governing narcotics production and export were even laxer than they had been in France. The Peruvian diplomat Bacula at one point reportedly bought three large trucks, each with secret compartments that could hold up to one hundred and fifty kilos, and simply loaded up at the factories and drove across Europe under his diplomatic cover. According to the turncoat Gourevidis, the Eliopolous gang bought two thousand kilos of heroin from one factory alone, with one thousand six hundred kilos sent on to Paris and four hundred kilos sent to Germany in 1931.

The drug traffickers experienced some problems unique to the environment in Istanbul. At one point it was estimated that every ship sailing for Egypt contained a hidden cargo of heroin or hashish. As a result, paying off corrupt Customs officials became a huge expense. A growing band of grifters then realised they could double their money by taking a bribe before subsequently double-crossing the gangsters. With the dirty money still warm in their pocket, they would tip off foreign countries about illicit loads and collect a reward. The next obvious step was to begin blackmailing the drugs barons literally at the factory gate. This had never happened in France and the factory owners took action. Paul Carbone established a major protection operation and the other factory owners preferred to pay off the gangster rather than the officials.

There was also official pressure being put on the government to close the factories. Partly as a result of the mounting problems in Turkey, Elie set in motion a plan to build the cartel's own drugs factory in Macedonia, well out of reach of officials in Britain, France, America and Egypt, all of which were closing in. Machinery for the extraction of opium alkaloids was found at Hamburg in 1931 and, although officially destined for Izmir, it would have been re-routed. But before Elie and his cartel of multimillionaire drug traffickers

— the real dope kings of Europe — could make their break for freedom, their empire came crashing down.

---

[15] Carbone, alias Venture, was a Corsican gangster based in Marseilles who had been kicked out of Egypt in 1924 for running a white slavery ring, and who later rose to notoriety for his role in the Stavisky affair.

[16] In November 1937, a man named George Eliopoulos sued the publisher Lovat Dickson and the printer, Latimer Trend and Co, for publishing a book by the late Baron Harry D'Erlanger, called "The Last Plague of Egypt". "A set of brothers of the same name as the plaintiff were described at considerable length," one report stated.

"And it was quite obvious that if the gang existed, and there was such a gang for all he [the plaintiff] knew, they were of a most iniquitous description and violated the criminal laws of almost every country." It was mere coincidence, George argued, that both he and the character described in the book, had worked for the Bank of Athens in London. He was duly awarded an undisclosed settlement.

[17] Polakiewitz was another Montreal-based villain who fraudulently obtained a British passport. He worked closely with Harry Davis, another associate of Max Faber.

# 12. DEATH ON THE NILE

**E**very criminal mastermind needs a foil, and in the case of the great Elie Eliopoulos his was an English police officer named Thomas Wentworth Russell. But Russell was no ordinary copper. In fact, this legendary lawman had never served a day on the streets of Britain.

Born in 1879 and educated at Trinity College, Cambridge, Russell joined the Egyptian civil service in 1902 as an inspector in the Ministry of the Interior. Even though Egypt was not formally a part of the Empire, the key organs of the state, including the police, were overseen by the partially-occupying British in an unusual arrangement that lasted until the swell of post-war nationalism led to a British exit in the 1950s.

During his early years in the country, Russell visited all but two of Egypt's police stations, travelling mostly by camel and railway. As a result, he developed a feel for the country and its criminal landscape unrivalled by almost any other Englishman, as well as a deep admiration for what he termed the "hardworking [Egyptian] people, happy and contented with so little relief from their daily toil".

Russell became the Assistant-Commandant of Police in Alexandria in 1911, and then later the Commandant of the Cairo Police, with the rank of Pasha, where he earned a reputation for fairness and crime-busting. But his driving passion was the elimination of the drugs scourge, which had hit Egypt particularly hard throughout the 1920s. One estimate suggested that by the end of the decade almost a quarter of working aged men — some 500,000 people — were hooked on dope, mainly heroin and hashish.

At the time, Egypt was one of the most cosmopolitan countries in the world, a magnet for Turks, Greeks, Britons, French and Italians, among others. This brought considerable wealth and mercantile opportunities, but also a determined group of usurers, fraudsters, thieves and drug traffickers who exploited the smuggling opportunities presented by the ports of Said and Alexandria. Hashish smuggling was also rife on the railways, where the drug was hidden in hollow axle boxes and other ingenious spots. Traffickers even made use of camels by clipping the hair from their humps and gluing it back on, with drugs hidden underneath.

One of the most infamous operators in Port Said went by the nom-de-crime "Keep it Dark". His real name was Mohammed Fawzi or Mohammed Abdel Kader Rahman. He was a Syrian ex-salesman for a local chemist, but evidently felt he could make more money by going it alone on the black market. Keep it Dark specialised in supplying drugs to ships' stewards, engineers and other seaman on liners flying the

British flag, almost exclusively. He would usually board the ship empty-handed and take orders, returning later with the goods and receiving a commission. This apparently kept him within the port's trading regulations.

One of the main attractions for criminals operating in Egypt was that the authorities could only enforce the laws of the suspect's home country. The Consular Court system often meant delays in obtaining search warrants so that incriminating material and suspects were no longer present by the time a raid was carried out, and that defendants experienced different levels of justice, often walking free where others faced prison, because what was illegal in one jurisdiction might not be in another. There was the additional problem that the courts dealing with foreigners sat only twice a year, leaving plenty of time for witnesses to be intimidated and evidence tampered with.

There were other problems with the Egyptian justice system, some of them noted by Sir Wasey Sterry, an English judge on the Supreme Court for Egypt. In a letter to a colleague, he pointed out that the lower, summary justice courts, could not impose a sentence of more than three months. Therefore, more serious cases had to be tried before a jury but, Sir Wasey noted, the juries in Egypt "are all so much more suspicious (and I don't say wrongly) of police evidence being manufactured than would be the case in England. For this reason I understand from the Crown Prosecutor that he often prefers to take summary proceedings rather than run the risk of a jury wrongly acquitting."[18]

Of course, these problems only arose if the criminals could be brought before a court in the first place. One case from

226

# DEATH ON THE NILE

Alexandria in 1928 involving British subjects Joseph Granna and Joseph Benzina illustrated just how dangerous it could be for officers trying to stop the traffickers. Granna, who began adult life as a taxi driver mired in poverty, became immensely rich in Egypt thanks to drug trafficking. He had been caught and imprisoned more than twenty times, a punishment that the chief of police laconically noted "does not seem to have had any effect on him".

Eventually, Granna's home was successfully raided and three kilos of heroin, cocaine and morphine were found. During the raid, Granna fired a revolver at the police but he was disarmed before causing any serious harm. Incredibly, the court granted him bail after Granna hired three of the country's best lawyers to argue his case, and he had to be hunted down again when his trial approached.

Benzina was also running a major operation. When police raided six properties linked to his gang, they found thirty-four drugged-up customers, including a fifteen-year-old boy and six British citizens. At another venue run by Benzina, his thugs beat a police officer with a stick and fired half a dozen bullets from a revolver, again thankfully all missing their targets.

By 1929, the drugs situation was out of control and required the attention of a single-minded problem solver. It was the Englishman Russell Pasha who became the natural choice to lead the country's new Central Narcotics Intelligence Bureau (CNIB). He saw that the issue could not be tackled simply by trying to bring prosecutions within Egypt itself. Investigations had to be proactive, international in scope and the resulting evidence absolutely watertight. Russell accepted from the beginning that some cases might go on to have little

227

or no bearing whatsoever on Egypt and that international traffickers had to be confronted wherever they were found. The force of his personality ensured that his superiors in the government came to see things the same way.

One of the Bureau's earliest investigations took its agents to Vienna and the activities of a gang of Polish Jews, all men who had previously been under investigation by the League of Nations' Opium Committee. Russell found they had been working with an Armenian named Thomas Zakarian, who had been convicted of drug trafficking in Egypt. The narcotics, usually about twenty five kilos of morphine per shipment, were sourced from legitimate French and Swiss factories.

Another early investigation involving Jewish gangsters, this time from Palestine and Vienna, became known as the Water Closet Case, after the gang smuggled heroin into Egypt hidden inside hollowed-out panels concealed by the hinges of wooden toilet seats. Each seat could hold two hundred grams of the drug.

One of the men sentenced to five years hard labour over the affair, Thomas Friedmann, was eventually released after serving just four thanks to Russell's compassion. Russell had been ambushed repeatedly at the League of Nations in Geneva by Friedmann's wife, who would throw herself at his feet and scream the place down. Eventually, Russell conceded that Friedmann might not have been aware of new, tougher sentencing laws passed in Egypt when he had committed his crimes. Owing to his good behaviour, Friedmann was allowed out and visited Russell to thank him personally although, it was claimed, he had lost the ability to speak any language other than Arabic.

Besides taking on the practical crime-fighting role with the CNIB, Russell also had a flair for diplomatic duties. He was an unflinching political lobbyist for greater international cooperation and lawmaking. This entailed much public speaking and behind-the-scenes bartering. But Russell was an enthralling speaker and used his own success stories at the CNIB to bolster his case.

When Russell made his first appearance before the League in 1930, he was able to boast not just of his success at dealing with the Jewish gangs, but also of smashing the hashish trade from Syria, which he said was producing some sixty thousand kilos a year in Lebanon. The crop had been burnt after he pleaded with the government to take action. Another success story was a case that had resulted in arrests in Switzerland, France, Italy, Germany and Greece.

"Is it fair that Europe should thus pour its tons of poison into my country?" Russell implored. "Europe is strict enough in its own countries to prevent their ruination by drugs...If you could see with your eyes, as I do every day, the abject misery and despair of our poor drug victims and their families, you would redouble, retriple your efforts to kill this vile traffic."

Russell's pleas eventually convinced France to clamp down on its wayward factory and license system. Next on his list was reform in Turkey. But at the same time, Russell held focus on his core mission — law enforcement. In his crosshairs were the heads of the world's premier drug trafficking cartel, men making the equivalent of tens of millions of pounds from the Istanbul factories, with customers from China to New York City. Elie Eliopoulos was about to have the smile wiped off his face.

---

[18] Sir Wasey also had scathing worlds for the European drugs manufacturers, writing, "It seems to me that the people who make and supply these drugs in Europe, chiefly I understand Swiss and German, are the worst scoundrels of all, and that the League of Nations should be urged to further exertions."

# 13. BROKEN

**R**ussell Pasha was well on top of the situation in Istanbul, even if he could initially do little about it other than to shame the Turkish government at the League of Nations. In his 1931 report to the League, he publicly named the three main producing factories and claimed six tons of white drugs had been exported to Egypt in the space of six months. The entire world's legitimate needs for one year amounted to just two tons, highlighting the scale of the problem.

In his speech at Geneva, Russell made a fresh plea for intervention in Turkey. "The country [Egypt] is still rotten with dope, but I believe that it can still be saved from the complete ruin that threatened it," he said. "Thanks to the role of the League and to the general tightening up of control in Europe, the stream of illicit drugs into Egypt is now limited to the Istanbul stream. During the year under review, I can say with assurance and conviction that not an ounce of illicit heroin has come into Egypt from the factories of central Europe."

While he acknowledged with some diplomacy the efforts being made by the Turkish authorities to stop the trade, Russell respectfully suggested that factories producing drugs should not be allowed to operate directly on the coast, where ships could easily spirit away illicit products. He also pointed out that while the Turkish government said nearly two thousand kilos of opium had been exported to Egypt officially in 1928, not a single kilo had been imported knowingly by the Egyptian government. Therefore, smugglers must have been behind the trade.

"Devastating is the physical ruin of a country given to drug addiction," he said, "still more disastrous is the complete moral ruin of so many of the Government officials whose services can be of value to the traffickers. Not only are all port officials exposed to this temptation, but also railway officials, postal officials, and all ranks of the police. The temptation is terrific and my only surprise is that more of them do not fall victims...The temptation is superhuman. Poisoners of bodies and poisoners of souls, that's what these dope traffickers are. And I wish I could sentence them to suffer the agonies of their victims."

Russell went on to show the League delegates a film illustrating the physical ravages of long-term drug addiction.

By the end of 1932, after both Russell and several American officials had travelled to Istanbul to personally put pressure on the government, the likes of Devinaeu and Mechelaere were facing deportation as President Mustafa Kemal Ataturk finally agreed to implement the various international conventions on narcotics. But by then, the Eliopoulos cartel had already faced a string of disasters.

\*\*\*

It was the type of bread and butter operation that had made Elie, George and Nassos extremely wealthy men. In August 1930, the cartel shipped seventy one kilos of opium on the SS Havelland from Hamburg to Tienjin, where it was to be picked up by Jean Voyatzis and his crony Dionisious Gelatis, another 'coffee importer' and owner of the General Trading Company — an obvious front operation. The drugs would have a wholesale value of about £5,000, just under £330,000 in today's money. But Gelatis never made the pick-up. Instead, the two trunks, packed with used clothing, including a suit decorated with the Legion d'Honneur, were seized at the Chinese port.

The name of the passenger who had booked the trunks on the ship at Istanbul, Paul Wolfheim, left a trail of breadcrumbs back to Elie. The German, a former croupier and general fixer, who lived with his wife Hildegarde on Dusseldorf-Strasse, Berlin, had been dispatched to Istanbul by one of the cartel's chief agents, a man named Seya Moses. Moses' real name was Rudulph Reiter, a Frenchman born in Bucharest, who nonetheless claimed to be an Afghan born in Beirut.[19] Moses had met with another cartel fixer, Kostas Belokas, in Istanbul, before travelling to see Wolfheim, although it was not clear whether he had lugged the trunks all the way to Germany or whether Wolfheim had picked them up in Turkey. In any case, Moses had an ulterior motive for personally travelling to Berlin to give Wolfheim his orders — the Frenchman was having an affair with the German's wife. As soon as Wolfheim was out the door the secret lovers picked up where they had left off some months previously. But the good times were not to last.

When no news was received of the seventy one kilos (clumsily code-named "81" by the gang) from China, Elie used Seya Moses and Kosta Belokas to send a series of panicked telegrams. Both men sent messages in October stating, "Telegraph here is 81 received in good order?"

Elie's little brother Nassos traveled to Moses' base in Berlin to find out what had gone wrong. He forced Moses to telegram George in London, stating, "I follow absolutely your instructions, but I have no initiative in the matter. My three telegrams to Jean remain unanswered." Four days later, Nassos sent a fourth telegram to Voyatzis, and later told George that again there had been no reply.

Ellie himself now arrived in Berlin, where he sent another flurry of telegrams via Moses. "What is the matter that you do not telegraph if you saved 81?" He demanded of Voyatzis. "Also please advise us where you addressed letter including our ten thousand dollars. Do not remit until further notice Athens. Retain money until further instructions. Telegraph at once Elie." Another message read: "81 must be saved at any sacrifice because we are exposed here." A further communication, apparently to family and friends in Greece, warned them that George would be returning to Athens and that they should "look after him well all of you together".

Finally, after Elie managed to confirm the drugs had been seized, he sent a message to Voyatzis confessing his fear of more trouble to come. "Must try to learn whether they had information from Paris or from London. Feeling morally broken. Afraid of much larger further catastrophe." Elie was right to be concerned, because a second disaster was indeed just around the corner.

In November 1931, customs officials seized four trunks marked as diplomatic baggage on a train from Istanbul to Berlin. Paul Carbone, Louis Lyon and the factory boss Paul Mechelaere were believed to be behind the shipment. Police also arrested the pair who had been destined to take control of the package onboard another train arriving from Switzerland — Little Augie Del Gracio and a Turkish national named Elie Abuisak. Little Augie would not normally have overseen delivery in person, and was only doing so on that occasion to avoid a double-cross.

It was a long and convoluted story. Del Gracio had previously placed an order with Mechelaere for two hundred and fifty kilos of morphine, which were to be hidden in a shipment of eight cases of machine parts. But the Belgian had a plan. He intended to double-cross the American gangster who, it was suspected, had played a part in the scam carried out by Legs Diamond in New York three years previously.

The crates were indeed sent to Hamburg but stored in a warehouse belonging to an underling of Mechelaere named Karl Frank. The plan was to remove the drugs and send the parts on to New York. Little Augie would later be told that the drugs must have been stolen en route. But Mechelaere decided not to tell Frank all the details of his plan, so when the German was told to remove the drugs and find a buyer, he began to ask around.

As luck would have it, George Eliopoulos's old flatmate and mutual friend of Frank's, David Gourevidis, had a suggestion. The New York mobster August Del Gracio was in Germany, he said, why don't I ask him? Little Augie must have thought he was suffering from déjà vu when Gourevidis relayed the quantity, the price, and even the packaging the drugs would arrive in, all of which tallied with the shipment he was already expecting from the devious Belgian.

Although privately Del Gracio was seething, he calmly went to view the goods in Hamburg and then traveled to Istanbul to confront Mechelaere. Although the factory boss tried to convince Del Gracio that his shipment had not even left the factory and was still being packaged, Del Gracio was not fooled. He demanded that Mechelaere send one of his cronies, Elie Abuisak, with him to Germany, to make sure this second shipment was not tampered with.

As the police closed in, Del Gracio desperately tried to hide some paperwork in the carriage, but it was recovered and linked him to Seya Moses. When police tracked Moses down in Berlin, his pocket book revealed he was a de facto employee of the Eliopoulos brothers. That tied the Greeks to the shipment seized in China, because the German police knew of Moses' relationship with Paul Wolfheim's wife.

Exactly why the police were on hand to arrest August Del Gracio on the train was never made clear. Perhaps he had issued one too many violent threats to Mechelaere and the Belgian had decided to get him out of the way by tipping off the authorities.

A third disaster befell the cartel in March 1932. By now, Jean Voyatzis had fled Tianjin and was spending time in Egypt.

# BROKEN

He was followed by agents from Russell Pasha's CNIB for nearly three weeks as he holidayed in Alexandria, where he avoided the city's underworld and instead spent his time dealing stocks and shares. Voyatzis set sail at the end of the month on a steamer bound for the Eliopoulos brothers' home town of Piraeus. The trip would become an incredibly successful operation for the CNIB.

Firstly, agents onboard the ship rifled through his luggage, uncovering a treasure trove of paperwork, including a remarkable thirty-five-page notebook containing the key to the cartel's extensive secret code. MD Perrins at the Home Office later hailed the book as "perhaps the most illuminating document ever seized in connection with the illicit drug traffic".

Written besides every name, supplier, company and other organisation involved in the trade was a five-digit number. Elie, George and Nassos were numbers 75000, 75001 and 75002 respectively. Factory bosses Mechelaere and Devineau both had entries, as did their respective factories. Louis Lyon, Gourevidis, Moses, as well as dozens of other traffickers and gang members from Japan to Greece were included. Front companies and otherwise respectable firms alike featured in the book and there were also codes for opium, its derivatives, various mixtures of the drugs and the equipment used to process them, as well as legitimate manufacturers such as CF Boehringer, (75321). The code for opium was "black" (75378) while heroin was "halawa", sweetmeat in Arabic, and number 75302.

Jean Voyatzis (75063) was also befriended on the steamer by an undercover agent, who complained of having his baggage rummaged through in the same way. It was enough to make Voyatzis suspect common thieves among the Customs officers, rather than a law enforcement operation. The code, he reasoned, would be useless to them. When the ship docked in Greece, Voyaztis and his new friend spent several balmy evenings drinking together in Athens, where Voyatzis introduced him to fellow drug traffickers. Russell Pasha viewed the discovery of the codebook as akin to finding the Holy Grail:

> For years we have been like an aviator flying above the clouds, and trying to make out the country lying below him: occasional gaps in the clouds gave us a glimpse now and then but it is only now that the clouds have rolled away and a clear panorama has been spread out beneath us. We can now see where the rivers rise in the mountains and wind their ways to the lakes and oceans! Our geographical dope map is clear, the manufacturing centres, the railroads and sea routes, the ports of departure and the ports of destination, all stand out: Not only so but we can see where rivers and roads have been and have been abandoned. Just as a landslide or an earthquake may alter the course of a river in the same way some 'show up' at Geneva or some new legislation due to an awakening of a national conscience has put obstacles in the way of the dope stream and forced it to seek a new channel.

Just a few days before Voyatzis' unfortunate voyage, Elie Eliopoulos had been followed around London by Special Branch officers. When he had arrived in Britain, he admitted to the immigration officer that there had been some publicity surrounding him and drug trafficking, but he claimed it was malicious information put about by the Paris police, who were trying to blackmail him. He said he was in the country to consult lawyers.

But he was in fact observed meeting with bankers and Greek businessmen, including the owners of a shipping company in St Mary Axe. He also spent much of his time window shopping, although he did buy a large quantity of women's underwear. In fact, Elie ended up leaving London for Rotterdam a day later than planned, "due to the non-delivery at the Imperial Hotel of certain articles of hosiery which had been expressly ordered on the afternoon of March 3, for delivery early that evening".

Further investigations found that Elie had lived in Britain back in 1919, when he arrived claiming to be a student. His Special Branch record stated, "Reported to be the head of the most important gang of drug traffickers in Europe, supplying large quantities of drugs regular to Tientsin and the United States."

Later that week, Elie was arrested in Mannheim en route to Switzerland, where he intended to withdraw some 450,000 francs deposited in a Swiss bank. Elie had been detained in connection with the Little Augie business, not the Tianjin seizure, and luckily for him the codebook had not yet been seized from Voyatzis. As a result, Elie was released on a ten thousand mark bail, at which point he immediately fled back to Greece.

Elie's arrest frightened Voyatzis, then still in Alexandria, and was undoubtedly the catalyst for his decision to head to Piraeus. He wrote to Gelatis back in Tianjin, "I am sure you have read the Reuters news at TIPOU (Elie) has been arrested in Germany. Before this arrest two of his collaborators, an

American and an Austrian [Del Gracio and Moses] who dealt with America were also arrested. This troubled me a lot but we cannot do anything...I am wondering what is the impression made upon the people at Tientsin...I hope you have started supplying the French. Take care of what you spend until we see what occurs."

While certain members of the cartel were now being rounded up by various authorities in America, Europe, Egypt and Turkey, its chief was a cannier operator. He took the bold move of contacting Russell Pasha and offering to make a statement, insisting that while he had been a drug trafficker in the past, he was not involved in the Hamburg fiasco. Agents of Russell's Bureau and the American Federal Bureau of Narcotics under Harry J Anslinger, travelled to Athens to hear him out.

Elie gave what he claimed was a full account of his life. He said his parents were respectable people and that he was sent to be educated in Istanbul. During the war, he said, he had been a contractor to the Greek Army, but he was left broke by the end of the conflict. That was when the drug trafficking began.

Elie described how he had first met Jean Voyatzis on a trip to China with David Gourevidis in 1927. The pair had drawn up a contract specifying each man's role in the cartel and, once back in Athens, had drafted George and Nassos to assist in the scheme. Start-up funds were supplied by a South American named Gonzales. Elie contested the amount of money he had made (£250,000 was, he insisted, too much). But he named names, and set out how the whole system worked, including how he paid bribes and who to. The one thing Elie denied most strenuously was any involvement in the Hamburg seizure. In other words, the one case where evidence existed which could see him put in prison.

Russell Pasha decided to give Elie the benefit of the doubt, writing, "This much might perhaps be added in pure justice to the man, that if one read his declaration of the Hamburg business in the light of his frank avowal of his past career in the narcotics trade, one could more readily appreciate his resentment at being accused of something he had not done when there were, in the past, so many things of which he might have been accused."

However, a second member of the cartel also made a statement, pouring scorn on Elie's protestations of innocence. Like David Gourevidis before him, Seya Moses now turned on his former employer.

"I have been to Athens where I lived with Elie, and he read his statement to me," he said. "It is such a monstrous distortion of the facts that I feel impelled to tell the whole truth regarding the arch criminal who has used me in every possible way, trampled upon me, and caused my imprisonment for eight months, through all of which he has amassed a huge fortune with impunity while I have had nothing in return."

Moses said Elie's story about how he acquired the funds to kick-start the cartel was a lie. He said that Elie and Gourividis had indeed used money supplied by a man named Gonzales to buy two hundred kilos of drugs in Germany, setting off in a car owned by the South American.

But the deal had been the first stage of a double-cross. On the way back, the car supposedly caught fire, destroying the drugs. Elie even showed Gonzales the charred remains but, of course, there had been no fire and the loss of the drugs was a scam.

Still, Gonzales seemed to be oblivious to Elie's ruse, and later accompanied him and a group of friends on a business trip to Cairo, with the South American again putting up the cash to buy drugs. This time, the goods were 'stolen' by bandits and Gonzales ended up falling ill, apparently from stress, in his hotel room.

Moses insisted that Elie's account of his war years was also riddled with untruths. According to his former crony, Elie, Louis Lyon and Bacula had been friends for more than fifteen years and previously travelled together as a gang of card sharps and confidence tricksters. Elie had at one point worked as an accountant for the Constantinople Gas Company, but he had swindled money and was also wanted in Romania for selling fake cheques and counterfeit money. It was said that Elie had even grassed up shipments being made by his own cartel because the reward money, in one case 120,000 francs, was greater than his share of the potential profits.

MD Perrins, who had spent years tracking the cartel and had supplied much of the information about them to Russell Pasha in the first place, later penned a report of the case. Sending it to the Metropolitan Police for distribution to other European forces, he asked for it not to be sent to the Paris police because, he wrote, "As you probably know, conditions in France in regard to the illicit drug traffic are far from satisfactory, and there is reason to believe that the principal suppliers of the drugs, such as the man Devineau, are able to exercise considerable political influence." Perrins had some final observations to make on the case:

# BROKEN

It will be observed that the smugglers moved about Europe, making their arrangements by telegram, telephone and letter so skillfully that it would not have been possible to detect any of the chief organisers actually handling the narcotics. To put a stop to their operations it would be necessary that the laws of each country should make it illegal for an unauthorised person to deal in narcotics even if those drugs do not enter the country in question....the case also brings out how the drug traffickers' path is made easy by the absence in some countries of any central official organisation...which can take prompt action on the receipt of information regarding the illicit traffic from central organisations in other countries...on the other hand, the case shows how much can be done to unmask the operations of the illicit drug traffickers by prompt interchange of information and cooperation between the authorities in various countries and gives some indication of how much more could be effected if international cooperation were more complete.

The Eliopoulos Cartel was finished, but Russell Pasha warned that even though the drug traffic had "reached its zenith and was now beginning to fall, an immediate crash to zero must not be expected".

Indeed, Elie Eliopoulos and Jean Voyatzis were allowed to walk away from the affair with their fortunes and liberty intact, but that was not quite the end of the story. After Germany invaded Greece in 1941, the Eliopoulos brothers moved to New York, where they continued to live the high life. They were, however, soon prosecuted over a shipment of one hundred kilos of morphine they had smuggled into Hoboken onboard the SS Innoko back in 1931. Although Elie and

George were initially found guilty after a trial in 1943, the decision was eventually overturned and the only punishment they suffered was deportation.

The tireless efforts of Russell Pasha had placed serious constraints on the activities of international dope syndicates. They could no longer source their goods from most of the European factories and trafficking drugs to places like Britain from Istanbul was considerably trickier than shipping them from mainland Europe. With the Turkish factories also closed down, trafficking in dope was now even more difficult. World War Two would soon bring so much disruption to the international order that drug trafficking was no longer a viable business. Yet there were still those who tried.

Back in Britain, Scotland Yard had no equivalent of Russell Pasha — a campaigning super-cop who would relentlessly pursue drug traffickers across borders and follow the clues, no matter where they might lead.

There was, of course, Special Branch, which had enjoyed some success in monitoring and bringing to justice drug traffickers based in Antwerp and elsewhere. Meanwhile, both MI5 and MI6 the nation's relatively young intelligence agencies, were also on the lookout for undesirable foreigners. So when allegations of a vast drug trafficking network led by Greeks and with a German man of mystery at its centre surfaced in the capital in 1932, all three agencies found themselves trying to break down a seemingly impenetrable wall of misinformation and mystery.

---

[19] Moses had been booted out of France in 1918 in connection with a spy scandal.

# 15. DUKE OF HAZARDS

By the early 1930s the dope menace was still making headlines in Britain, but they were not as frequent nor as prominent as those generated by the likes of Brilliant Chang or Eddie Manning in the first half of the Roaring Twenties.

Brilliant Chang's arrest and deportation had coincided with a remarkable drop in the capital's drugs cases — there had been an average of sixty five cocaine prosecutions and one hundred and forty eight opium cases a year from 1921 to 1923. That figure fell to just five cocaine and thirty six opium cases for the years 1927-1929. According to some accounts, London's clubland had become practically drugs free by 1930.

But in February 1931, *The People* began asking questions about the identity of London's "new dope king," claiming that Scotland Yard was hunting a "syndicate, at the head of which is someone wealthy enough to be able to provide all the financial backing necessary". It said a new, large supply of cocaine had begun to circulate in London, Manchester, Glasgow and Cardiff, and it was once again being sold openly in nightclubs. Airplanes were believed to be a new method of smuggling.

The *Daily Herald* also ran an expose of the "huge profits of the big gangs". International syndicates, it said, could make returns of as much as six hundred percent on cocaine, smuggled into the country unwittingly by innocent merchants who believed they were bringing in cosmetics.

One example of such an organisation was given as a Russian doctor and two merchant countrymen, who conspired to ship drugs from the Far East into Britain. The illicit goods went to a company of unsuspecting forwarding agents in Berlin, which easily got them past Customs throughout Europe. The drugs were then removed by corrupt agents and replaced with legitimate goods.

In another case, twelve police forces worked together to make near-simultaneous arrests in Berlin, Berne, Paris, Copenhagen, London, and other European cities. The profits in that case had run into the millions. The police dubbed the organisation "The Black Hierarchy" and, while dozens of its members were arrested, the heads evaded justice with their secret identities intact.

Amid this rampant speculation, a bizarre trio headed to New Scotland Yard to make a series of extraordinary claims about an alleged criminal network with links to the highest levels of the British aristocracy. As investigators chipped away at the truth, the case would require the attention of both MI5 and MI6, making it the intelligence agencies' first drugs case.

London's police headquarters had welcomed more than its fair share of strange characters over the years — and that was just the police officers. But rarely did someone arrive at the Yard accompanied by both his wife and his mistress. He may well have felt the need to stifle a giggle, but the officer on the front desk dutifully showed Mr Stanley William Curtis and the two women through to an interview room, where they awaited the arrival of Detective Sergeant George Hatherill.

At the time, with the world still reeling from the effects of the stock market crash of 1929, unemployment was high and crime was also on the rise. But organised crime usually revolved around the racetracks, general racketeering and forgery, of which Hatherill was an expert. What Curtis was about to allege was an altogether different type of illicit business — a sprawling international drugs plot hatched by a duke, a journalist, a notorious gun runner and a cast of shady hangers-on.

Not much was known about Stanley William Curtis, ostensibly a financier, on October 22, 1932. And in the days, months and years that followed, precious little else was uncovered. Or at least, if it was, the details were not committed to paper.

Curtis was probably in his early thirties at the time, and may have been the same Stanley William Curtis mentioned in the

# DUKE OF HAZARDS

*London Gazette* in February 1924, which carried the announcement of his promotion to 2nd lieutenant in the 17th Battalion of the London Infantry Regiment of the Territorial Army.

Curtis was certainly married to a woman named Lilian who, in 1932, petitioned for divorce. Why she accompanied her erstwhile husband on that day was never clear, because she apparently made no further contribution to the story. At the time, Lilian was living on her own in Ilford, East London, while Curtis was shacked up with a widow named Maud Christian Stewart, who had lost her RAF squadron leader husband Harry in a crash over Iraq two years previously, leaving her to raise the couple's two children.

Curtis and Maud spent their time living in West End hotels and travelling backwards and forwards between Paris and Berlin, apparently financing and arranging numerous property deals, the exact details of which were never established. The only thing that can be certain about Curtis today was that he moved in decidedly bohemian circles and didn't particularly care who knew it.

Sergeant George Hatherill also had extensive experience of Europe, although for different reasons. He had served in France and Flanders during the war and spoke French and German fluently. It was partly for that reason that he was recruited by Special Branch and sent to Brussels to act as liaison with the Belgian police where, he later wrote, he "acquired a taste for wine". He would also have learnt much about the international drug trade.[20] Hatherill never spoke publicly about the case Curtis brought to him, but he would have listened intently as this unusual story unfolded.

Curtis told Hatherill that he had been telephoned from the King George V hotel in Paris by a wealthy, aristocratic acquaintance, William Angus Drogo Montagu, otherwise known as the Ninth Duke of Manchester, asking for his help in a business transaction with the Portuguese government.

The Duke of Manchester — known to his friends as Kim — was a notorious bounder and cad whose various failed business schemes had already come to the attention of the police and the intelligence services, although Curtis was not to know that. Most of the duke's ventures had flopped, leaving a string of angry creditors in their wake. Despite his financial problems, the duke owned three castles and had been married to two beautiful women, first wife Helena Zimmerman and the actress Kathleen Dawes.

The duke's relationship with the American heiress Helena Zimmerman, who he married in 1900, caused controversy when her father Eugene, president of the Cincinnati, Hamilton and Dayton railway lines, revealed the duke was planning to join the family business. One newspaper article from the time called it "as extraordinary an episode in the annals of the British peerage as has ever been recorded".

The plan was for the Duke to learn the ropes of running a railway from the bottom up, starting out among the lowliest employees. "President Zimmerman is a hard and practical man and will have no hesitancy in casting the Duke aside as a successor to the Zimmerman railway properties should the young man fail in the test," the article continued. "On the other hand, Mr Zimmerman will be filled with pride and gratification if he finds that his noble son-in-law has in him the making of a first-class American railway man."

DUKE OF HAZARDS

The couple went on to have four children, but the relationship did not last long enough for the duke to take the reins of the company. They divorced in 1931 and Montagu eventually married his lover Kathleen Dawes, a well-known former actress who had appeared in West End shows 'Oh Joy' and 'Tilly of Bloomsbury', although she had not been on stage since 1919. Besides his two wives, the duke had also once challenged the Crown Prince of Germany to a duel over the affections of a girl in a Mayfair Hotel.

At the time of the approach to Curtis, Manchester had recently published a book, *Candid Recollections*, in which he regaled readers with details of his friendship with the late King Edward VII and bemoaned the failings of his commercial projects. "The chief danger when an inexperienced man attempts to take up commerce is that, not having been trained in it from his youth, he becomes an easy prey for financial sharks," he wrote. It was a sentiment that would surely have been recognized by Richard Cadbury Butler, had he chanced upon the tome.

The duke's own experiences in failure were best illustrated a few years later when, in August 1935, he faced proceedings for his third bankruptcy in thirty five years. The case shone a light on his finances at the time of the meeting with Curtis. Until 1929, Manchester had received a stipend from his mother's estate of up to £9,000 a year, but that slumped to 'only' £3,500 during the Great Depression. The sum was paid to his wife, who gave him an allowance. The duke then began to earn money through commissions, as a result of buying and selling ships, but ended up losing his entire £52,000 fortune. He went to Canada in 1925 and invested in a mining company, where he

251

also lost money. Despite these financial disasters, Manchester revelled in the title "Britain's most happy-go-lucky duke." He was reported once to have said, "My trouble is I have been a mug — always been too trustful and willing to help others."

While the prospect of Manchester doing genuine business with the Portuguese government was unlikely, although not impossible because as a nobleman he still exuded a certain gravitas, it was perfectly possible that he had informed Curtis of such a scheme, real or not. In any case, Curtis went to France the following day, as requested.

Almost as soon as he had arrived, the duke informed him solemnly that the business had been cancelled and that he had already phoned Maud to say both men would be returning on the 4pm train from Paris, via Boulogne and Folkestone. "On arrival at Folkestone," Curtis explained, "the Duke of Manchester gave me a small parcel which he told me contained half a dozen pairs of silk stockings and asked me to smuggle them in for him."

Curtis took the parcel without examining it, asked no further questions, hid it under his waistcoat and handed it back once they were on the train. In hindsight, the entire affair seemed to be a ruse to entice Curtis to Paris simply so that he could smuggle something back into Britain for the duke. We will never know if the package really contained only stockings, or something more sinister.

Curtis returned to Paris later that month, supposedly in connection with another real estate transaction. He offered Hatherill a somewhat wooly version of events. Curtis said a man named Charles Leese was a party to the deal. He had met Leese through Henry James Bellingham, another toff introduced to him by Manchester about one month previously. Curtis checked in to the Hotel Avenida. He was there just a few hours before Bellingham phoned and asked him to meet a Greek named Soulidi, a mutual friend of Leese, who was also involved somehow with the business. In his garbled version of events, Curtis failed to expand on exactly what was discussed and quickly moved on to what he saw as the meat of the tale — his next trip to Paris on October 5.

This time the visit would take longer, because Curtis had to conclude the real estate business, the deal with the Portuguese government and the proposed acquisition of a French bank. As a result, he decided this time to invite Maud, who would accompany him as his wife.

A few days into the trip, Soulidi called at the hotel with a man named Rousseau, who proposed a business importing wood pulp boxes to England. Curtis promised to consider his idea. But within minutes of Soulidi and Rousseau making their exit, Curtis received a visit from a Dr Georges Serafides, yet another acquaintance of the Duke of Manchester, who told him that Soulidi was "no good". If Curtis had an opinion about what had been going on with this whirlwind of new friends, he kept it to himself during his police interview.

He did explain that during both visits, from Soulidi and Serafides, Curtis and Maud had more than a few drinks. The next morning, the pair awoke feeling unwell, tired and Maud "very sick". She slept all through the day, the following night and the next day. Curtis got up and went about his business, but felt unwell all day. He believed they had been drugged, possibly with opium.

Maud Stewart gave a more lucid and altogether more colourful account of the trip with her husband and his strange friends in a separate interview with George Hatherill.

She suggested the sojourn had been an extremely boozy affair, going to lunch on two consecutive days with Soulidi, then enjoying an evening of cocktails at the Ritz and the Hotel Scribe with a gaggle of his female acquaintances, with all drinks paid for by the Greek.

On the third night, the trio and their new friends visited the Follies Bergeres — a racy cabaret show famed for its risqué and sometimes nude performances. According to Maud's account, all three stormed out "owing to the disgraceful performance we had seen". On the way back to the hotel, Curtis apparently "flew into a most violent temper" and "accused me of knowing the type of performance we had seen". The couple quickly made up, but on the Sunday night, while having dinner, Maud "passed an unnecessary remark". What exactly it was that she said remains a mystery, but Curtis "lost his temper completely". He was sick on arrival back at the hotel but quickly regained his health.

Maud said she returned to London alone on October 10, carrying business papers for Curtis, then travelled back to Paris in the afternoon, staying until October 15, when they both came back to London.

The intrigue continued almost as soon as the couple arrived back at the West End's Vernon Court Hotel, where they were staying indefinitely. Bellingham called at their rooms on October 16 and Curtis, suspicious, asked him whether they had been given drugs by either of his two friends in Paris. He told Bellingham that he wanted nothing more to do with

Manchester and "would take whatever steps I considered necessary to expose them". Bellingham left but later returned with another man — a German whose surname was Stahl.

The introduction of Stahl to the story would go on to form the basis of an intelligence file that would be developed over the course of at least two decades. Curtis described this man as: "Age 26, height 5 feet 11.5, complexion sallow, eyes blue, hair light brown, clean shaven, oval face, slight build. Was dressed in a double-breasted suit in medium gray of good quality and cut. Speaks English with a slight foreign accent. Has a knowledge of many foreign languages. He has long tapering fingers and moves his hands while talking. He informed me he is partial to hashish." Curtis added that he knew Stahl's first initial was H, but at that time he was not sure whether the name was Hubert or Herbert.

Stahl said he was the son of a German ambassador, while Bellingham apparently lied to Stahl, "I have known Curtis all my life. We were at school together and you can talk to him as if you were talking to me." With this assurance, Stahl began to explain his purpose at the meeting. Like Soulidi's friend Rousseau, he too had a proposal for this financier from London.

"I can supply you with any commodity you require," he began, "including guns, gas, liquid fire, ammunition, opium, heroin, cocaine, morphia or any other drug you require, and I can give an undertaking that I can produce any of these things in large quantities in bulk and deliver in any city or town in this country or on the continent. I can also obtain for you a passport of any country, if you don't wish to travel on your own." It was quite a proposal, and an extensive list of goods.

Intrigued by the offer, Curtis asked for evidence that Stahl could indeed provide such services. Stahl left for his rooms and returned within twelve minutes, carrying two large bundles of papers. Curtis read them thoroughly.

Enclosed were two letters from a Mr Christofrides in Cyprus to various small bankers throughout Europe and America, purportedly dealing with ordinary business. But, Stahl explained, "All this correspondence is in code and deals with drugs. The head of the organisation is Christofrides in Cyprus, who has several aeroplanes which are used in the traffic. I am prepared, if you are serious, to take you to Cyprus to discuss the whole business with Christofrides. I also have a man in the United States who has a new explosive which is stronger than TNT and which gives off gas and liquid fire on explosion."

Stahl produced further documents showing tests carried out by a New York chemist, as well as two passports, one German and one Mexican — apparently a diplomatic passport bearing the signature of President Cailles. Stahl suggested Curtis should come into the trafficking ring for an investment of £10,000. Curtis said he would think it over and get back to him via Bellingham. Stahl added, "It is of course understood that in the event of our not doing business together the whole conversation is forgotten by us both. This, as you know, is the rule of the ring." Curtis agreed.

Maud Stewart was able to shine some further light on this initial meeting with Mr H Stahl. She explained how shortly after Bellingham arrived at their rooms the conversation turned to dope trafficking. "Bellingham said that he was in a position to show the source of supply of drugs coming into France, also the route," she said. "I do not remember the reason why Mr Bellingham spoke about drug trafficking but it may have been because Mr Curtis and I were furious at the Duke of Manchester taking away our car and causing other trouble during our absence in Paris." This was in reference to a separate, but perhaps related drama, in which Curtis claimed to have bought a car from Manchester, who had subsequently snatched it back.[21]

Maud also elaborated on Stahl's arrival at the hotel. She told how Curtis ordered her to remain in her room, which she did. At one point, she claimed, Bellingham told her that Stahl "does what I tell him". "I might say here," she added, "that Bellingham has been the right-hand man of the Duke of Manchester, and Bellingham has said that he is his cousin, or some other relation. I know it as a fact that the Duke of Manchester has described Bellingham as his secretary. The Duke has from time to time hindered Mr Curtis in his business. I know that Mr Curtis told Bellingham that he would have nothing further to do with the dope subject."

According to Curtis, following the discussions with Stahl the duke's cousin Bellingham turned up at the hotel on three consecutive days, asking immediately on the first, "Are you going on with the dope business?" Curtis said he was still thinking about it, but on the second day he told Bellingham that he wanted "the ring" to "leave me alone".

On October 19, Bellingham arrived at Vernon Court again, but this time made no mention of drugs. Instead, he said he intended to go to Munich in connection with a mortgage on a Roman Catholic monastery. But for whatever reason Bellingham didn't leave the country. Instead, he returned at about 4pm for a chat, and then again at 9.30pm, by which time

Curtis was dining with a Captain Boddington of the Intelligence Dept War Office. Boddington was a mutual acquaintance of them both, Curtis explained, so Bellingham joined them for dinner.[22] Curtis now made another bizarre claim. While he admitted that he had not seen Bellingham since the meal, he suspected that he had been drugged by Bellingham or his agents as recently as the previous evening.

"This morning I awoke in a slight stupor and I also found that Mrs Stewart was in a worse condition," he said. "The only reason I can ascribe to this is that some drug may have been put in a glass of whisky just before I went to bed. The whisky was obtained only yesterday morning by my sending the porter of my present address to purchase a bottle of Haig and Haig whisky."

The couple had two or three drinks and were not drunk, he elaborated, yet in the morning he noticed a "sediment" in the glasses. "Due to her condition and mine this morning I was under the impression that the sediment was some kind of dope," he insisted.

Curtis said he had taken the glass to an East London chemist and was still awaiting results at the time of the interview. On the question of the second "poisoning" Maud added, "Personally I can give no explanation as to what the sediment is. I have never taken drugs of any kind in my life, neither have I seen any."

Having spent the best part of the day listening to all this, George Hatherill would have been excused for pouring *himself* a large glass of whisky. What exactly had Curtis and Maud been telling him? Was it the truth? Their accounts differed slightly in places, but the core story about Manchester,

Bellingham, Stahl and the other characters remained largely consistent. And what crime or crimes had been alleged? Motor theft? Poisoning? Illegal drug possession? Certainly, there was nothing in their statements that would stand up in court and, as yet, no corroborating evidence. And the political implications of opening an investigation that would drag the likes of Duke of Manchester, Bellingham and Captain Boddington into it would have to be thought through. Curtis could well be a crank, a drug addict perhaps.

Yet as fantastic as the story sounded to George Hatherill, Curtis's visit to Scotland Yard would spark a decades-long investigation involving Special Branch, MI5, MI6 and — when alleged dope peddler Herbert Stahl later became a celebrated American journalist under the name Johannes Steel — even the FBI.

_____

[20] Hatherill's work in Europe also saw him meet Hitler, Goering, Himmler and other Nazis, as well as visit the Gestapo headquarters in Prinz Albrechstrasse, where he was given a tour by Heydrich. "It was not simply personal curiosity that prompted these visits," he later wrote in his autobiography, *A Detective's Story*. "They enabled me to see and learn a good deal about what was going on, particularly with regard to the Nazi's anti-Jewish activities." When he returned from his posting in 1931 he was transferred to the CID at Scotland Yard and by 1939 was in charge of the department in the West End. Throughout his career, Hatherill investigated fifty murders, complex frauds (which sometimes spanned the continent) and the 1963 Great Train Robbery. He retired as a Deputy Assistant Commissioner.

[21] In November 1932, the duke reached a settlement with a claimant in the High Court, with no details released to the press,

other than that the claimant's name was Curtis. This case most probably referred to the car.

[22] Who was Captain Boddington? The files do not make it clear. One possibility is Herbert 'Con' Boddington, a veteran of the private intelligence group the Makgill Organisation and an MI5 agent tasked with monitoring Communists. What was he doing dining with both Curtis, who police thought suspect, and Bellingham, who most certainly was? The files do not say.

# 16. A DANGEROUS INTERNATIONAL ADVENTURER

**H**erbert Johannes Stahl arrived in America as a political exile from Hitler's Germany intending to forge a career as one of the nation's great journalists. Stahl certainly made his mark, and by the time of his death in 1988, Johannes Steel, as he was then known, was famous enough to warrant an obituary in the *New York Times*:

> Johannes Steel, a newspaperman and radio commentator whose career was marked by controversy over his outspoken left-wing views and his often sensational political and economic predictions, died on Wednesday at his home in Newtown, Conn. He was 80 years old.

# DOPE KINGS OF LONDON

Mr Steel, who came to the United States from Germany in the early 1930's, was foreign editor of The New York Post and a columnist for the short-lived Daily Compass. He was a political commentator for the radio stations WMCA and WHN and in recent years wrote a syndicated column on financial matters that appeared in The Waterbury Republican-American in Connecticut and in other newspapers.

In 1965 he was convicted of 14 counts of stock fraud and sentenced to a year in prison for selling 1.2 million unregistered shares in Alaska International Corporation, which acquired oil, gas and mineral claims that were never successfully developed. Federal prosecutors contended that investors lost $3 million, most of which went to Mr. Steel.

In 1946, Mr Steel ran unsuccessfully for the House of Representatives in a bitterly contested election in a district covering Manhattan's Lower East Side. He was the candidate of the American Labor Party, which arose from a split in the left wing of New York politics. Mr. Steel lost narrowly to a Democratic-Liberal opponent, Arthur G. Klein.

Born Herbert Stahl, the son of an affluent German-Dutch landowner on the border between the two countries, he fled when Hitler took power. In 1934 he wrote for The Nation before joining The Post, where he gained the job of foreign editor by writing articles predicting, correctly, that Hitler would conduct a series of purges.

Not all of his predictions were borne out; early in the Hitler years he said the downfall of the German dictator was imminent. But his crystal ball could be sensationally accurate: he predicted the Japanese attack on Pearl Harbor a week before it occurred on Dec. 7, 1941. Forty-six years later, on Oct. 16, 1987, he wrote in his financial column that the stock market would crash. Three days later it did.

# A DANGEROUS INTERNATIONAL ADVENTURER

Mr Steel is survived by his wife, the former Rhys Caparn, a sculptor.

On the face of it, the stock fraud appeared to be a somewhat incongruous blip in an otherwise successful career. But it was only during the 1990s that further unsavoury details about Steel began to emerge.

For example, in 1995 the United States declassified most of the Venona cables — intercepted Soviet intelligence reports from the war and the early Cold War years. The intelligence had exposed the British spies Guy Burgess and Donald McClean, and American moles including Klaus Fuchs, Alger Hiss and Harry Dexter White. The same files showed that in July 1944, Johannes Steel had told Vladimir Pravdin, a KGB agent in New York, that Roman Moczulski, the director of the Polish Telegraphic Agency, was secretly pro-Communist. He also told Moczulski that he should remain in place with the agency, which could set up a meeting with the KGB. Steel's code names assigned by Soviet intelligence and deciphered by cryptographers were DICKY, DICKI and DIKI.

But the real dirt on Steel remained buried in MI5's top secret archives for decades, and until now has never been published. They show that the feted journalist's criminality ran far deeper than his colleagues would ever have believed.

\*\*\*

Before the British government's file on Herbert Stahl could get going, Sgt George Hatherill needed more information. Fortunately, Stanley William Curtis showed up at New Scotland Yard again on November 2, 1932, demanding to see him. This time, Curtis wanted to make even more dramatic allegations.

Rather than avoid the clutches of "the ring," Curtis had found it irresistible not to contact Bellingham again. Perhaps he simply wanted to obtain further evidence to help Hatherill's investigation. Or maybe he really was curious about drug trafficking and had decided to give the ring one more shot. In any case, he tried to reach Bellingham but was told that the aristocrat had finally made his trip to Berlin. On the off chance that he would be back soon, Curtis told their mutual acquaintance, Charles Leese, that he would wait at the Grosvenor Hotel for a few days.

Bellingham didn't show up, but Herbert Stahl did. "We discussed dope, rifles, ammunition and the high explosive which gives off poison gas and liquid fire," Curtis alleged. "Stahl said that if I was serious about the dope and wished to satisfy myself that it is quite a genuine affair I could go with him to Constantinople where I would be put into touch with Christofrides in Cyprus and receive £8,000 worth of dope, cocaine, morphia, etc, and, with him and another man, travel by their underground railway to Paris and London. I partly agreed to this, but said I should have to be satisfied as to how the stuff would travel as I did not want to be arrested."

The underground railway was not literally a series of secret tunnels, but rather a normal Istanbul to Paris express train staffed with corrupt conductors, who would be paid to conceal the drugs inside seat cushions. From Paris, the drugs would be taken to the coast and then shipped to the Isle of Wight, before being brought to London.

# A DANGEROUS INTERNATIONAL ADVENTURER

Curtis was not appraised of all the details, but Stahl said he would tell him more if he committed. Stahl said he would receive ten per cent of the purchase price, £800, and then thirty-three per cent of the profits. Curtis agreed on the proviso that he would not hand over a penny until the drugs were in Paris. Stahl said he would organise diplomatic passports, perhaps from the Vatican, for Curtis to travel.

During a subsequent meeting at the Savoy Hotel, Stahl also discussed an arms deal. He said there was £400,000 worth of rifles and ammunition waiting to be shipped. In addition, he claimed that the new explosive he had mentioned was worth $3m. And the German introduced a new name to the conspiracy — Sir Basil Zaharoff, one of the most famous international adventurers of all time.

According to Stahl, the aforementioned Christofrides was in the number two in a "powerful Greek syndicate controlled and headed" in actual fact by Zaharoff, with credit amounting to $50m. Zaharoff was a name that would certainly have raised eyebrows at Scotland Yard. Known as "the mystery man of Europe" and the "merchant of death," Zaharoff was by turns a swindler, suspected spy, agent provocateur, arms dealer and war profiteer.

Born Vasileios Zacharias in Mugla, Turkey, in 1849, Zaharoff was well into his eighties and only four years away from his eventual death at the time of the intrigue unfolding at Scotland Yard. Yet anything was possible from this extraordinary figure, who was both celebrated for his philanthropy and war efforts and reviled for his dubious business practices and machinations, to the extent that Sir Ian Fleming would later base his supervillain Ernst Stavros Blofeld on him.[23]

While Zaharoff would go on to inspire countless writers, appearing as characters in numerous novels and movies throughout the twentieth century, he played no further part in the investigation sparked by Curtis's complaint. Intriguingly, while a wealth of police and intelligence memos and reports would go on to discuss the activities of the Duke of Manchester, Bellingham, Stahl and their associates, Zaharoff was never mentioned again, at least in writing. Nevertheless, his name would almost certainly have piqued the interest of anyone who later read Hatherill's report.

For his part, Stahl did not go into detail about Zaharoff's role in the alleged ring and may only have mentioned his name to boost the credentials of Christofrides. To prove he was indeed in touch with the Constantinople-based merchant, Stahl produced a telegram sent to his lodgings at 131 Ebury Street, Belgravia. It read, "Have credit 200,000 USER dollars cash waiting you here, balance usual terms. Christo." Another, purportedly from Rotterdam, said: "Referring transaction, you have done good business and terms agreed."

Stahl then suggested that if Curtis put up £250 in cash, or £150 and a private plane, he would fly from London and Brindisi and then get a boat to Cyprus. He would take with him a man nominated by Curtis. They would see Christofrides, pick up the dope, bring it to Paris and hand it to Curtis. When Curtis asked if he would bring it over personally, Stahl replied ambiguously that "everyone is scared at the moment of bringing in white stuff to London, Paris and Berlin".

# A DANGEROUS INTERNATIONAL ADVENTURER

In return for the £250, Stahl would repay him £1,000 out of his commission on the sale of the drugs. Curtis again said he would think about it and discuss how to raise the money with his solicitors. Instead, he went to Scotland Yard to report the conversation.

George Hatherill made a list of the names that had cropped up during the course of his conversations with Curtis. The leader of this drug trafficking ring, he wrote, appeared to be the Duke of Manchester, at least on the British end. His right-hand man was Henry James Bellingham. Then there was Charles Leese, another man named as HA Huntley, D Soulidi, Dr Georges Serafides, Christofrides of Cyprus, and Cynthia Humes, proprietress of Cymie's Club, in Grosvenor Street. She was, at least, part of Manchester's crowd and was involved in some way in the ring, Curtis alleged, probably as a dealer to her bohemian customers. Then there was Herbert Stahl, who appeared to be the lynchpin between these various characters on the British and Greek ends.[24]

"Records have been searched but apart from complaints re suspected cheque frauds and unsatisfactory money transactions by William Angus Drogo Montagu, Duke of Manchester, nothing has been traced of persons who appear to be identical with the persons mentioned by Curtis in his statement," Hatherill wrote. Chief Inspector Reid, who had sat in on the interviews, also weighed in on the affair in an addendum to Hatherill's report, which was sent to MD Perrins at the Home Office:

I have seen the man Curtis and his mistress, Mrs Stewart, myself at this office on two or three occasions. They are undoubtedly a mysterious couple, and many of their statements should be accepted with great reserve. My opinion of Curtis is not by any means a good one, and evidently he has some ulterior motive for making these allegations. However, if there is any truth in what he says regarding Stahl, Bellingham, Leese and the Duke of Manchester, it would be worthwhile for Home Office to take their usual steps regarding persons suspected of trafficking in drugs. It is to be seen that Stahl has asked Curtis to advance the sum of £250. In reply to my question, Curtis says he does not think that Stahl is trying to fraudulently obtain that sum from him. Regarding Curtis's information in respect to his suspicions that attempts are being made to drug his mistress and himself, also to the dispute between him and the Duke of Manchester regarding a motor car, further enquiries are being made by Detective Inspector Sharp and PS Hatherhill.

Two days after Curtis had visited Scotland Yard for his second interview with George Hatherill, an intriguing letter made its way to the news desk of the *News of the World* offering a most sensational story. It was marked "Strictly Confidential" and signed by JS Blacklock, a Scottish solicitor who gave as a return address the Regency Club in Piccadilly. "[The story] can be used in toto," Blacklock wrote, "but on no account must my name be mentioned."

The general tone and style of the letter would be familiar to generations of newspaper journalists. Tipsters offering up what they believe to be an earth-shattering exclusive can often come across as pompous and verbose. On this occasion, while the letter was clearly penned by Blacklock, he had decided to write the bulk of it in the third person. In addition, any written submission usually leaves so many points unexplained that it is impossible to publish without much more information. On this occasion, Blacklock had unhelpfully named one of the key figures "Mr X". But this wasn't really a problem for the editors, who did not intend to publish and immediately contacted Special Branch.

"About the beginning of October, 1932, a friend of Mr Blacklock's whose name and designation are Captain GA Gamble, DSC, MC, was introduced to a German named Herr Herbert Stahl by a mutual acquaintance," Blacklock wrote. "During a subsequent social meeting between the two, Herr Stahl, who has only recently returned from Mexico, via New York, to London, mentioned to Captain Gamble that, while in the latter city, he had been relieved of some £9,000 in a business deal with a certain English nobleman and his friends."

This was how the letter began. Stahl, it elaborated, said that he had come to England to meet business friends en route to Rotterdam in connection with a shipment of German machinery. Stahl told Captain Gamble that he needed £1,000 to charter a plane so that he could deliver the Bill of Lading to Cyprus, where the cargo was heading. Gamble said he might be able to find the money and, in return, Stahl would pay him a commission. It was at this point that Gamble introduced Stahl to his solicitor, Blacklock. The lawyer, in turn, introduced Stahl to "Mr X", who Blacklock described as "ostensibly a financier, but actually brought in to check off Stahl's statements".

When probed on why he must deliver the Bill of Lading by hand, Stahl eventually admitted that the cargo of "machinery" was actually arms and ammunition which had come from a German factory, in contravention of the Treaty of Versailles, and that after passing through Cyprus the illicit cargo would transit to the Near East. As the transaction was an offence against Britain, he could not disclose the type of cargo to Lloyds or to any bank, and consequently had to try and raise the cash he needed "in manner sub rosa".

Stahl insisted that he had previously handled Bills of Lading for similar cargoes for Cyprus, Mexico and elsewhere and that the value of this particular shipment was approximately $460,000, which was to be handed to him at Cyprus in the shape of an Ottoman Bank draft. "At this stage," the letter said, "Captain Gamble and Mr Blacklock decided that the facts disclosed a conspiracy and that they were distinctly valuable as a newspaper story. They proceeded to obtain as much additional information from Stahl as possible, leaving him under the impression that they were still trying to find his £1,000."

According to this account of Stahl's activities, the German phoned Blacklock on October 23 and told him that he had secured a plane from a friend, so no longer needed the money. The privately chartered 1929 Fokker was due to leave from Croydon in the coming days. Blacklock was officially out of the picture, but wanting to gain further evidence to sell to the papers, he asked Captain Gamble and Mr X to keep in touch with Stahl. Mr X, acting on Blacklock's instructions, got in touch with Stahl at his rooms in Ebury Street and a meeting took place between them at the Ritz Hotel on October 26. Hatherill would have noted that this was the date of the last known meeting between Curtis and Stahl.

At this meeting, Mr X told Stahl that he wanted in on the deal and might be able to put up the £1,000. Stahl said he still wanted the money and would be prepared to put all his cards on the table — Bill of Lading included — if the cash could be produced.

"After some difficulty, Mr X obtained the name of the ship and the owners thereof," Blacklock wrote. "The ship is the Dutch steamer 'Zaandam 11'. The owners are Wilhelm Hoos and Craaten of Rotterdam. The ship is to sail for Vigo on or about Wednesday November 9. Stahl's brother will travel to Vigo onboard as super-cargo and the vessel will remain in Port of Vigo with him on board until Stahl cables his super-cargo that he has exchanged the Bill of Lading in Cyprus and has returned to London, duly cashed it and settled with his Principals. Then his brother steps ashore and the consignee's super-cargo come aboard. The vessel thereafter sails for Cyprus. Stahl draws a commission of £4,000."

Blacklock said a further meeting was scheduled for the coming Saturday and a newspaper reporter could accompany Mr X, posing as a friend, and bring along £1,000 in cash so that he could view the Bill of Lading.

"Captain Gamble is prepared, if necessary, to go to Cyprus in the interests of the newspaper purchasing the story, but he would like some assurance of newspaper protection if Stahl falls foul of the British or other authorities during this operation," the letter added. "The arms, which are Mausers and Maxims, with two thousand rounds of ammunition to each rifle, (there are forty thousand of the latter), flow from Krupps and other German armament firms, to Holland, thence via Stahl's principals, to various parts of the world."

According to Blacklock, the ultimate head of the "Greek syndicate" running the show was a man named Contemichalos. He also offered up some further biographical details about

271

Stahl, who had claimed that his father was a retired secretary to the German Embassy in London until 1914 and Food Controller in Germany during part of the war:

> Stahl is about thirty and an excellent linguist. He has acted for the syndicate engaged in running German guns (it is believed with the cognizance of the German and Dutch governments) for some years. While in Mexico two or three years ago on a similar venture, he purchased privately certain lands with silver and other concessions from the estate of the late Lord Balfour (AJ). At that time, he was engaged to the daughter of General Caisu, minister of finance and interior in Mexico. That individual arranged for Stahl a cheap purchase of the lands in question (Paplants, Vera Cruz).

Not only that, but the letter said Stahl had also been in negotiations with the Anglo-South America Bank in London. Stahl claimed the bank had floated a private company to acquire his Mexican lands from him. Stahl was to receive £2,500 in cash, forty-nine per cent of the ordinary shares and a seat on the board, with a salary of £600 per annum. Blacklock suggested this story in itself might be another line of enquiry for the newspaper. The letter concluded:

> Captain Gamble and Mr Blacklock and Mr X are all convinced that this is not an attempt at a 'confidence trick' and that the newspaper concerned in purchasing the story will be in a position to put before the Government and the Public, facts pointing to a direct contravention by Germany, of the Treaty of Versailles, a matter of intense interest to this country, France and the League of Nations. All this apart from the fact that the arms and ammunition go to, among

other countries, British Protectorates. There is the added news value of a German agent operating in London in connection therewith.

Despite the wordy nature of the letter, the missing information and the complex and frankly unlikely nature of the allegations, George Hatherill was intrigued. What on earth was going on?

Blacklock was the second person to accuse Herbert Stahl of wrongdoing. While he seemed convinced the scheme was not a confidence trick, it had all the hallmarks of an 'advance fraud' scam, where cash is paid up front for supposed admin purposes in order to secure a payment at the end of the business. That being said, even if Stahl was trying to defraud Blacklock and his friends, that was not to say he was not also genuinely involved in arms and drugs trafficking. It was something that both MI5 and MI6 would be interested in.

Special Branch immediately made discreet inquiries at Croydon Airport and with the Lloyd's Registry of Shipping, to find out both about the Fokker and the Zaandam 11. While there was indeed a Fokker ready to leave for Europe, it had been chartered by the Marconi Wireless Co to take an official to Brussels, and it was not leaving on the date Stahl had suggested.

The Head of Special Branch, Superintendent Albert Canning, sent a note to the Assistant Chief Constable, alerting him to the plot but adding, "This appears to be a confidence trick or an effort to make up a sensational story for sale to a newspaper. If, however, this story is genuine, it seems strange that Captain Gamble and Mr Blacklock, solicitor, have not communicated with the authorities direct."

# DOPE KINGS OF LONDON

Having been passed the letter from Blacklock and been present during Hatherill's interviews with Curtis, Chief Inspector Reid had his own views on what had been going on, concluding that Curtis must be Mr X:

> It is difficult for one to believe the allegations made by Curtis, who does not appeal to me as trustworthy. He is a pseudo-financier and it is more than likely that he is the person referred to as 'Mr X' in the attached papers, whom, it will be seen, is stated to be 'ostensibly a financier'. Curtis, in his statement, also refers to the Duke of Manchester, and it is highly probable that he is identical with the person referred to in the attached papers as a 'certain English nobleman'. A copy of the report dealing with Curtis's visits to this office and of statements made by him and his mistress have been handed to Mr Perrins, Home Office, but evidently he does not place much value on the disclosures made by Curtis and his mistress.

If it was the case that Curtis was Mr X, then why had he made no mention of Blacklock or Captain Gamble in his statements? Was this all part of a single con-job by Stahl, or had he targeted multiple potential victims? And who were Blacklock and Gamble? Special Branch certainly had no file on them and there is no evidence that officers ever bothered to speak to them, or indeed sought to re-interview Curtis about the new information that had come to light.

It sounded, to the authorities, that while there was something there, neither Curtis, Blacklock, Gamble or any of the other characters could be trusted to give a truthful version of events — and even if they did, how could the detectives be certain? Some indication of the attitude taken by the authorities can be found in a memo written by Perrins to the Deputy Assistant Commissioner RM Howe. "I feel certain that Curtis is suffering from persecution mania," he wrote, "and as far as the drug side of his story is concerned, it would be a waste of time to pursue the investigations further, although I can imagine that you may think it desirable to investigate the doings of the German, Stahl, who appears likely to be an undesirable alien."

It might be thought strange that Perrins so easily discounted the drug trafficking claims, which had the ring of truth about them. After all, the dope was supposedly being shipped along what was then the principal route into Europe – by train from Istanbul. The alleged syndicate was headed by Greeks, who were, as the Eliopoulos case had shown, among some of the most sophisticated traffickers. The group also apparently used a code and airplanes which traffickers, including the Eliopoulos brothers and Paul Stone, had been known to do. Stahl must certainly have had some knowledge of drug trafficking to have got so much correct.

While the Home Office was not particularly interested in the drugs claims, both Special Branch and MI5 made considerable efforts to investigate Stahl's other activities. Their findings would indeed go on to suggest his genuine involvement in arms trafficking, in turn raising the prospect that a drugs probe might not have been "a waste of time" after all.

Investigations found that Herbert Stahl had arrived in Plymouth on September 1, 1932, after sailing from New York.

His landing card showed that he was German, aged twenty-five, and a journalist. His stated reason for the trip was "to visit friends". Stahl was landed with no conditions, other than "not to take up employment". Stahl gave as a reference a Captain Webster of the Black Watch, although police could find no trace of such a man. Stahl also gave his address as the Savoy Hotel, but he never actually stayed there, lodging instead in Ebury Street (some documents suggest the property itself was owned by a man named Christofrides).

It wasn't until December 12 that Stahl went to register himself at Bow Street Aliens Office, a requirement at the time. The following day, Inspector Frederick Copley called at the Ebury Street address to speak to Stahl, but he was told by a neighbour that Stahl had left for Birmingham on business and would be back in a week. Ten days later, the officer went back, but was told that a woman who described herself as the secretary for the Duke of Manchester had called to say Stahl had left for Egypt and paid his bills. Further enquiries found Stahl had in fact flown from Croydon to Rotterdam on December 13.

By December 28, George Hatherill had been able to gather some basic details about three of the other characters mentioned by Curtis in his statements. Georges Serafides was born in June 1882 in Athens and had arrived in England in August 1931, stating he was to sell his interests in a British glass manufacturer, with help from a HA Huntley, another financial agent. Serafides left the UK the same month and had apparently not returned. Meanwhile, Demosthenes Soulidi — the fun-loving Greek based in Paris — was a partner in a

# A DANGEROUS INTERNATIONAL ADVENTURER

London-based shipping firm called McAllum Soulidi & Co, which was "suspect during the Great War".

"It would appear that Stahl is a dangerous international adventurer," Hatherill wrote, "and if there is any truth in the information received regarding him, his activities in this country during his three month visit would stamp him as an undesirable alien. It is noticeable that as soon as he was aware police wished to see him, he left the country. Serafides and Soulidi also have an unsavoury reputation, the former being suspected by the French Police of drug trafficking and fraud."

The trail on Stahl initially went cold, but things heated up again on Valentine's Day, 1933. A glamorous young woman named Delila Rogers-Hatherton turned up at Bow Street Aliens Office claiming a German named Herbert Stahl was refusing to repay £17 she had lent him in December. Rogers-Hatherton, an actress, said she had almost forgotten all about it — until she saw Stahl arm-in-arm with a woman on the Strand two nights previously.

Delila described meeting Stahl in the lounge of the Savoy Hotel in December. She had found him charming and the pair met on several further occasions, when he repeatedly spoke of his "friend" the Duke of Manchester. Stahl also showed her papers suggesting he was owed £2,000 by a Greek named Christofrides. But Stahl never seemed to have any money and repeatedly borrowed small sums from her. When she tried to get the money back by visiting Ebury Street on December 13, she was told Stahl had gone to Egypt.

After she bumped into him on the Strand, Stahl said he would meet her later with the money in the Waldorf Hotel, but he never showed up. Instead, she saw him later that night in the Savoy, with a young woman, and she and a male friend followed them into a cinema. Inspector Copley, who took the statement, wrote, "She thought that the young woman whom she saw him with was being victimised in the same way, as she paid for the admission to the pictures." Copley sent his report on to Special Branch.

Meanwhile, MI5 and MI6 had made some progress on the arms trafficking front. Spies had intercepted a letter apparently sent from Stahl to the German-Jewish arms dealer Benny Spiro on February 13.[25] Like Sir Basil Zaharoff, Spiro was a veteran operator. He had established his arms manufacturing firm in 1864 and was best known for helping to supply the UVF in Ireland in 1914.

Stahl had written to Spiro in Berlin, inquiring about a particular catalogue item for "aircraft defence," meaning machine guns to be mounted on aircraft. Stahl also apologised for being "so busy" in the United States that he had not sent him any messages for two months. It implied a long-term relationship. Two days after Stahl sent the letter, Captain Booth from MI5 sent a note to the General Post Office, asking for a list of letters sent to Stahl at both the Ritz and 131 Ebury Street. The agency also found that his latest visit to Britain had been extraordinarily short — he had landed in Newhaven on February 11, saying he was here to visit his fiancé, a Miss Walker, for four weeks. He had given his address as Ebury Street but then left for Dieppe on February 14.

Another MI6 note headed "secret" and written in late February 1933, said that information received via a "trustworthy source" showed Stahl had chartered a freight ship in Rotterdam to carry two thousand five hundred tons of machinery to Haifa, Palestine. Stahl had said that he was financed by a group in New York.

"Stahl was in a very great hurry to ship," the informant claimed. "Actually, the goods left Rotterdam about a week ago. He would not consider anything but a ship to himself. He insisted on inspecting the ship and seeing the captain, and placing two 'machinery experts' on board. The 'machinery' is split into a number of cases all weighing exactly the same, two tons. When asked the weight of the cases, Stahl gave it promptly without reference. It might be interesting to verify the contents."

It sounded as though the plan Stahl had concocted with Christofrides and tried to recruit Captain Gamble for was going ahead — and Gamble's decision to steer well clear was probably a wise one. The ship never made it to Haifa and the goods were clearly offloaded somewhere else.

A further note to Colonel Menzies on March 3 made reference to sources named only as Kastell and Don, the latter the codename of the source who had provided the information about the ship. "Don had mentioned vaguely that the yacht from which the goods were dumped had belonged to the Duke of Westminster, but he was uncertain. Kastell may have said the Duke of Manchester, who would be much more in the picture." It fitted because Manchester had previously been involved in buying and selling ships.

Later, in another memo to Menzies from the Home Office, the author suggested taking no further action. "Regarding this report," it said, "please note that the Germans have undertaken to the Home Office here to keep a watch on the activities of Stahl should he return to Berlin. It would clearly, therefore, be undesirable for your people to do anything in this matter."

The Germans, now under the Chancellorship of Adolf Hitler, had provided some extra intelligence on Stahl, in a letter dated March 9, 1933. They said Stahl had been an agent for a firm of necktie manufacturers but had fallen out with his bosses, leaving in debt.

"A few weeks ago he was recommended by a certain Captain Simons of London to a large Berlin arms dealer to whom he represented himself as being connected with a number of highly-placed personages, saying that he was in a position to introduce customers," the memo said, presumably referencing Benny Spiro. "He gave himself out as a journalist writing for American papers," it continued. "He also alleged that he had been defrauded of a matter of $40,000 by the Duke of Manchester, but this is regarded as a flight of his own imagination, as it is hardly conceivable that he could ever have possessed such a large sum. Up to the present he is not known to have either purchased or offered arms for sale, neither is there any evidence that he is engaged in the illicit drug traffic."[26]

In an example of the bureaucracy that plagues even the intelligence services, the investigation was about to come full circle, with MI5 now writing to Special Branch advising Superintendent Albert Canning about this suspicious foreigner:

A German named Herbert STAHL...has been giving a good deal of trouble by dealing, or pretending to deal in arms. He also deals, or pretends to deal, in drugs. When he comes here he gives as his address 131 Ebury Street, which is apparently the home of a Cypriot named CRISTOFRIDES. We were thinking of making very quiet enquiry [of] the individuals frequenting this address, but I hear from Mr Perrins at the Home Office that there has been some enquiry into it before. I wonder if you could very kindly let us have any reports that there may be. I should think that it was the Drug Section of the CID who went into the matter.

The expanding Stahl file was now passed back to Detective Inspector Copley, who in turn sent it on to MI5, whose officers until now had only read a summary of the case. Copley agreed that he would carry out the new enquiries into Stahl.

The officer called twice at the Ebury Street address, but Stahl was absent on both occasions. Eventually, the two men met by appointment on April 22, 1933. Finally, the mysterious German necktie agent-turned-journalist-turned-drug-dealer-turned-gun-runner would give his side of the story. Unsurprisingly, Stahl expressed absolute shock at the allegations.

Stahl insisted that he was in the country to visit his fiancée, a Miss Walker, for four weeks, and that he was working for the Co-Op Newspaper Syndicate based in the United States. The officer reprimanded him for not taking a photo to be registered with the police when he had last visited the Aliens Office on December 12, 1932, and Stahl apologised, saying he did not think it was urgent, but that he would do it within the three-month period.

Stahl then explained that he was in London to speak to the publishers Wishart about his planned book on Hitler, later to be published under the title *Hitler as Frankenstein*. As proof,

Stahl produced a £35 cheque from the firm. In total, he said, he earned around £350 from writing per year.

The officer asked about his dealings with the Duke of Manchester, Henry James Bellingham and others, and Stahl explained some of the history. As the officer wrote, "He appeared to be very bitter towards them, and alleged he had been financially ruined, and almost morally ruined by them."

Stahl was interviewed by Copley and Chief Inspector Reid at Scotland Yard two days later, giving a much fuller statement about his relationship with the Duke of Manchester. Stahl disclosed that he had two passports, one issued in Berlin and one at Krefeld. The latter he had kept because, despite being full up with visas, some had yet to expire. They included visas for France, Argentina, Chile and Colombia. He said his father was a retired shipping merchant and had no ties with the German government, contrary to the story spun by Curtis.

Stahl said he first met Manchester in New York in February 1932, having just returned from a tour of South American countries on behalf of some German textile firms. He returned to New York to take up journalism contracts offered by *Textile Zeitung* and *Die Muehle*, as well as to give six broadcast lectures about the economic situation in South America.

"While I was in New York, a man who called himself Count Renarto Zepponi Biondini made my acquaintance at a party and said that he knew my father," he said. "A few days later he telephoned me and asked me if I was willing to take on a job. I asked what the job was, and he said that he wanted to introduce me to someone who wanted a man with a good knowledge of languages and the position in South America and the Far East."

# A DANGEROUS INTERNATIONAL ADVENTURER

The Count introduced Stahl to the Duke of Manchester and his friend, Henry James Bellingham. The potential schemes included the sale of Arizona bonds in England, the purchase of silver in Mexico for the Bank of England — "he produced a lot of documents which seemed to support that" — and Manchester also said he was interested in selling arms to the Far East, asking if he knew of any Germans who could supply.

"I was very impressed at the time, because the Duke of Manchester was living in good style with his wife, giving parties, and all that kind of thing," Stahl said. In fact, he was so impressed that he lent him $1,200 on post-dated cheques, $400 personally and $800 which he gave to Biondini. Montagu repaid him with post-dated cheques, but when it later transpired that he had issued dishonoured cheques to a hoard of lenders totalling $60,000, Stahl realised his were among them. On top of all that, he had given Bellingham around $200 in several installments.

"Suddenly the Duke of Manchester and Bellingham left New York for England," Stahl said. "I did not know they were going. All the schemes that they mentioned to me did not materialise, and I was left in a very bad financial state as my six-year savings were gone."

Stahl remained in New York working as a reporter but his sense of injustice festered. He saved up enough money to travel and arrived in Plymouth on September 1, 1932, aiming to track down Manchester. "It took me about five weeks to find out where he was, and found him living in a nicely furnished house in Park Street," he said. This is where the intrigue about drug trafficking and arms dealing began.

Stahl pestered Manchester for his money and eventually got some of it back in £5 and £10 installments, with the promise of more to come. The first meeting with Curtis came in October, at the duke's Park Street address.

"Bellingham was there at the time and told me that he and Curtis were at school together and they were very great friends," Stahl explained. "There was some conversation about the Duke of Manchester's schemes, and I was told that if he owed me money I should get it in time. There were several meetings at Park Street in connection with these schemes, and I met several other men at various times, but I do not remember their names."

Stahl said that as a result of the discussions he made a few enquiries in Berlin about purchasing arms, after being introduced by Manchester to a representative of the government of Romania or Yugoslavia who might wish to buy them, "but I certainly did not make much effort". Stahl said he boasted at the party of knowing people in Beirut, Syria, Jerusalem and Cyprus, one of them a "well-respected trader", CM Christofrides, of Nicosia, who Stahl revealed was an agent for Messrs A Wander Ltd of London (the makers of Ovaltine).

By December, Stahl said he had realised that the plans were going nowhere, so he began to ask again for his money. He was sent a post-dated cheque for £200 and invited to a meeting in Paris, where, Manchester promised, he would see that the schemes would soon pay off. Stahl first visited his brother in Rotterdam, to discuss their sick mother, then he went on to Paris by train, where he met Manchester at the Scribe Hotel. The duke was with a group of about ten people, some Greeks,

Stahl claimed. The pair had dinner, where Manchester refused to discuss business matters, until the next day.

But when Stahl phoned the hotel the following morning he was told that Manchester had left. Stahl said he had not seen the duke since. The cheque was dishonored and he had not received any further payment. Of the $1,200 he had lent to the aristocrat, he had only received about £25 back.

"I emphatically deny that I have ever discussed the question of dealing in dope or drugs of any kind," Stahl insisted. "Curtis asked me about arms and ammunition, and I certainly discussed that, telling him I could arrange about them with German firms. Of course, it is quite possible that 'dope' has been mentioned at the Duke of Manchester's place, because they spoke about so many subjects. He had a bar at the place, and we all used to have quite a lot of drink. I do not remember talking about the subject, and if I did, I certainly would not have had anything to do with that traffic, because I know nothing about it and do not want to."

Stahl said he had had no further involvement with arms dealing, but had previously been given an introduction to a Berlin firm, via Captain Simons, of Regent Street. Also, he said, while waiting for Manchester in the Savoy Hotel, he had met the actress Delila Rogers-Hatherton, or Harrison, he wasn't sure, who asked about Manchester and said she had recently returned from Hollywood.

According to Stahl's version of events, they began a short-lived relationship and he even visited her mother's home in Elstree, but he claimed to have walked out after hearing that her father "was in some sort of trouble in South Africa". Later, the actress had accosted him on the Strand when he was with Miss Walker. Stahl claimed her male friend had told him, "I am an inspector from Scotland Yard, you owe this lady money. Pay it, or we tell your lady friend [about the previous relationship]."

Stahl said he had marched to the policeman on the next corner and reported the matter, with the officer advising her to take civil action, but Stahl said he had not heard from her since. "I again deny having dealt with or attempted to deal in drugs of any description," Stahl reiterated.

Was it a convincing performance? There was clearly much Stahl had left out about his contact with Benny Spiro and the alleged one-on-one meetings with Curtis. He had also not addressed the situation with Blacklock and Captain Gamble, or what had happened in Rotterdam with the missing freight ship. Then again, it is not clear from the police report exactly what he was asked, nor for that matter how much Copley or Reid knew about the enquiries undertaken overseas by MI6 and Special Branch. Copley, perhaps naturally, probed Stahl over the dispute with the actress because it was probably the most likely way to bring a prosecution. But again, there was no clear proof of any wrongdoing. In any case, very little of the substance of Curtis's allegation was explored.

"Stahl strongly denies having ever dealt in Dangerous Drugs, or having discussed the matter, but he admits that he has made some enquiries in Berlin for the purchase of arms and ammunition on behalf of the Duke of Manchester," Copley wrote in his report:

> His passports show that he has travelled extensively in South America, and he produced documents shewing that his tour was at the instance of a group of German textile traders, for

the purpose of investigating German trade possibilities there. He is only twenty five years of age, but undoubtedly clever. He speaks English fluently, and also speaks German, French, Italian, and Spanish....As a result of my two lengthy interviews with Stahl, I am inclined to believe his statement that he has been victimised by the Duke of Manchester and his associates, who probably wanted to use Stahl's knowledge of languages, and his trade associations in South America and the Far East to further their nefarious schemes. If Stahl's statements are correct he has not trafficked in drugs, and has only discussed trading in arms and ammunition without anything having materialised. He appeared to be genuinely anxious to convince us of his bona fides, and I think that his story is correct. On the other hand, I realise that a man of his undoubted intelligence and ability is not easily led, and his association with the Duke of Manchester and others creates a deal of suspicion which is not easily disposed of.

Chief Inspector Reid added his own thoughts to the report. "Stahl's version of his association with the Duke of Manchester and others is entirely different to that given by Curtis," he wrote. "Of the two men, Curtis and Stahl, I would say that the latter appears to be more reliable than the former."

Herbert Stahl appeared to be off the hook as far as Special Branch and MI5 were concerned, and there is no record of further enquiries being made regarding the Duke of Manchester and his associates by the domestic agencies. But MI6 was still keeping tabs on his group.

On May 18, 1933, an internal memo discussed a new development in the case. "The Duke of Manchester, who has been giving out that he is the 'head of the secret service for the Orient' is now trying to raise money by alleged deals in arms for China," it said. "The group consists of Colonel Bellingham in London, and Jim Aspinall, son of Joe Aspinall, who is at present in prison in Paris. The activities in question seem to centre around the address of 79 Harley Street." This was later shown to be a mistake and the address was amended by hand to 72 Curzon Street, where a German named Herbert Stahl was now living. "Informant's belief is that the present business is all to raise some money to pay for the defalcations of Joe Aspinall, whom they think the French authorities will release if the amounts of his frauds are made good."

The intelligence was relayed to Special Branch, with a report sent to Colonel Menzies on May 23, 1933 stating that Stahl had previously been seen by a CID inspector and claimed to have broken off the relationship with Manchester. The author noted that "his statement that as far as he was concerned the whole thing had come to an end do not quite tally with letters which we have seen showing Stahl to have been quite recently active in arms deals, actual or alleged. We propose to pursue the matter further and will let you know what comes of it".

· In June 1933, a Home Office Warrant was granted to intercept all post going to Stahl's Curzon Street address, with the reason given that "this German, in association with several accomplices, has been engaged in arms deals which may be fraudulent".[27]

New information about Stahl continued to come to light. In a Sept 4, 1933, note to MI5's Captain Cecil Lidell, older brother of Guy Lidell, a CJ Norton from the Foreign Office made mention of a publication called *The Week* and its apparent access to sensitive information. The source, it had been suggested, was a "young German refugee" named Herbert Stahl. The source believed there was a "clearing house of official secrets" giving information to *The Week* and *The Express*. A reply came directly from Colonel Sir Vernon Kell, known as K, MI5's then-director general. "We have Stahl under close observation and as soon as we get anything substantial shall recommend to the Home Office that he should be asked to leave," he wrote.[28]

On October 4, 1933, Stahl was finally interviewed by George Hatherill at a new address of 22 Monmouth Road, Westbourne Square, where he once again gave an innocent explanation for his presence in the country. Stahl said he was now the foreign correspondent for the *Amsterdam Freie Press*. He also discussed his book, *Hitler as Frankenstein*, which had overcome its initial difficulties. The book had been published by Wishart and Co, with fifteen thousand copies printed. Stahl had received £65 as payment, plus £20 for excerpts published in America. He was on a £2-a-week retainer from the Dutch paper and also picked up a few more pounds a week by writing articles for other publications in England, Germany and America. He had recently hit upon a new income stream, translating German plays into English.

Stahl told Hatherill that he "dared not go back to Germany, as his book violently attacks Hitler and his regime and his newspaper articles have been of a similar nature". Hatherill, having himself developed a strong dislike of the Nazis, could well understand.[29]

Stahl said that he aimed to become a US citizen and had asked to be allowed to enter the country in the next quota. As soon as he received a reply, Hatherill wrote, he intended to leave. The officer asked about the Duke of Manchester and Stahl replied that he had not seen him nor any of his associates since the end of the previous year, having realised it was "hopeless" to try and recover his money.

Stahl sailed back to New York on February 2, 1934, without reporting his departure to the Bow Street Aliens Office. It was the final time that Stahl would be interviewed by British police, who had made no headway in establishing whether any of the original allegations made by Curtis and Blacklock were true. But with a new war in Europe on the horizon, the focus shifted from Stahl's criminal leanings to his political ideas.

Shortly after the publication of his book, Stahl's Home Office file was updated to say his work "seems to be a clever mixture of truth and sensationalism. There seems to be no reason for requiring this man to leave UK but MI5 should see the papers and be asked for their observations."

In a summary of the case written in May 1934, an MI5 officer noted how Stahl had been in touch with Benny Spiro — "the notorious arms dealer" — and Gerald Hamilton, of the League Against Imperialism, a journalist and fixer who, like Sir Basil Zaharoff, had earned the nickname "the wickedest man in Europe".

The report made several conclusions:

> A/ Stahl has without doubt been actively connected with arms traffic in the past, possibly with the Far East, or more certainly with the establishment of an agency in Cyprus — no proof of the ultimate destination of the arms being available.

# A DANGEROUS INTERNATIONAL ADVENTURER

B/ Whether or not his active interest was prompted by a genuine interest in the scheme, or by a desire to regain his loans to the Duke of Manchester by means to active co-operation, cannot definitely be decided.

C/ Since his stated break with the Duke of Manchester's activities, there has been no concrete reason to suppose that he has taken any further interest in this line, though it is possible his press interests in America may well be serving as a cloak for activities in other directions.

MI6 also managed to establish a link between Stahl and the short-lived New Britain movement, a socialist group advocating for world federalism and the abolition of world banks which also published a variety of newsletters. Spooks obtained dozens of letters sent to Stahl at a C/O Thomas Cook address in West Tenth Street, New York, signed by a woman called Ruth who wrote with an obvious passion for Stahl. All her letters appeared on headed "New Britain" notepaper, although her surname remains a mystery. It is more than likely that "Ruth" might also have been Stahl's "Miss Walker".

One typical example begins, "Darling. Thank you for your letter," and goes on:

I have been so mean lately in not writing to you. I am sorry. It is more that I have had every single minute filled up that I haven't wanted to, also perhaps I have felt the last two or three weeks you haven't wanted to receive my letters. I felt no response and no warmth from your side, but your letter this morning reassures me, so I am writing just a word to get my sins off my chest. My dear, the things that have been happening here would amaze you. You must come back and see for yourself. We are a mass of manifestos and Big Things which I feel are a million miles away from me, but I don't think any evil will get into my system from it. I am not, as you know, sufficiently 'politically conscious' for it to have much effect. I am happy or unhappy according to the individual I have around me, and whether they are anarchists or Christian Scientists doesn't make any difference. I expect you want to scream at my hopelessness, but you see you have ambition and I have none, absolutely none, and that's where the difference lies. It's awful I know, but what can I do? I simply haven't any ambition except to have a son.[30]

But love letters were not the only notes dropping onto Stahl's doormat. A letter dated June 7, 1934, was received from the General Products Trading Co Ltd in London. It read, "I have a new inquiry for 7.92mm calibre New Maxims with ammunition and spare parts for delivery F.o.b. Antwerp, also for 1,000,000 pairs of military boots. The inquiry seems to be serious, and my correspondent says definitely that their buyer has ample funds in Brussels to pay for the goods. As you are in the US perhaps you could put me into direct touch with your friends, in which case I would cover you for a reasonable share on any business. PS, I hear that a firm 'Prenglau' in Hamburg may do the business. Are these your friends?"

The letter was signed "L Edmunds," one of the firm's directors. A note to Menzies suggested that the firm 'Prenglau' in Hamburg should be Prenzlau, "in which case the goods will be for the Far East". It showed that Stahl had remained in the arms business even after moving permanently to New York.

On December 12, 1934, police received a tip about a Johannes Steel, or John Steel, described as "German; aged about 28; medium build; fair hair; clean shaven; speaks almost perfect English." It went on to say: "Press agent; recently escaped from the Nazis; has recently been in London and is now doing his work in New York. While he was in London frequently flew from London to France; stayed at a good hotel; appears to have plenty of money. Did no genuine work on London affair while he was here, as far as can be ascertained; rather a mysterious individual. While in London he used the offices of Agency Havas; talks of receiving enormous fees for his work. Are you interested?"

Officers did further digging on his press duties while in Britain, and found that on one occasion Stahl "tried to put over the story of a revolution in Berlin, claiming he had seen it 'coming over the tape'" of a newspaper office he had visited. Police thought it was probably the *Evening Standard*, where he was well-known and was always "nosing around," according to an informant. "He impressed informant as being keener to pick up information than to do business. He had nothing to sell and did not wish to buy."[31]

Herbert Stahl, now widely known as Johannes Steel, arrived back in Britain on October 13, 1935, and stayed in London for about ten days before leaving for Paris. He came back to London on November 10, landing at Croydon Airport for what was supposed to be a two-week holiday. Charlotte Mary Young, a barrister, had met Stahl about eighteen months previously, after he arrived at her chambers with a letter of introduction from a mutual friend in New York. When Stahl arrived back on October 13, he called on Charlotte with his new wife Rhys Caparn, to ask if she knew anyone with rooms for a couple of weeks. In turn, she passed him onto another barrister, F Howard Collier, who let him a furnished flat at Essex Court, Middle Temple, until November 20. Charlotte was later visited by Special Branch. All she could tell the officers was that Stahl was now the foreign editor of the *New York Post*, a well-known journalist in New York and that he had been forced to leave Germany because of his anti-Hitler writings. She also said he was well-known at the Havana News Agency in Carmelite Street and visited acquaintances there during his stay. As far as she knew, he was visiting Europe for a holiday.

The latest report on Stahl, signed by Insp A Davis, concluded that while the German had entered the country under his correct name, he had sailed from Southampton to New York on the SS Champlain with his wife on November 20 under the names Johannes and Rhys Steel. Davis concluded, "Stahl has been under the notice of Metropolitan Police as a suspected drug trafficker and is regarded as a dangerous international adventurer. The aliens officer at Bow Street is desirous of interviewing this man when he is next seen, regarding his failure to notify his departure from this country on 2nd February 1934."

Stahl's name was later published in the Nazi's newspaper, the *Volkischer Beobachter*, on March 4, 1936, in a list of twenty-five people condemned by the Third Reich as traitors. He was described as a "Jewish editor. Connected with anti-German propaganda in American newspapers." During the conflict, Stahl flew into Britain at least twice, in 1941 and 1945, in transit to cover the war in Europe.

# A DANGEROUS INTERNATIONAL ADVENTURER

After the war, Steel was openly socialist, if not Communist, in his politics — and almost certainly a Soviet agent. As an extract from his FBI file said in 1952:

> Steel has gained certain recognition as a radio commentator and foreign news analyst. He has been described as pro-Communist and pro-Soviet. He has made several trips to Europe and has reportedly interviewed Molotov and Tito. He has also been reported in contact with leading Communists in France, Czechoslovakia and Poland. Steel has appeared as a speaker before Communist-front groups and in 1946 received the support of the Communist Party in his unsuccessful campaign as a congressional candidate. He associates with numerous Communists and Communist sympathizers.[32]

In May 1949, Sir Percy Sillitoe, the new director-general of MI5, wrote to E. Thistlewaite at the British Embassy in Washington, to say: "You may care to know that a copy of *'Report on World Affairs'* [a newsletter] edited by Johannes Steel has been sent to Tang Man Chiu, who is well known to you." Another note addressed to a PO Box in Singapore, asked for no more copies of the report to be sent as "we now receive them from our representative in Washington" but the spooks would "be grateful for the names and addresses of the recipients of this report, if such information becomes available".

Despite the reams of information gathered on Herbert Johannes Stahl, the man remains a mystery. Was he a spy? Almost certainly. An arms trafficker? Probably. A dope dealer?

Again, he probably was but no concrete evidence was gathered to support the claim.

The question remains as to why, given the evidence that Stahl was involved in illegal arms deals, the Home Office considered it a "waste of time" to investigate the drugs allegations. It's reasonable to assume that if the German was not bluffing about the guns and ammunition, then neither was he trying to pull a fast one where the dope was concerned.

There seems to be no satisfactory explanation for this, other than that MD Perrins simply did not believe the admittedly extraordinary claims made by the two informants. Perrins had collected a wealth of information on European drug traffickers, and neither Stahl nor any of the characters associated with him had cropped up before. As a result, the intelligence agencies decided to focus only on arms trafficking.

Of course, we only know the aspects of the case that were committed to paper (and then released into the public domain). We don't know what was said in person, between the men who discussed the case in their smoky offices and gentleman's clubs, or what any still-secret papers might reveal (MI6 has never declassified its archives, except for snippets contained in the available files of other organisations).

Perhaps there was a cover-up of sorts. An arms trafficking operation could, if necessary, be disrupted discreetly by the security services without dragging the affair into court. A police-led drugs sting could have exposed the activities of Manchester, Bellingham and others, placing them before the Press at the Old Bailey. It is notable that Sir Basil Zaharoff was never mentioned in the reports again, not necessarily because he was or was not involved in the plot, but because it illustrates that officers could always be selective about what they chose to put on the record.

In any case, while Stahl never faced charges, the Duke of Manchester did, at least, face some form of justice. In early April 1935, he suffered a serious heart attack, after being arrested on suspicion of fraud. Then, in May, 1935, William Angus Drogo Montagu, the ninth Duke of Manchester, was found guilty at the Old Bailey of obtaining £650 from pawnbrokers by false pretenses.

Aged fifty eight, the duke was sentenced to nine months in jail and remanded into Brixton Prison, although less than one month later the conviction was quashed, on the grounds that the summing up had been insufficient to direct the jury on a matter of law. Manchester was freed. He died in February 1947, aged sixty-nine, at Seaford in Suffolk.[33]

After his death, one newspaper published a quote that seemed to sum up his life. "People think that being a duke must be great fun," the nobleman had once observed. "Well it has its advantages and disadvantages. But I am not quite sure if I am glad I was born to be a duke. I have been so broke at one time and another that I have only just been able to pay for my valet's meals."

It remains a distinct possibility that the Duke of Manchester had, at one point, turned to drug trafficking as a solution. We will never know, because it was never fully investigated.

---

[23] Zaharoff was the son a Greek merchant, who assumed the surname while living in Russia. He was later suspected of being an arsonist employed by unscrupulous Istanbul firefighters, who were

paid for rescuing goods from burnt out properties. His name cropped up in the British courts during a dispute with a Greek merchant about exports from Turkey (he was ordered to hand over £100 to the claimant) and he later inveigled his way into becoming an agent for the Swedish arms manufacturer Thorsten Nordenfelt. During this time, he was suspected of a number of underhand and corrupt practices, including sabotaging rivals, notably at a machine gun display for potential buyers where Nordenfelt and his rival, Hiram Maxim, were vying for business. Through his schemes, Maxim ended up signing his firm over to Nordenfelt and being forced out of the company, although Zaharoff continued to work with Maxim for years, notably on one of the very first prototype aircraft.

Zaharoff also managed to sell Nordenfelt's first submarine to a number of rival nations. The first model went to the Greeks. Zaharoff then persuaded the Turks that the Greek submarine would be a threat to them. The Turks subsequently bought two. On the same basis, the Russians bought another two. None ever saw action because the steam-driven propulsion system turned out to be inadequate for going underwater and several of the vessels sunk. In the early 1880s, Zaharoff emerged in Galway, Ireland, where he recruited young women to work in American factories, and he solidified his US connection in 1885 by marrying a Philadelphia heiress, Jennie Billings. Zaharoff had married under the pseudonym Prince Zacharias Basileus Zacharoff and was later exposed as a bigamist who had also married an English girl a few years previously. He fled to Rotterdam, pursued by private detectives.

Then came the career move that would define his life. Zaharoff joined the British engineering and munitions firm Vickers in 1897, a job he would hold for the next thirty years. How much he earned in backhanders, graft and genuine commission is unknown, but the years running up to and including World war One were certainly profitable. Following the end of the conflict, *The Times* suggested he had personally spent at least £50 million funding the Allies. He had also, on behalf of the British government, been instrumental in convincing Greece to join the effort, even helping to depose King Constantine, a brother-in-law of the Kaiser. As a result, he was given an honorary knighthood.

During the 1920s, he married a member of the Spanish aristocracy, inheriting her enormous wealth when she died from an infection eighteen months later. He also bought Monaco's biggest bank, funded Greece's conflict with Turkey and set up the forerunner of British Petroleum, predicting that oil would become a hugely valuable substance in the coming years.

[24] There is a discrepancy with one of the dates mentioned in Hatherill's report. He wrote that after one meeting between Curtis and Stahl at the Savoy Hotel on October 20, a PC Hislop followed Stahl back to his Ebury Street lodgings. Not only did Curtis make no mention of a meeting with Stahl at the Savoy, or elsewhere on October 20, but the date fell before the allegations had even been brought to Scotland Yard. There are a number of explanations for this, including that Hatherill wrote the wrong date or hotel, or Curtis lied, or the police had already been given information about Stahl from another source.

[25] Stahl had written "1932" at the foot of the letter, thought possibly to be an effort at misdirection. The letter had been forwarded from "HMM" to Colonel Stewart Menzies of MI6, soon to become the intelligence agency's chief, or C. The author, probably the station chief in the German capital, added that Stahl "has been in touch with the Chinese delegation here regarding the purchase of war material and is to meet them later on in Berlin". HMM also pointed out the discrepancy with the date on the letter, suggesting

Stahl may have intentionally tried to hide the fact he had recently been in the country, knowing Special Branch was on his trail.

[26] Interestingly, in the same week that the Germans compiled their report, the Duke of Manchester was facing his own difficulties. He was found to have passed a dishonoured cheque for £350, with a judge in the Chancery Division ordering him to pay back £50 a month on March 6.

[27] The intercept turned up at least one interesting tidbit — the preparations for Stahl's book were not going well. A letter from his publisher's office in John Street, Adelphi, contained scathing criticisms from the proofreader, who pointed out several mistakes. "I notice a bad slip at the beginning of chapter five with regard to the Edict of Nantes," he wrote. "This edict expelled Hugenots from France, and not Jews from Spain. There are a considerable number of misprints of names, and my son, who looked at the proofs last night, tells me that in one place it is stated that Schleeicher succeeded Bruening as Chancellor, instead of Papen. On galley 5 you use the German name Pommern for Pomerania. It is obvious that the proofs need very careful revision."

[28] Stahl managed to annoy the editors of *The Week* by claiming to work for them — they put around a note to journalists in London stating that Herbert Stahl, otherwise known as Johannes Steel, had supplied some items in the past but is not "an active and constant correspondent".

[29] One passage from the book sums up Stahl's feelings about Hitler: "So the leaders of a movement which claims to have a monopoly of all that is desirable in ethics, morals, and high thinking, are in the overwhelming majority nothing but a collection of

madmen, drug fiends, crooks, and murderers, whom a trick of fate has made the masters of more than sixty million people." A review by the critic Cecil Roberts in The Sphere, August 1933, praised the tome as a "virulent attack" although he belied his own prejudices, adding, "This book is the work of a Socialist Jew. It is prefaced by Professor Harold Laski, himself a Socialist Jew. Even so, there are charges in this book which cannot be ignored by any self-respecting nation."

[30] Other notes revealed the internal strife at New Britain, with "friction" between the new and old editors, one of which was Charles Purdom, pioneer of Britain's garden cities. Ruth also mentioned a "terrific" rise in sales.

"I have been made editor of the Indian Forum of the New Albion, which you know is a thankless task," Ruth wrote in one note. Another, undated letter, relayed a personal disaster. Ruth said she "would have sent you my foolish work had it not been for a most dreadful accident which has made me almost frantic with despair". All of Ruth's manuscripts were in a brown, attaché case left in her hallway, which was inadvertently picked up by departing friends and subsequently left in Victoria Station. "I have not been able to trace it back and it has made me terribly upset," she wrote.

Other letters, some typed, some handwritten, were addressed "Dear Herbert". One dated April 6, 1934, apologized for losing a letter before she had managed to post it. "I am hoping to atone for this misfortune by sending you my copy of 'The New Albion'. And I kiss the furrows on your wrath-ridden brow and hope for the best. I'm sorry to hear your autb. Has made you balder than ever. Alas, you will soon be an unmistakable Duitscher."

She told how the editor "CBP" — meaning Purdom — and Andrew Campbell, had walked out along with sixteen others. "It is a mess," she said. "Conferences and meetings have been thick and they have all been at each other's throats." The letter also mentions that Purdom pulled her aside to ask if she was in love with an organiser, Samuel Lohan. "I would like to write much more about it all, but don't like to put it in writing." And on the subject of Stahl's article being re-printed from the Nation in LU she said: "I have the vague notion that LU reprints the best articles from all periodicals. I am glad to hear you are working so hard. It gives me such a great thrill of pride in you and a big warmth in my heart." In another, she mentioned some "Mexican business" and trouble he was having apparently arranging a trip, but that he should focus on the News Service, a newsletter he planned to send to subscribers. "That, as far as my understanding goes, is the most important of your activities." She signed off, "Goodbye. Keep well, and get some relaxation when you can, and when that relaxation is accompanied by soft music, please think of me."

[31] In May 1934, an article by Stahl, known as Johannes Steel, on the subject of German colonising policy appearing in American "Nation" was reproduced in an issue of *Pravda*, proving that he did in fact carry out some genuine work.

[32] This biography continues in a similar vein in an MI6 extract from November 1953, "Johannes Steel was on a list of sponsors and sympathizers of the National Committee to Win the Peace which was a Communist Front organisation set up in the USA in 1946 under the direction of Abbott Simon. Steel was at one time the foreign editor of a magazine named 'Redders Scope'. He visited Paris in August 1948 in company with Otto Katz, Andre Simone and Louis Dolivet as reported in our {…} of 25.8.48 to MI5. Dolivet was said to intend using Steel to cover the Paris session of UN in Paris during the Autumn."

# A DANGEROUS INTERNATIONAL ADVENTURER

MI6 also found out details about Steel from its Washington agent, who reported back on information given to the FBI in 1951, about his dealings with the KGB spy Vladimir Pravdin: "Roman Joseph Moczulski recently informed the FBI that in 1944 in order to discover what type of information the Russians were attempting to obtain in this country, he obtained an introduction to [Vladimir] Pravdin through Johannes Steel, whom he had previously known in newspaper circles. Moczulski says that after receiving this introduction he met Pravdin in New York City on three occasions. On one of these occasions Pravdin asked Moczulski to provide a list of names of pro-Russian Poles in this country. According to Moczulski, Pravdin throughout the conversation gave him the impression that he was interested in obtaining political information and caused Moczulski to believe that Pravdin might be a 'secret agent' in this country. It might also be mentioned that in December 1945 a former employee of Johannes Steel, when interviewed by the FBI, said that she believes Steel was one of the highest paid espionage agents in the United States. She stated that there were a number of people who frequented Steel's office 'with whom he conversed in a foreign language in a whisper'. Named as one of these frequent visitors a Mr Pravdin of the Tass Agency."

The atomic spy Klaus Fuchs was also questioned in 1950 about speaking to Steel, bur denied ever doing so or meeting him.

[33] There had been numerous other court cases. In February 1933, the duke was jailed for forty two days and fined £10 for contempt for refusing to appear in Margate County Court after being sued by North Foreland Hotel Ltd, the owners of Kingsgate Castle. The sentence was never imposed. In October 1933, Manchester was sued by a man named Albert Atkinson, an engineer, in the High Court after the duke bounced a £1,000 cheque put down as a deposit on a £20,000 fee to by the American rights to a ventilator he had

invented. Bellingham was the middleman, but the duke denied Bellingham was his agent and insisted he told Atkinson the cheque would be cancelled if he later found no interest on the American market. Manchester won the case.

# 17. THE WRONG POWDER

**W**orld War Two devastated the international drug trafficking industry just as it did most other sectors of commerce. But shortly before transatlantic travel became one of the most perilous activities on earth, Britain did have one more notable success story in the war on drugs — a straightforward but impressive case that ran in parallel with the mystery of the Stahl-Manchester affair. And the villains at the heart of the plot formed one of the most amateurish drug smuggling gangs on record.

John 'Jack' Albert Deeble was as far from an international drugs baron as it was possible to be. Born in December 1911,

Deeble lived with his parents in Streathfields Street, Poplar, until joining Canadian Pacific's SS Beaverdale as a cook's boy. He later signed up with one of the firm's other five 'Beaver' steamships, the SS Beaverburn, having lost his first job thanks to a bout of tonsillitis.

The ships sailed regularly between Antwerp, London, Liverpool and Montreal. It was a classic drug smuggler's route, one exploited many times by villains such as Max Faber and Laurent Deleglise. Before long, Deeble was presented with his opportunity to enter the dope game.

According to his later version of events, Deeble had been sitting in the Café Balfour in St Lawrence Boulevard, Montreal, in May 1932, with a crewmate, Robert 'Bob' Adams, when they were approached by a man named Jack, who Deeble described as "a Jew, aged about 45, five foot four inches, dark complexion, dark hair, but almost bald".

The three men made small talk, which quickly moved on to the subject of drugs and the question of whether the sailors would be willing to ship narcotics in from Europe. The next day, Deeble and Adams met Jack again. This time, the shady Canadian took the pair for a ride in his car and asked whether they could get cocaine from Antwerp. In return, he said, he would pay $1,500 per kilo. Such a sizable sum must have been hard to turn down. Deeble and Adams talked it over on the voyage back to Antwerp. Deeble also spoke to a mutual friend, a twenty-five-year-old greaser named Walter Cain, and invited him into the proposed conspiracy.

While in Antwerp, about two weeks after the meeting with Jack, the trio tracked down a former colleague named Charles Chovau, who had once been a steward on the Beaverburn and was now running a boot repair business in the city. Chovau said he would introduce the sailors to a man who could supply their cocaine.

The meeting itself did not take place until the next time the men were in Antwerp, in June 1932. This time, Chovau introduced the friends to man named only as Pole, supposedly a Frenchman aged about forty-five or fifty.

The meeting took place in a cafe and Pole said he could supply the drug at £135 a kilo. Notwithstanding the exchange rate, the potential profits were huge. Deeble handed over £25, Cain £35 and Adams £75. In return, Pole handed over ten bottles of white powder, which they divided amongst themselves. Adams, as second steward, was responsible for the store room and so the trio hid the drugs there in a wooden box.

Back in Montreal, the sailors went in search of Jack. But when they found him, Jack said he could now pay just £85 for the cocaine, claiming "there is so much stuff in the place I can't pay you the price I promised". After hoping for a huge profit, the lads were now staring at a massive loss.

Jack nevertheless took two of the bottles as a sample and promised to meet them the next day. However, at the subsequent meeting he claimed the bottles had smashed in the car and he now offered just thirty-five Canadian dollars for the powder he had been able to retrieve. Adams accepted the cash, but as he had already spent it on refreshments in the café over the previous two days, it wasn't much of a deal. The trio kept the remaining eight bottles.

By August 1932, the Beaverburn was in the Surrey Docks in London and Deeble, Adams and Cain resolved to sell the drugs in the city. Another crew member, pantry boy Frank Cole, nineteen, was enlisted for this task. Cole had originally been asked to join the scheme, but had to decline because he was broke.

The next day, all four went out into the city armed with the cocaine. Cain had three bottles, Cole one, Adams three and Deeble one. They met up in Southwark Park and handed them all to Cain who said he knew a place where they could be stored. This turned out to be at the East London home of another former crewmate, Allen Mattocks. A few days later, Cole, Cain and Deeble had to leave again on the Beaverburn for Antwerp, but Adams was re-assigned to the Beaverford. This would prove to be the group's undoing, because now they were forced to communicate by letter. The cocaine would stay with Mattocks as they continued to search for a buyer.

A crew member on the Beaverburn had previously given confidential information about both people smuggling and drug trafficking to Captain Henry George Kendall. The information then found its way to MD Perrins at the Home Office.[34] The same informant now chose to grass up Adams and Deeble.

Famous for having spotted the presence of Dr Crippen onboard the SS Montrose in 1910, Captain Kendall was keen to help with the case. As MD Perrins wrote, "Captain Kendall has been an enthusiastic amateur detective ever since he brought about the arrest of Crippin and Miss Le Neve by the first use of wireless in the history of crime."

Kendall passed on his information to the Home Office and Perrins was able to arrange the interception of the conspirator's mail, the contents of which cast doubt on certain aspects of Deeble's story.

For example, Deeble later claimed that the group, minus Adams, had met Chovau in Antwerp again and agreed to take a pound of opium to Montreal which Adams had paid for on a separate visit. This was later sold to Jack in Montreal and the $43 from that deal was later left in an envelope in Antwerp for Adams to collect. But Deeble's letters proved he was a far more proactive member of the plot. One of his letters from Montreal to Adams in London said:

> Well Bob, the situation stands like this, your £18 and the money we took over to Charles [Chovau] is still in Antwerp and will buy about 12 lbs of Gum which will be ready in Charles's house waiting for you to pick up and remember do not let this go under 45 USA a pound. So when you reach London do not take any money from Allan [Mattocks], leave it there for me to pick up as Charlie is getting a kilo of H cheap to sell here at 1.250 dollars so that I can make a big scoop being on the last voyage. Charles is also of the opinion to leave all the cash in London for us as he thinks 12 lbs of Gum will be quite a lot for one to manage so think it over whether you will buy more Gum or let Wally and I take the H.

Another letter, from Jack to Chovau, said, "Up to present no luck with sale of C in London." Shifting the gear was obviously more difficult than the group had anticipated. The gang even resorted to trying to offload the drugs to a disgraced doctor who had been convicted under the Dangerous Drugs Act after supplying cocaine to a woman who later died. One letter, found in Walter Cain's possession, directed him to Dr Harold Gamlen:

> Be very careful. This man is very hot. Has been in trouble, he was living with a woman and she took an overdose and cashed in, but it's worth trying. I know for sure that he has a very big market as he is a doctor and used to get it through prescriptions, but since this he can't get a sniff. He will pay any price so long as it the right stuff. Well go to this place and if you work right and box clever it ought not to be so hard.

MD Perrins planned to bring the entire gang down in one go, or as close as possible. He arranged to have the Beaverburn searched in London, and the Beaverford, carrying Adams, raided in Montreal at roughly the same time. He hoped the Belgian police would swoop on Chovau within days.

It was a masterclass in law enforcement cooperation in a time without the benefits of instant communication. Throughout the investigation, Perrins kept Colonel Charles Sharman informed. On the British side, Perrins brought the police and Customs officials together for the raid. They searched the Beaverburn as it sat in the Surrey Docks on October 27, 1932. No cocaine was found, but Perrins had the letters and Deeble cracked under the pressure of the police interview, giving a full confession and stating, "I would like to add that I should never have entered into this business at all, but for the fact that I wanted some extra money to pay for treatment for my mother who is ill with arthritis."

Deeble admitted that the remainder of the bottles were at the home of Allen Mattocks in Greenwich. Police arrested the ex-seaman and brought him, the bottles, and a small amount of opium found in his home, to Scotland Yard.

Deeble, Cain and Cole, apparently without lawyers, were kept in the dark as MD Perrins and the police weighed up what to do about a slight snag in the investigation — the powder found in the eight bottles was not cocaine, but novocaine, a substance not covered by the Dangerous Drugs Act.

The men were unexpectedly released while the Director of Public Prosecutions (DPP) considered whether there was enough evidence to charge them with conspiracy. Eventually, Deeble, Cole and Cain were charged with *attempting* to import cocaine. Mattocks was not charged over the opium, because the police wanted him to give evidence against the others.

It was another case in which a canny lawyer might well have found grounds for appeal. The DPP decided to try the case summarily, that is, in the lower magistrates' court, rather than on indictment in the crown court, meaning the case could be handled quickly. As a result, the men pleaded guilty. However, they were not informed that the powder was novocaine until after they had done so and the prosecutor began explaining the case to the magistrate for sentencing. If they had known that they had not, in fact, been dealing in cocaine, then they might well have pleaded differently. Perrins took some delight in this.

"It is evident that Pole and Chovau deluded the gang into thinking it was cocaine and obtained £135 from them!" He wrote gleefully. "It was not until the case came into court and after they had pleaded guilty that the smugglers realised that the stuff was not cocaine!"

Even though the way the prosecution was handled verged on the unethical, if not illegal, the outcome of the case did have the desired effect. As Perrins pointed out, "I think the result of this case has been very satisfactory. We have evidently nipped in the bud what was likely to become a regular line of traffic, and I understand that the prosecutions have created an impression with the crews of the Canadian Pacific boats." Deeble was jailed for five months, Cain for six and Cole for four months.

As planned, the Beaverford was searched as it sat in Montreal docks three days after the London raid. After being told that his friends had been arrested in London, Bob Adams admitted to smuggling opium and handed over a large square tin containing six bricks wrapped in chocolate packaging, stating they had been given to him in Antwerp by Chovau. Adams said he has originally been approached by Deeble. Adams was tried in Montreal, found guilty and sentenced to eight months in prison, with a $200 fine.

It transpired that Jack was a low-level hood named Jack Melnic, who was later arrested alongside his brother during a drug deal. Melnic had been duped into selling some of the fake cocaine to an undercover agent.

However, as Colonel Sharman wrote, this would make no difference in a Canadian court. "There would not appear to be much difficulty in being able to convict them both," he gloated. "The fact that the sale involved novocaine is immaterial, in view of the Section 4 (f) of our Act which refers not only to the selling, giving away or distributing of any drug, but of any substance represented or held out to be a drug." The case was the first involving novocaine in Montreal "for a long time," he added.

# THE WRONG POWDER

The Antwerp police failed to bring a charge against Chovau, although he was arrested and questioned. He told police in Antwerp that he knew Deeble and Adams after sailing with them in the past. But he claimed it was they who had introduced him to a man named "Charlie" for whom he wrote letters (but signed in his own name) to Deeble and Adams. He also claimed to have collected parcels for 'Charlie' and handed them to Adams. Chovau had no idea of Charlie's real name, all he knew was that he was an Italian who spoke French and English. It was not a very convincing story. But the Belgian police found no drugs at his house and therefore they felt they had insufficient evidence to bring charges.

Incidentally, in one letter sent to Perrins concerning Chovau from the police in Rotterdam, the chief commissioner said the matter was now in the hands of the Belgian police and added, "Many thanks for your letter...respecting STAHL. Any further information received here regarding this individual will be forwarded on in due course." It would suggest that Perrins was influenced into focusing on the Deeble, Cole and Cain case, rather than the Stahl investigation, because there was more available evidence.

Even though it probably went down as one of the most successful operations in Perrins' career, he did get a severe ticking off from the Met's assistant commissioner Sir Norman Kendal. Of all the various authorities involved in the arrests, both Perrins and the officer in charge of the operation, Det Insp Robert Donaldson of the CID, had forgotten to tell the Port of London Authority what they were up to. It was only when Donaldson was already on the Beaverburn that he thought to ask the authority to put guards in place around the docks to stop the suspects slipping away.

This prompted a furious missive from its chief, WHA Webster, to Sir Norman. "I confess to feeling a little surprised at having received no official communication of any sort respecting this matter from Scotland Yard," Webster wrote. "The attempted bringing of drugs into London via the Port Authority's Docks would appear, prima facie, to concern the Chief of the Port Authority's Police. Perhaps you will look into it. I shall be grateful if you will."

Sir Norman was forced into offering a humiliating apology. "There has been a very bad botch," he wrote to Webster, "but I hope you will take it from me that the rudeness to you and your force was quite unintentional. I am really savage over this as, on the whole, our forces have got on so well with each other in the past."

To add insult to injury, in Sir Norman's eyes, MD Perrins *had* been present at the raid when the authority had not. "This kind of thing will not do," he wrote in an internal memo:

It is no part of the business of the Home Office officials to give directions to our officers as to how they should carry out their duties or to ask for assistance in any type of case from particular named officers. It is our business to select the right officer for the right case, nor should Home Office or any other officials be taken with our officers when they are going out on duty. I have spoken to Mr Maxwell at the Home Office and, I hope, put the matter right with them. On our side we must see that this kind of thing does not happen again. I do not like having to send groveling letters of apology.

# THE WRONG POWDER

Webster accepted Kendal's apology in full, replying, "I guessed it was a 'blog' on someone's part and felt sure that you would take steps to prevent it happening again. Believe me it would take more than this to disturb the good relations that, I am happy to say, exist at present between our respective forces."

There is no record of Perrins' reaction, but the row did not put him off investigating smuggling among sailors. Almost one year later, in September 1933, a ship's engineer on the SS Beaverhill named Jack James Johns, aged twenty-five, appeared at Tower Bridge police court charged with possession of seven ounces of opium.

Johns, who earned around £14 a month, had been under suspicion for about a year. At the direction of Perrins, his ship was carefully searched in Montreal, but nothing was found. Johns was then watched when he arrived back in Britain. Insp Edward Griffey, who had been involved in the previous case and was now overseeing the Met's drug work after Walter Burmby's retirement, roped in Sgt George Hatherill for the task.

Griffey and Hatherill followed Johns as he left the ship in Surrey Docks and headed to his favourite spot for lunch, a restaurant attached to the New Cross Cinema. Griffey was late due to a traffic breakdown in the Rotherhithe Tunnel, proving that in London nothing much really changes. Johns was spotted after lunch walking down Redriff Road in Bermondsey fiddling with the bottom of his waistcoat and Griffey decided to stop him. "What have you got here?" he demanded.

"A man named Joe gave it to me at New Cross and asked me to take it aboard. I think they are cigarettes," Johns replied unconvincingly, as he handed over the package of drugs. Griffey made it clear that he didn't believe this unlikely tale and took him to Rotherhithe police station, where he would be charged. "This will be a terrible thing for me," Johns answered back.

In his cabin was found a slip of paper bearing the name of one Karl Jorgensen, also known as Charlie Emile Jorgenson, a Dane living in Belgium. Jorgensen was later convicted of drug trafficking and sentenced to six months in a Belgian prison, although he had the conviction overturned on appeal.

As he sentenced Johns to three months in prison, the magistrate WH Oulten told him, "You and a lot more like you, chiefly officers on ships, cargo and otherwise, have an exceptional opportunity for dealing in the drugs and it is little excuse for you that you were receiving small pay. It is a very serious offence against society and against the laws of any country."

There is a tragic footnote to the case. On November 5, 1942, the SS Beaverford was part of Convoy HX 84 sailing from Halifax, Nova Scotia, to Britain with a cargo of metals, meats, cheeses and ammunition. The convoy was attacked by the German heavy cruiser the Admiral Scheer.

Although it put up a brave fight, making possible the escape of all but five of the other ships in the thirty-eight-strong convoy, the Beaverford and all seventy-seven lives onboard were lost when a torpedo ripped through the hull and ignited the ammunition. Neither Deeble, Adams, Cain, Cole nor Johns were on the ship as they had been dismissed and blacklisted by the company. Ironically, their convictions for drug trafficking might have saved their lives.

# THE WRONG POWDER

[34] Perrins duly passed the information to Colonel Charles Sharman, head of Canada's narcotics bureau. Perrins wrote in June 1933 about being told of illegal immigration taking place via the ship. "Some time ago," he wrote, "a member of the crew of the SS Beaverburn privately told a chief officer that illegal immigration was being carried on the ship both into this country and Canada. It appears that two or three months ago, there were two men said to be Russian brought across in one of the vessels of the Canadian Pacific from Hamburg." The men involved in the plot were three firemen called Connor, Wicken, and Harper, and a donkeyman named Lynch. All were also smuggling drugs.

# 18. PROBLEM SOLVED?

By the time war broke out in Europe in 1939, Britain's first war on drugs had been relatively successful. Homegrown suppliers of illicit narcotics — dodgy chemists, doctors and large companies such as T Whiffen — had been largely brought under control. When the drug dealers had turned to European factories for their supplies, pressure from the likes of Sir Malcolm Delevingne and Russell Pasha had seen more stringent measures put into place to stop controlled substances from entering the black market. Russell Pasha had achieved even greater success by having the gangsters' factories in Turkey shut down.

By the end of World War Two, the drugs issue in Britain was thought to be more or less solved. It had rarely, if ever, occurred to lawmakers that organised criminals would, in the decades to come, simply switch to growing their own crops of opium, cocaine and cannabis to feed a resurgence in demand.

# PROBLEM SOLVED

This was despite the fact that, according to Harry Anslinger, by 1941 Mexico was producing five tons of opium a year, mostly for consumption in America. There was also the fact that, thanks to the factory closures in Turkey and the lack of availability of raw materials in Europe, the rest of the world's opium and heroin supplies were now being produced in China.

To be fair to the experts, they had accepted that drug trafficking would remain a problem for some time to come. After the factory closures in Turkey, Bulgaria briefly became the worldwide centre of heroin production, churning out about three tons a year. Illegal operations were also set up in Tirana, Albania, with the help of Italian crime groups. This shift to Eastern Europe presented an opportunity to create, in May 1937, what would have been the world's first criminal intelligence-sharing system, under the auspices of the International Criminal Police Commission, founded in 1923 in Vienna and later to be known as Interpol.

Each nation, it was proposed, would send all details of foreign-born drugs convicts, including photographs and fingerprints, to the ICPC to be circulated among members. This way, aliases could be uncovered and each member could be made aware of those suspects likely to evade justice by crossing into other territories to carry out their crimes.

Czechoslovakia was an early adopter of the system and papers stored in Britain's National Archives include the names of a dozen or so individuals wanted there for smuggling drugs into North America (photographs were originally attached to the files but sadly have not survived). They include Moritz Bliuds-Bliudzas, a Latvian, and his brother Serjeg. Another name on the list was a Polish woman named Lia Katz, said to be Serjeg's lover. A man named Wilhelm Sherler, a Pole, who was also known by his Spanish name Guillermo Chelrer y Mariano and a Frenchwoman named Suzanne Feldman were also on the list. These were the new generation of traffickers, similar in background to so many who had come before. An accompanying report gave instructions to monitor them carefully and gather evidence rather than to arrest:

> In the event of the journey over the frontier (in and out) of one of these persons being ascertained, it would be desirable that the Customs should unostentatiously make a thorough search of their belongings, and ascertain the amount of money brought into or taken out of the country, but these persons are not to be detained, unless there is some other ground for doing so, but in no case are they allowed to suppose that their identities are known and that they are being [put] under supervision.

An example of how this monitoring system would work in practice came in the case of the "known international smuggler" Harry Kessler (born on March 12, 1873). Kessler was a naturalised American subject born in Odessa, Ukraine, thought to be a supplier to New York's Newman brothers, among others. He was spotted in March 1937 in Stolpce, Poland, and followed to Breclav in Czechoslovakia, where agents notified the Austrian authorities that from there he planned to head to Vienna.

Kessler was then shadowed by agents as he made his way first to Paris and then to Le Havre, where he left for America. It was assumed, rather than proved, that Kessler had been on a smuggling run, but the case illustrates the level of international cooperation taking place to combat and gather intelligence on traffickers.

As the tracking system was being planned, Nikola Manoloff, the chief of police in Bulgaria, wrote an impassioned and prescient screed about the inherent difficulties in pursuing a war on drugs, which he said was "very difficult and connected with great dangers".

He noted how the illicit trade was comprised of "chain transactions" where it was often impossible to pinpoint the true buyers and sellers, where middlemen frequently muddied the waters further by using their own sub-agents, and where those agents were often entirely ignorant of the other links in the chain. "If to these difficulties in the way of the investigation of the police is added the fact that the traffickers in narcotic drugs dispose of very large funds, it becomes evident that the war which the police authorities wage against the illicit trade, is fought only with great difficulties on the part of the police," he wrote.

To make arrests, he added, the Bulgarian police preferred to use civilian undercover agents to act as buyers. But there were inherent dangers in this, not least that the buyer usually had to provide large sums of cash upfront and was liable to be robbed or even killed. The other possibility was that the agent could disappear with the money.

In 1938 however, the ICPC fell under the control of the Nazis and the intelligence-sharing system was never properly implemented. The body re-emerged as the International Criminal Police Organization in 1946, but by then the global drugs trade had been wrecked by the war. Even if demand had been maintained throughout the conflict, the disruption to international freedom of movement was simply too great for the traffickers to overcome.

Even after the war, the drugs issue would not re-emerge as a major societal problem — at least in the West — for years. And when it did, Europe was no longer the most important source for drug traffickers. Instead, places such as Mexico, Colombia, Peru, Bolivia, Iran, Afghanistan and Turkey — and much later Eastern Europe — would see the growth of narco-trafficking organisations with unprecedented criminal power.

None of this is to say that the type of drug use and trafficking seen during the interwar period simply ended when World War Two broke out. There was fierce and often bloody competition between Chinese and Japanese traffickers throughout the war. In February 1939 it was reported that Japanese farmers had stopped growing soya beans in favour of the far more profitable poppies. The resulting drugs were then sold to Chinese dealers. There were said to be drug dens in cities such as Harbin and Mukden where addicts could put their bare arms through a hole in a door clutching twenty cents and be greeted with a shot to the arm.

Many of the old school traffickers simply adapted. For example, the Peruvian diplomat Carlos Bacula continued to smuggle throughout Europe until he was arrested and jailed in Austria, and then France, between 1939 and 1943. Louis Lyon was also active until at least 1938. His long-term business partner, Paul Carbone, alias Venture, continued his life of crime throughout most of the war. He joined the Nazi-aligned Carlingue organization in Marseille, also known as the Bonny-

# PROBLEM SOLVED

Lafont gang, which aided the Gestapo. He died in December 1943 in a train sabotage carried out by the Resistance.

In Britain, a few notable drug cases made the papers in the run-up to war, but not many. Smuggling gangs were said to be using speedboats on the Thames to bring in their wares. The dope was dropped off the side in waterproof wrapping and tied to blocks of rock salt. When the salt dissolved, the packages floated to the surface and were collected by other gang members. The police by that point had their own speedboats to patrol the river, but it was unclear whether anybody had yet been caught and prosecuted.

Russell Pasha's CNIB provided inspiration for the authorities in Jerusalem, who opened a similar drugs bureau in 1939. Smugglers there were still using the old camel hair trick, as well as some newer ploys. One case came to light in July 1939, after a car travelling into the territory from Syria suffered a flat tyre. The driver swiftly changed it but police noticed a subsequent trail of white dust, leading to the car being stopped. The driver had been forced to use a spare tyre which had its inner tubes stuffed with opium. Another operation saw an undercover agent asked by a smuggler if he knew a girl who could dress up as a nun. A second agent was provided and she was eventually asked to travel to Egypt with a party of men dressed as Franciscan friars. Drugs were bound around her legs and under the robes of the 'friars'. They were arrested when the 'nun' made a signal on landing.

The inconclusive end to the story of Brilliant Chang did provide another criminal with an opportunity for making money. In 1939 — nearly fifteen years after Chang had last set foot in Britain — his name was once again on the front pages.

This time, a fraudster named Hartley George Grail found himself in court on ten charges of obtaining money by false pretenses. Grail had claimed he was secretly importing drugs on behalf of Brilliant Chang and had induced several desperate men to join him in this conspiracy, with the promise of fantastic returns. Cash upfront, he insisted, was needed to pay bribes and other expenses. In 1932, one of the men had allowed Grail to deposit a large trunk at his bank, telling him mysteriously that it contained "something to be shared with somebody else". The man withdrew it in June 1934 and found it contained nothing but sticks of firewood covered with a blanket. Grail was sentenced to five years in prison for fraud in 1939, although the conviction was quashed in 1944.

The history of Britain's first war on drugs is a mixture of fact, myth and mystery. To a certain extent, it was a law enforcement success story, because notorious figures like Brilliant Chang and Eddie Manning were taken off the streets, not to be replaced for decades. Not only that, but the corrupt system whereby legitimate manufacturers were able to sell products to smugglers and gangsters was fully abolished. This took money-making opportunities out of the hands of amateurs like Richard Cadbury Butler and Jack Deeble and ensured such men could never evolve into major criminals.

But we will never know how the campaign would have played out if the world had not been torn apart by war. The next logical steps — entirely criminal factory operations set up closer to the source of the drugs —- were already in motion. With the amateurs and risk-taking businessmen eliminated, it would have left only the professional criminals — ruthless and brutal men such as Paul Carbone and Lucky Luciano — in full control of the drugs underworld.

We can see today how such a scenario has come to pass. Drug lords can become billionaires and inter-gang conflicts leave thousands dead each year. The likes of Walter Burmby, MD Perrins and Sir Malcolm Delevingne would hardly be able to comprehend what is happening today in places like Mexico and, indeed, on the streets of London, where a new generation of young men and women are risking their lives on the front line of both sides in an ever-evolving war on drugs.

# INDEX

Abuisak, Elie, 162, 226-227
Adams, Harry, 96
Adams, Robert, 295-305
Admiral Scheer, 305
Afghanistan, 310
Ahern, Dr Maurice, 91
Albert Hall, 23
Alexandria, 216, 228, 230
Ali, Mohamed, 147-151, 182, 185-186
American Labour Party, 252
Amsterdam, 102, 137, 281
Amsterdam Frie Press, 281
Anslinger, Harry, 63, 231, 307
Antwerp, 45, 61, 103, 133, 137, 173, 178, 206, 235, 286, 295-298, 301-302
Albania, 307
Argentina, 274
Aspinall, Joe, 279
Aspinall, Jim, 279

Ataturk, Mustafa Kemal, 223
Athens, 204, 209, 210, 225, 229, 231-232 268
Atkinson, Albert, 292
Avory, Horace, 200
Bacula, Carlos, 203-205, 213, 233, 310
Balfour, Lord AJ, 263
Banque d'Hochelaga, 63
Barron, Ernest Bosworth, 96-97
Basel, 42
Bayer, 10, 44
Beaverburn, SS, 295-297, 299, 302
Beaverdale, SS, 295
Beaverford, SS, 165, 297, 299, 301, 305
Bechet, Sidney, 183
Belcher, Lionel, 22-25

Belgium, 23, 45, 53, 56, 60, 103, 179, 180

Bellingham, Henry James, 243- 250, 254, 257-259, 274-276, 279, 291-292

Belokas, Kostas, 224

Benjamin, Alfy, 15

Benjamin, Frances, 82-83

Benzina, Joseph, 218

Berlin, 133, 137, 206, 224, 225, 237, 239, 254, 258, 270, 271-272, 274, 276-278, 287

Best, Henry Cadogan, 124-125, 134

Biondini, Renarto, 274

Birmingham, 110, 151, 168-170, 186-190, 192-193, 196, 197, 199, 267

Blacklock, JS, 260-264, 291

Black Man's Café, 144-145

Bloomsbury, 20

Boan, Harry, 86

Boddington, Herbert 'Con', 248-249

Boehringer, CH and CF, (of Hamburg and Mannheim), 42, 43, 141, 142, 206

Bolivia, 41 310

Bolton, Edward, 129-130

Booth, Charles Henry, 46, 58

Bow Street, 34, 35, 267, 268, 283, 288

Boston, 59

Bourneville, 151, 168, 197

Boy, The, 21

Bradley, William, 148-151, 186- 188, 190-192, 194, 197

Braun, 206

Brentano, Lilly, 139

Brett's Dance Hall, 19, 95-99, 112, 118, 128, 172

Brighton, 171

Bright Young Things, 3, 12, 20

Brindisi, 258

British Empire, 4, 23

British Expeditionary Force, 16

British Library, 4

British Medical Journal, 13

British Newspaper Archive, 4

British System, 28

Brixton Prison, 25, 292

Brussels, 60, 84

Bubeck and Dolder, 141-142

Bulgaria, 307, 309

Burgess, Guy, 253

Burgess, Harry, 106-107

Burke, Thomas, 101

Burmby, Walter, 29-30, 40-41, 44-47, 49-57, 61-64, 76-85, 88-90.149-150, 210, 304, 313

Burnby, Mary and James, 129

Burnham-on-Crouch, Essex, 46

Butcher, Violet, 148

Butler, Arnold, 158 (pics) 168-202
Butler, Richard Cadbury, 3, 5, 146-151, 168-202, 242, 312
Buzzi, Malvine, 56
Cadbury, Edith, 167-169, 197
Cadbury, George, 168
Cadbury, Richard Barrow, 168-169
Cadbury, John, 168
Cain, Walter, 295-303
Cairns, JAR, 39
Cairo, 169, 206, 216, 232
Calcutta, 45
Callaghan, Sarah, 12
Canada, 3, 19, 46-47, 56-65, 96, 242, 297
Canadian Pacific, 295
Canning, Albert, 272-273
Canvey Island, Essex, 174
Caparn, Rhys, 252, 288
Capone, Al, 5
Carbone, Paul, 207, 213, 310
Cardiff, 107, 237
Carlingue Organisation, 311
Central Narcotics Intelligence Bureau, 218-221, 228
C Division, 145
Chamberlain, Neville, 205
Chamberlain, Sir Austen, 206
Champlain, SS, 288
Chenk, Lon, 127
Chovau, Charles, 296-302

Chow, Kum Tack (George Kentwell), 108-109
Chicago, 105
Chile, 274
Christofrides, 246, 254, 255, 257-258, 267, 269, 270-271 276
Cohen, Same, 62
Coleman, James, 148-151, 197
Collins, Alfred, 193-195, 199
Collins, Sarah, 89
Cologne, 151, 178, 182
Colombia, 41, 274, 310
Commercial Tavern, 129-130
Cooper. Lady Diana, 91
Co-Op Newspapers, 273
Copley, Fredderick, 267, 269, 272, 274, 278
Covent Garden, 70
Carleton, Billie, 4, 20-27, 86-87, 90, 97, 99, 101, 112, 124
Castle, Irene, 23
Charring Cross Hospital, 72, 73
Charring Cross Road, 15, 19, 20, 67
Chang, Brilliant, 3, 22, 80, 90, 94, 99-145, 157 (pic), 186, 236, 311-312
Charlot, Andre, 21
Chaplin, Charlie, 55, 84
Childs, Sir Wyndham, 46

China, 8, 16, 27, 36, 38, 43, 44, 53, 103-104, 108-111, 119, 133, 137, 139-141, 210-211, 221, 225, 227, 231, 255, 279, 307
Chinese Labour Corps, 35
Chong, Lum, 52, 63, 103, 105-109
Choy Loy, 37, 51-54, 62, 103-105, 139, 153 (pic)
Choy, Violet, 52
Ciro's nightclub, 73, 172
Clements, George, 85, 87
Cleveland, SS, 51
Clubs (Temporary Provisions) Act, 18
Cochrane, Charls B, 21
Coldstream Guards, 29
Colombia, 41
Connor, Samuel Grahame, 29
Convention for Limiting Manufacture, 8
Convention for the Suppression, 8
Cornelis, Leon, 173-184, 190-197
Crawford Street police station, 86
Crippin, Dr, 298
Croydon Airport, 262
Cuba, 180
Cunard Line, 48, 57

Curtis, Stanley William, 238-250, 253-255, 258-267, 291
Cyprus, 246, 254, 258, 261-263, 276, 283
Czechoslovakia, 309
D'aeth, RH, 89
Dangerous Drugs Act 1920, 7, 27-29, 41, 78, 81, 85-86, 136, 192, 299-300
Dangerous Drugs Act 1964, 28
Davis, Harry, 211
Davis, Maud, 81
Davis, Robert, 67-73
Dawes, Kathleen, 240
Dawes, Lillian, 148
D Division, 41
Deeble, John Albert, 295-303
Defence of the Realm Act (DORA), 7, 17-20, 27, 29
Deleglise, Laurent, 39, 40, 55-64, 154 (pic), 295
Delevingne, Sir Malcolm, 16, 30, 44, 57, 59, 106, 141-142, 210, 306, 313
Del Gracio, August, 162, 204-205, 208, 226, 227, 230
D'Erlanger, Baron Harry, 209
Dethier, Catherine, 61
De Veulle, Pauline, 23
De Veulle, Reggie, 21-25, 31, 72

Devineau, G, 207, 212, 228, 233

Diamond, Jack 'Legs', 205, 226

Domenico, Antoniani, 111

Donaldson, Robert, 303-304

Dover, 182

Dutch East Indies, 43

East African Rifles, 186

Edward VIII, 45

Edwards, Rose, 14

Egypt, 44, 106, 169-170, 207, 209, 212-214, 215-222, 231, 268-269, 311

Eliopolous, Elias, 42, 205-215, 221-235

Eliopoulos, George, 209-210, 224, 225, 227-228, 231, 234

Eliopoulos, Nassos, 210-211, 224-225, 228, 231

Ellis, Albert, 32-36, 46, 49, 52, 62-63

Ellis, David, 49-51

Elstree, 277

Empire Theatre, 21

Empress of France, SS, 55, 59

Escobar, Pablo, 1

Evening Standard, 287

Express, Daily, 26, 110, 122, 123, 128, 133, 281

Faber, Max, 39, 46-55, 58, 60, 62-64, 139, 153 (pic), 211, 295

Fabian, Robert, 91-92

Fairbanks, Douglas, 172

Farley, Joseph, 61

Fawzi, Mohammed 'Keep it Dark', 216-217

Federal Bureau of Investigations (FBI), 250, 289-290

Fleet Street, 32

Fleming, Ian, 255

Florentine, Juliette, 60

Flying Squad, 87

Folkestone, Kent, 14, 55, 242-243

Follies Bergeres, 244

Fong, Sim, 127

Foo, Lo Li, 126-127

Ford, Charles, 85

Forty Three Club, 19, 112, 121

Fox, Elizabeth, 66, 69-72, 75

France, 8

Freedom of the Seas, 21

Freud, Sigmund, 12

Friendmann, Thomas, 219-220

Fuchs, Klaus, 253, 290, 292

Fu Manchu, 101-102, 136

Gaikwar, Sitaram Sampatro, 149-150

Gelatis, Dionisious, 224, 230

Gamble, Captain GA, 260-271

Gamlen, Harold, 299

Germany, 8
Gerrard Street, 19
Gestapo, 311
Glasgow, 57, 109
Goddard, George, 30-31
Goodwin, Eric, 75-76, 81, 93
Gourevidis, David, 162, 211, 213227-228, 231-232
Graham-Cutts, Jack, 125
Grail, Hartley George, 312-313
Granna, Joseph, 218
Grapes, The, 72
Gray, Herbert, 130
Great Depression, 28, 242
Great Train Robbery, 239-240
Greece, 220, 225, 228-229, 234, 256-257
Greek Street, 68, 87
Griffey, Edward, 304-305
Grosvenor Hotel, 254
Guzman, Joaquin 'El Chapo', 1
Hall, George, 171
Hall, Mary 'Queenie', 171-177, 179-180, 185, 189, 196
Hamburg, 29, 37, 42, 47, 49, 51, 53-54, 63, 104, 142, 173, 206, 214, 224, 226-227, 231, 232, 286, 297
Hamilton, Gerald, 283
Hammersmith, 96
Haifa, 270-271

Halifax, Nova Scotia, 305
Harley Street, 108
Horne, Richard, 169
Harrods, 13
Harrison Act 1914, 7
Harris, Thomas, 88
Harwich, 51, 127
Hatherill, George, 164 (pic), 239-240, 243-244, 249, 253-254, 257-268, 281-282, 304
Havas Agency, 287
Havelland, SS, 224
Haymarket Theatre, 21
Heckel, Sadie, 99, 113-114
Heckel, Sarah, 99, 113-114
Heinberg, Rose, 98, 111-115, 120
Herald, Daily, 183
Hicks, Mary, 24
Hill, CV, 80, 119
Hing, William, 106-109
Hiss, Alger, 253
Hitchcock, Alfred, 125
Hitler, Adolf, 239, 249, 252, 271, 273, 281, 282, 288, 310
Hennessey, Basil, 118
Hoffman La Roche, 41
Holland, 8
Holmes, Sherlock ,12
Home Office, 16, 30, 44, 46, 52, 53, 54, 88, 109, 103, 118, 139, 188, 192, 199, 201, 209, 228, 259-260, 266-267, 271,

273, 280-281, 283, 291, 297-298, 303
Hong Kong, 49, 52, 103, 109, 139-140
Howard, Charles, 70
Howe, George, 59-62
Howe, RM, 266
Hugo Bursch Company, 178, 188, 198
Humes, Cynthia, 258
Humphrey, Howard, 139-140
Hymie's Club, 258
Iassonides, Alexandre, 77-78, 83
Iassonides, Zenovia, 76-85
Illustrated Police News, 83
Illustrated Sunday Herald, 123
India, 8, 16, 19, 34, 38, 43, 44, 98, 101, 141
Innoko, SS, 234
International Opium Convention 1912, 6-7, 27
International Opium Convention 1925, 7-8, 213
International Criminal Police Commission (Interpol), 307
Iran, 310
Isle of Wight, 91, 254
Istanbul, 160, 212-214, 221-227, 231, 234, 254, 255, 267
Italy, 6, 8, 43, 56, 87, 220
Ivaldi, Carlo, 87
Jamaica, 65, 73, 88-89

Janes, Percy, 102104, 130-132
Japan, 8
Jazz, 5, 19, 21, 73-74, 84, 90,117, 143, 172, 201
Jenkins, Huntly, 25, 72, 80-81
Jersey, 197-198
Jerusalem, 169, 276, 311
John Bull, 106, 200-201
Johns, Jack James, 304-306
Jones, Arthur, 68
Johnson, Willy, 15-16
Jorgenson, Karl, 305
K Division, 52-54
KGB, 253
Kell, Sir Vernon, 17, 281.
Kelson, Jack, 93-94, 138
Kempton, Freda, 19, 76, 90, 95-99, 111-125, 130, 132, 134, 136, 148, 158
Kempton, Jessie, 134-136
Kendall, Captain Henry, 297-298
Kendal, Sir Norman, 53-54, 302-304
Kennedy, Frank, 201
Kessler, Harry, 308-309
Ket, Ah, 138
Kildare, Dan, 73, 183
King Constantine, 257
Kingsley, Horace Dennis, 14-15
Kitchener, Maisie, 74

Kitt, Choy Ah, 37, 52-53, 63, 104

Kitt, Julia, 32-39, 49-50, 52, 62-63, 94, 138, 152 (pic)

Kitten, Jim, 146-148, 150, 183,

Klein, Arthur, 252

Knowles-Harrison, Audrey, 98, 113

Kofler, Wilhelm, 203-205

Kohn, Marek, 4, 25

Krumm, Louis, 176

Krupp, 263

Latin America, 8, 104, 264, 274, 278-279

Laurier, John, 140

League Against Imperialism, 283

League of Nations, 6-8, 16, 30, 206, 212, 218, 219, 220, 222, 264

Lebanon, 220

Lee, Chan Chun, 107-109

Leese, Charles, 243, 254, 258-259

Leicester Square, 19, 20

Lemarchand, Celina, 74

Levey, Ethel, 21

Lewis, Gertrude, 127

Lidell, Cecil, 281

Lidell, Guy, 281

Limehouse, 13, 22, 32, 34, 37-38, 51-52, 93, 100-103, 109, 128-132, 136, 138-139, 143

Lisle Street, 15, 22 92

Lippack, Dora, 91

Liverpool, 35, 37, 48, 103, 106-109, 295

Lloyd, Sir Francis, 16

Loftus, Cissie, 41

London Gazette, 238

Loo, Wun, 35

Lortie, Antoine, 59

Lucas, Morris, 67-68

Luciano, Charles 'Lucky', 3, 5, 58, 204-205, 313

Lyon, Louis, 208, 211-212, 226, 228, 233, 310

Macedonia, 214

Mackay, Nancy, 149

Maharaj of Baroda, 149-150

Mail, Daily, 26

Manchester, 237

Mann, Charles, 148-151, 197

Manning, Eddie, 3, 5, 22, 41, 66-94, 100, 138, 142-143, 156 (pic), 172, 186, 236-237, 312

Manolof, Nikola, 309

Marconi, 265

Margate, Kent, 53, 292

Marlborough Street police court, 30, 72, 77, 80, 96, 124, 136, 184-185

Marsh, John Darlington, 21, 23
Mason, 142-143
Mattocks, Alan, 297
Mauser, 263
Maxim, 256, 263
McAllum & Soulidi, 268
McBean, Robert, 148-151, 197
McBrien, James, 59-60
McLaughlin, JJ, 63
McLean, Donald, 253
Mechelaere, Paul, 207, 212, 226,-228,
Melita, SS, 48
Melnic, Jack, 301-302
Menzies, Stewart, 269, 271, 280, 286,
Meyrick, Kate, 19, 30-31, 95, 112, 128,
Mexico, 246, 260-261, 264, 275, 307, 310, 313
Miles, John Nelson, 124-125
Miller, Frank, 65-75
Misuse of Drugs Act 1971, 28
Miyagawa, Yasukichi, 141-142
MI5, 4, 235, 238, 248, 250, 253, 265, 267, 269-290
MI6, 4, 45, 235, 238, 250, 265, 269-270, 279, 284, 289, 291
Moczulski, Roman, 253, 289, 294

Montagu, Wiliam Angus Drogo (Duke of Manchester), 164 (pic), 240-250, 257-259, 265, 268-269, 271-272, 274-282, 291-293, 294
Montmatre Café, 77
Montclare, SS, 51
Montreal, 46-64, 204, 211, 295-304
Moody's, 96
Moses, Seya (Rudulph Reiter), 163, 224-228, 230-233,
Murhard, Karl, 178-183, 188-196, 199
Murray, Dalton, 19
Nam, Chan, 52
National Archives, 4, 307
New Britain, 284-287
New Court Club, 96, 99, 119-120
Newman Brothers, 208, 308
News of the World, 86, 260
New York, 46, 48, 50-51, 56, 58-62, 71, 101, 104, 203-204, 208, 212, 221, 226, 237, 243, 246, 251-253, 267, 270, 274, 275, 283-284, 287-290,
New York Post, 252, 288
New York Times, 251
Nitch Smith, Reginald, 29
Notting Hill, 22, 99, 112, 120
Nordenfelt, 256

NYPD, 56-57
O'Brien, Molly, 66-67
O'Connor, Edmund, 36
Old Bailey, 25, 70, 72, 91, 104, 131, 141, 292
Opium Wars, 101
Oporto Tavern, 130
Orleans, SS, 71
Ostend, 61
Oswald, HR, 119, 123
Overbury, RL, 198
Owen, Charles, 34-35, 77, 81-82, 94, 149
Oxford, 86
Palace Theatre, 67-68
Palais de Dance, 96
Pall Mall Gazette, 34, 118
Palm Court Club, 128
Parkhurst Prison, 91
Paris, 13, 45, 55, 59, 84, 87, 133, 137, 140, 149, 208, 210, 213, 226, 229, 233, 237, 239-240242-247, 254-255, 258, 276, 280, 287, 289, 309
Paul, Brenda Dean, 20
Payne, Violet, 129-131
Pearce, Peggy, 85
Pearl Harbor, 252
People, The, 137-138, 237
Pennyfields, 13, 38, 54, 130, 142
Perrins, MD, 30, 44, 46, 53-54, 59-63, 139, 201, 228, 233,

260, 266-267, 273, 291, 297-304, 313
Peru, 41, 310
Pharmacy Act, 6, 11, 13-15
Philibert, Alexander, 68-69
Piccadilly, 111, 117, 180, 260
Piraeus, 208, 228, 230
Platt, Deborah, 29
Polakiewitz, Jacob, 210-211, 213-214
Poland, 47, 309
Polish Telegraphic Agency, 253
Pond, Gerald, 130
Porter, William, 142-143
Port of London Authority, 303-304
Port Said, 216
Pravdin, Vladimir, 253, 289
Primrose Hill, 76
Probert, John, 61
Prohibition, 4-5
Purdom, Charles, 285
Quebec, 59-60
Queen Victoria, 168
Rector's Nightclub, 183
Referee, The, 12-13
Regent Street, 99, 110, 119-120, 126-127, 134, 277
Reilly, William, 59
Reuters, 230
Reynolds News, 36
Richardson, Olive, 23

Rich, James, 143-144
Riou, Edgard, 61
Ritz Hotel, 262
Roberts, Cecil, 282
Roberts, May, 32-39, 52, 62-63, 94, 103, 105, 138, 152 (pic)
Roessler, 207
Rogers-Hatherton, Delila, 268-270, 277
Rohmer, Sax, p.101-102
Rolleston, Sir Humphrey (Rolleston Committee), 28
Romania, 233, 276
Roome, HD, 141
Rosen, Louis, 62
Ross, Robert, 44-45
Ross, Walter 'Wally', 44-45, 299
Rothstein, Arnold, 205
Rotterdam, 29, 37, 45, 103-104, 206, 230, 256-257, 261-262, 268, 270, 276, 278, 302
Royal Canadian Mounted Police, 46
Royal Flying Corps, 170
Russell Square, 81, 173, 208
Russell, Thomas Wentworth (Russell Pasha), 159, 212-221, 227-235, 306, 311
Russian, 8
Ryan, Edward, 59
Ryno's Hay Fever, 10-11

San Francisco, 43
Saturnia, SS, 57
Savory & Moore, 9, 13
Savoy Hotel, 23, 255, 258, 267, 269, 277
Schiefer, Wilhelm, 197
Scotland Yard, 24, 41, 77, 86, 136, 188-192, 201, 209, 235, 237, 240, 250, 253, 255, 258, 259, 274, 278, 300
S Division, 81
Seligman, Oscar, 175-177, 190
Serafides, Georges, 244, 258, 268
Seven Dials, 20, 127, 143-144, 146
Shanghai, 6, 109, 129,
Sharman, Colonel Charles, 64, 297-299, 301-302
Shields Daily News, 43
Soho, 15, 30, 38, 77, 80, 82, 87, 90-91, 117, 146
Soulidi, Demosthenes, 243-246, 258, 268
South Africa, 277
Shaftesbury Avenue, 15, 67, 71, 144, 182
Sillitoe, Sir Percy, 290
Sing, Ah, 126
Smith, Mabel, 127
Smith, Reginald, 197
Smith, Victor, 174
Spanish Flu, 19, 24, 51

Special Branch, 45, 51-55, 59, 61, 84, 102-103, 209, 230, 235, 239, 250, 260, 265-272, 279,-280, 288,

Sphere, The, 282

Spiro, Benny, 269-270, 278, 283

St Albans, 74

Stallman, Rudolf, 45-46

Starnes, Cortlandt, 46-49

Stavisky Affair, 207

Steel (Stahl), Herbert Johannes, 3-4, 5, 164 (pic), 245-293, 294, 302

Sterry, Sir Wasey, 217, 220-221

Stewart, Maud, 239

Stone, Paul alias Harry, 47, 51, 60, 62-63, 267

Straker, Jean, 74

Strand, 34, 269, 277

Stretton, Gordon, 84-85

Surete, 211

Stuart, Dr Frederick, 21-25

Sunday Post, 114-117

Surrey Docks, 299, 304

Switzerland, 8

Syria, 216, 220, 276, 311

Tabloid cocaine tablets, 11

Tass Agency, 290

Taylor, Doreen, 74-75

Tchai, Ah Kiu, 102

Thompson Line, 57

Thurston, John, 68

Tienjin, 212, 224

Tilbury, 71

Times, The, 9, 13-14, 41, 256

Tip, Won, 103

Tongs, 102. 105-109

Tong Say Company, 140

Tottenham Court Road, 96, 99, 143, 172, 174, 186,

Treaty of Versailles, 7, 27, 104, 261, 264

Trinidad, 93

Tunnick, Charles, 67-73

Turkey, 8

Twaddle, Dr JB, 62

Ukraine, 308

United States, 6-8

Umpire, The, 20

USSR, 8

Vaughan, Keith Harrison, 61-64

Venona cables, 253

Veidt, Conrad, 208

Vernon Court Hotel, 245

Vickers, 73, 256-257

Vienna, 204, 219, 307-308

Vine Street, 30, 69, 148, 167, 190

Volkischer Beobachter, 288

Voyatzis, Jean, 162, 212, 224-231, 234

Waldorf Hotel, 35, 269

Walvish, Henry, 82

Warren, William Charles, 46
Watch Your Step, 21
Webster, WHA, 303-304
Week, The, 281
White, Harry Dexter, 253
Wild, Sir Ernest, 131-133
Williams, Claude, 150, 183
Wintner, George, 62
Whiffen, Thomas and Sons, 27, 140-142, 201, 306
Wolfheim, Paul, 224-225, 227
Won, Mum, 102
Wong, Ah, 142
Woolridge's, 22
World's Pictoral News, 89, 109
World War One, 10, 73, 75-76, 101
World War Two, 8, 102, 306-312
Yau, Ada, 22-25
Yau, Lau Ping, 22-25
Yau, Yong, 127
Yeoland, Ida and Edith, 11-12
Young, Charlotte, 287
Young, Olive, 116
Yugoslavia, 276
Zaharoff, Sir Basil, 255-257, 269, 283, 292
Zakarian, Thomas, 219
Eugene Zimmerman, 240-241
Zimmerman, Helena, 240-241
Zurich, 57, 137

## IF YOU HAVE ENJOYED THIS BOOK OR FOUND IT INFORMATIVE THEN PLEASE CONSIDER LEAVING A SHORT REVIEW ON AMAZON.

## ABOUT THE AUTHOR

John Lucas has written for some of Britain's best-selling national newspapers, including *The Sun*, *The Daily Mirror*, the *Mail on Sunday* and *The Times*. He is also the author of two more true crime books:

*Britain's Forgotten Serial Killer* — Tells the chilling life story of one of Britain's most notorious murderers, Patrick Mackay, and a string of unsolved crimes for which he remains the prime suspect.

*Albanian Mafia Wars: The Rise of Europe's Deadliest Narcos* — Exposes the untold saga of one of the world's newest and most dangerous criminal societies, from the civil strife of the Balkans to the streets of New York and the tower blocks of East London.

## ABOUT ABERFELDY LONDON

Aberfeldy London is an independent publisher based in the capital's East End.

We specialise in investigative journalism, true crime and history. For submissions or more information, please contact us at info@aberfeldylondon.com.

Printed in Great Britain
by Amazon